The Knowledge Economy at Work

The Knowledge Economy at Work

Skills and Innovation in Knowledge Intensive Service Activities

Edited by

Cristina Martinez-Fernandez

Urban Research Centre, University of Western Sydney, Australia

Ian Miles

Manchester Institute of Innovation Research/Centre for Service Research, University of Manchester, UK

Tamara Weyman

Urban Research Centre, University of Western Sydney, Australia

Edward Elgar
Cheltenham, UK • Northampton, MA, USA

Published by
Edward Elgar Publishing Limited
The Lypiatts
15 Lansdown Road
Cheltenham
Glos GL50 2JA
UK

Edward Elgar Publishing, Inc.
William Pratt House
9 Dewey Court
Northampton
Massachusetts 01060
USA

A catalogue record for this book
is available from the British Library

Library of Congress Control Number: 2011924156

ISBN 978 1 84720 049 5

Printed and bound by MPG Books Group, UK

Contents

Figures

Tables

Contributors

Prof. José Albors-Garrigos – Professor of Technology Management, at Universidad Politecnica de Valencia, Spain.

Dr. Marianne Broch – Researcher at NIFU STEP – Norwegian Institute for Studies in Innovation, Research and Education and PhD Candidate at the Norwegian School of Management, specialization of Innovation and Entrepreneurship.

Prof. Jose Luis Hervas-Oliver – Associate Professor at Universidad Politecnica de Valencia.

Dr. Patricia Marquez Rodriguez – An industrial engineer from Colombia working professionally in Mexico.

Prof. Cristina Martinez-Fernandez – Associate Professor and Senior Research Fellow at the Urban Research Centre, University of Western Sydney, Australia. Policy Analyst at the Organisation for Economic Co-operation and Development (OECD).

Dr. Laura E. Martinez-Solano – IARC, Warwick Manufacturing Group, University of Warwick, UK; Senior Researcher appointed to a RCUK research fellowship in Healthcare Systems Improvement at the IMC.

Prof. Ian Miles – Professor of Technological Innovation and Social Change at the Manchester Institute of Innovation Research, Manchester Business School, University of Manchester, United Kingdom, where he is Co-Director of the Centre for Service Research. He is also, since 2011, Head of the Research Laboratory for Economics of Innovation, Higher School of Economics, Moscow.

Dr. Tavis Potts – Principal Investigator: Oceans Governance and Theme Leader: Prosperity from Marine Ecosystems, Centre for Coastal and Oceans Governance Scottish Association for Marine Science (SAMS), Oban, Argyll, Northern Scotland, U.K.

Dr. Samantha Sharpe – Research Fellow at the Centre for Business Research at Cambridge University.

Dr. Tamara Weyman – Research Associate at the Urban Research Centre, University of Western Sydney.

Prof. Heidi Wiig Aslesen – Associate Professor at the Norwegian School of Management (BI).

Abbreviations

ABARE	Australian Bureau of Agriculture and Resources Economics
ABS	Australian Bureau of Statistics
AEGIS	Australian Expert Group in Industry Studies
AIIA	Australian Information Industry Association
AIMS	Australian Institute of Marine Science
ANSTO	Australia National Nuclear Science and Technology Organisation
ARC	Australian Research Council
ATC	Atlantic Technology Corridor
BASIX	NSW Building Sustainability Index
BMBA	Blue Mountains Business Advantage
CCB	Centre of Ceramics of Bologna
COFOG	Classification of the Functions of Government
CRCs	Cooperative Research Centres
CSIRO	Commonwealth Scientific and Research Organisation
DSTO	Defense Science and Technology Organisation
EU	European Union
FAQs	Frequently Asked Questions
FESC	Framework for Procuring External Support for Commissioning
FDI	Foreign Direct Investment
FTE	Full-time Equivalents
GDP	Gross Domestic Product
HEIs	Higher Education Institutions
IATA	Instituto Agronomico de Tecnologia Alimentaria
ICT	Information and Communication Technology
IDA	Industrial Development Agency
IP	Intellectual Property
IPOs	Initial Public Offerings
IPR	Intellectual Property Rights
ISO	International Standards Organization
IT	Information Technology
ITC	Institute of Ceramic Technology
IVIA	Insituto Valenciano de Investigaciones Agronomicas
KBTEN	Knowledge-based techno-economic network
KIBS	Knowledge Intensive Business Service
KIS	Knowledge Intensive Services

KISA	Knowledge Intensive Service Activities
KPIs	Key Performance Indicators
KS	Kommunenes Sentralforbund (The Association of Local Government and Regional Authorities)
LGA	Local Government Area
MIP	Most Important Innovative Product
MNCs	Multinational Corporations
MTS	Mining Technology Services
MTSAA	Mining Technology Services Action Agenda
NAO	National Audit Office
NHS	National Health Service
NICE	National Institute for Health and Clinical Excellence
NPM	New public management
NSW	New South Wales
NTBFs	New Technology-based Firms
OECD	Organisation for Economic Co-operation and Development
OGs	Other Graduates
OH&S	Occupational Health & Safety
PCTs	Primary Care Trusts
PPBS	Planning, Programming, and Budgeting System
PPP	Purchasing Power Parity
PSI	Public Services Industry
PSRs	Public Sector Research
R&D	Research and Development
RAC	Regional Absorptive Capacity
RBV	Resource-based Value
REIN	Regional Environmental Innovation Network
ROE	Return on Equity
ROA	Return on Assets
RTOs	Research and Technology Organisations
SAAS	Software-as-a-service
SBAs	Sustainable Business Activities
SEC	South East Coast
SMEs	Small and Medium Enterprises
UN	United Nations
VC	Venture Capital

Acknowledgements

The editors are grateful to Mr Robert Strauss, Head of Employment Analysis, European Commission, Directorate General for Employment, Social Affairs and Inclusion for his helpful comments and suggestions on the different chapters of this book. Thank you also to anonymous reviewers and proofreaders. Alexander W. Gomez-Martinez and Mateo Dorvan provided very useful ideas for the final format of the book.

1 Knowledge Intensive Service Activities: Integrating Knowledge for Innovation

Cristina Martinez-Fernandez and Ian Miles

Knowledge Intensive Service Activities (KISA) are undertaken within firms in the course of innovation. Knowledge is produced and co-produced among actors within the firm through KISA. This chapter will set out approaches to understanding the role of KISA, discussing also such other elements in the innovation process as Knowledge Intensive Business Service (KIBS), Research and Technology Organisations (RTOs), and the wider network within which the firm is embedded. The analysis of KISA is important for understanding firms' innovation practices and opportunities, and is thus relevant for policy analysis and management strategy.

INTRODUCTION

Innovation research grew explosively in the last quarter of the twentieth century and continued to do so in the opening decade of the twenty-first. International research into firms' innovative activity has clearly indicated its multiple dimensions (for a review, see Fagerberg et al, 2004). Moving on from an initial focus on product innovation, and mainly on radical product innovation in high-tech manufacturing industries, there is now widespread understanding that innovation encompasses not only radical and incremental product development. It also encompasses new production methods and new organisational forms taken up by productive enterprises in all sectors of the economy. Product innovation includes service innovation as well as innovation of new and improved goods; and service firms also display innovation in service processes and delivery. Public sector innovation is also of major importance, alongside that in the private sector. While firms may vary in their emphases on product, process and organisational innovation, these are often closely intertwined.[1] It has become clear that all these aspects of change characterise innovative firms and influence competitive success.

Notably, we see both manufacturing and services sectors as increasing their use of inputs from Knowledge Intensive Business Services (KIBS) (Tidd and Hull, 2002; Miles and Boden, 2000; AEGIS, 2003). The innovation features of some KIBS (especially technology-related KIBS such as computer and engineering services) are in many ways similar to those of high-tech manufacturing industries (Tether, et al, 2001; Sundbo and Gallouj, 2000). For instance, they undertake formal research and development (R&D) and make use of Intellectual Property Rights (IPR) methods such as patents, they invest considerably in innovation activities, and so on. Much recent literature has been documented the role of KIBS as organisations critical to the modern economy (Hauknes, 2000; Hales, 2000; Miles, 1999; Murphy and Vickery, 1999). These firms are now a critical element of the service sector and innovation systems in most OECD (Organisation for Economic Co-operation and Development) member nations. They assist innovation in both manufacturing and other service firms, and can act as linking agents between these two sectors. For example, consultants, computer services, systems integrators, and others play roles in helping users in all sectors identify, acquire, and apply the new systems and techniques flowing from high-tech manufacturing. The sorts of services supplied by KIBS may be provided by organisations that are not specifically identified as KIBS – for instance, systems integration, after sales and other forms of assistance may be provided by manufacturing firms (AEGIS, 2003), and Universities and public laboratories are active in providing some forms of business support. Recent research has explored the KIBS sectors in some depth, not least because statistics are available on the supply-side of KIBS: employment and turnover of the firms concerned, the size of various subsectors, and their innovation activities, for instance (Miles 2005).

However, there is relatively limited literature concerning the use of KIBS. This underdevelopment reflects a more general limited paucity of analysis of how firms engage in a process of learning that facilitates continuous product, service or process innovations. The pioneering work of Nonaka and Takeuchi (1995) showed that innovating firms indeed draw on a range of providers of expertise – they note, for example, R&D, testing, prototyping and other technical and engineering services; and IT (Information Technology), legal (especially Intellectual Property (IP)-related), financial, marketing and training services. However, critical questions remain about how, when or why firms choose to use particular kinds of innovation-related services, from among the variety available from public, private (and academic) sources, let alone from in-house sources. Even less is known about how firms transform the innovation services they receive from outside to build their own capabilities and support sustained innovation at firm level. The lack of detailed information on how firms use the services available is liable to mean that innovation policies are less well targeted and effective than they should be.

One of the major developments in innovation research has been the idea of innovation systems that link together providers and users of knowledge and other innovation-related resources (for example finance, marketing) within national and regional economies, and/or in sectors and value clusters. Analysis of National Innovation Systems has rarely considered how firms who are seeking to innovate go about determining how and how far to combine their own expertise with the use of expertise from private firms and other external sources. There are some studies of collaborative arrangements (often undertaken in the course of evaluating public research support programmes that have promoted such collaboration); and recently there has been a great deal of celebration of 'open innovation' (Chesbrough, 2003a,b; Chesbrough, Vanhaverbeke and West, 2006; Kirschbaum, 2005; Laursen and Salter, 2006; Perkmann and Walsh, 2007; van der meer, 2007; West and Gallagher, 2006; West and Lakhani, 2008). The KISA project, conducted under the auspices of the OECD was the first study to our knowledge to set out to analyse this complex issue (OECD, 2002) in terms of the whole range of knowledge sources used by firms.

The KISA project was conducted at several levels of analysis and industries, as will be seen in later chapters. This provided the context for a firm-level investigation of innovation knowledge-seeking choices. KISA in a firm are those activities which are undertaken with the aim of achieving appropriate combinations of in-house and external expertise. This is not to say that all KISA are used by firms for innovation purposes. For example, firms will use services for translation, locating specialist staff, logistics, legal support, accountancy, and much else. But many KISA are highly relevant to innovation activity, for instance R&D and engineering consultancy services, product and process design services, intellectual property protection, market intelligence, and support for the creation of knowledge networks. Conversely, while innovation requires a great deal of KISA, it does not consist entirely of KISA. Most professional workers are supported by paraprofessionals and technicians, of course, but also by more routine workers who provide various clerical and operational services. The implementation of innovation is liable to require support from a wide range of services, including transport and storage, repair and maintenance, disposal of waste and obsolete systems, and much more.

The KISA research project examined the interfaces between organisations providing and receiving innovation services, and the ways in which KISA can be used to build competitive capabilities. Understanding how firms access and use the variety of innovation-related KISA available to them, in different industries, at different times, is not just of academic interest. It is intended to help policy makers design policies and programmes to actively stimulate innovation, or at least reduce barriers to it. The analyses can be used by policy makers to increase their effectiveness of innovation programmes (and thus increase returns to the National Innovation Systems); the insights may even help in the elaboration of completely new policy directions). The study should furnish organisations providing innovation services with better understanding of how their services work in practice. It may thus indicate areas for improvement in the range of service provision, and in the ways in which innovation services may be accessed and used.

This chapter aims to explain the meaning of KISA and its field of analysis. We first discuss the context of KISA, the importance of KIBS and then, other elements involved in the co-production of knowledge and innovation.

THE CONTEXT OF KISA: CO-PRODUCTION OF KNOWLEDGE FROM DIFFERENT ACTORS

Recent research on innovation focuses attention on understanding particular patterns of innovative activity seen in an economy (Fagerberg et al, 2004; Soosay, 2003). It relates these to the characteristics of major players (public institutions and private firms), and their linkages (see also Hales, 2000; Hales, 2001; Martinez-Fernandez, 2004). The players may be linked in different ways at different spatial levels (national, regional or local), through activities such as R&D provided through public and/or private enterprises, or through the development and use of management and other business-related skills and expertise. Again, they may be linked in supply chains through their entrepreneurial activities as suppliers and customers. This extension of our view of the learning space of the firm – from the organisational unit to the wider community – has been recently addressed by Amin and Cohendet (2004); this new view is encapsulated by Hales (2004) when he says the 'community should be given central status as the all-important site of knowledge formation'. The rise of 'society' as a key element of innovation activity is now more systematically taken into account by the framework of open innovation and the social innovation approach (Noya, 2009).

The focus on this wider space in which the firm operates has brought more understanding of the elements involved in the co-production of knowledge by different actors. The main formal external intermediaries of knowledge linked to firm-level innovation and capability building, that act as functions in the co-production of knowledge in the firm, are KIBS[2] and public and hybrid RTOs. For the purpose of this chapter these knowledge intensive services, whether they are sourced internally or externally, are referred to as 'KISA contributions'.

In recent work, KIBS are the most intensively studied knowledge and innovation intermediaries. The literature on KIBS discusses many issues relevant for understanding the context of KISA, so a brief and very selective review of this literature is presented below. First, what are KIBS?

Den Hertog (2000) expands upon the initial discussion of KIBS in Miles et al (1995); he defines KIBS as 'private companies or organisations who rely heavily on professional knowledge and skills, that is, knowledge or expertise related to a specific (technical) discipline or (technical) functional domain to supply intermediate products and services that are knowledge-based' (den Hertog, 2000:505). Although the knowledge may cover practically any sort of activity, KIBS often need to engage in high levels of interaction with their clients, for whom they play consulting and problem-solving functions. They can be very actively integrated into innovation by jointly developing knowledge with their clients. KIBS play multiple roles within national and other innovation systems. They serve as innovators themselves, as well as being facilitators, carriers, or sources of innovation (Muller and Zenker, 2001; Wong and He, 2002; den Hertog, 2000).

The Importance of KIBS

Research into KIBS has noted two broad classes of such services: those dealing with social and institutional knowledge (many traditional professional services), and those dealing with knowledge of science and technology.[3] Similar broad classifications may apply to KISA, as well. In the case of KIBS, one indicator of knowledge-intensity is the prevalence of people with higher educational qualifications in firms. Among the first to examine this were Tether and Swann (2003), who used data from the UK's third Community Innovation Survey (2000). The data differentiate between Science and Engineering – S&E, science (including social science) and engineering – graduates, on one hand, and other graduates (OGs – including arts and humanities, and so on) on the other. KIBS sectors emerge as outstandingly graduate-intensive. For most sets of KIBS, more than two-thirds of firms employ graduates. Some are particularly heavy employers only of S&E graduates (for example R&D and testing services). Some mainly employ OGs only (some Financial Services, Professional Services, and 'Other Transport Services'[4]). Some are heavy employers of both types of graduate (for example IT services, architecture and engineering services). Of course, this broad-brush sectoral account is bound to meet with exceptions; there are certainly some firms with many graduates in sectors that generally employ few, and vice versa. In Chapter 11 we consider evidence on the skill requirements of KISA jobs, where a broadly similar picture is apparent.

KIBS employ people with higher education and professional qualifications to help their clients solve what are typically highly specific and/or complex problems, which demand more than relatively routine solutions. Even so, KIBS may often find themselves engaged in activities that are quite routine. In one project a firm may be providing marketing consultancy, for example, in another just running an opinion poll using standard instruments and tabulations. There is little evidence on the distribution of standard and non-routine work in firms. One analysis used German survey data to explore how far services provide standardised solutions, as opposed to ones that are specially produced or adapted to specific clients (Hipp et al, 2000). Firms were asked how far their activities were standardised, as opposed to being customised to the requirements of specific clients. Technology-related KIBS were much more likely than other service firms to produce specialised service outputs, although they still reported a surprising amount of more standardised work. Twenty-seven per cent of Technical Services, and 18 per cent of Software firms, reported that at least a third of their output was specialised – contrasting with 10 per cent for Other Business Services, 5 per cent for Trade, 4 per cent for Banking and Insurance (but 18 per cent for Other Financial Services), 2 per cent for Transport and Communication, and 4 per cent for a Residual category. The more specialised services can be expected to require greater exchange and co-production of knowledge between service firm and client. Figure 1.1 depicts the relationship between client and KIBS. This creates opportunities for mutual learning. The clients can gain new understanding of their problems and how to avoid or overcome them; this may trigger further innovation in the clients, or at least adoption of solutions from the KIBS. The service supplier, too, may learn about new ways to meet client requirements, as well as possibly deepening generic knowledge about business processes or their own markets and ways of relating to the client.

Tordoir (1996) distinguished between 'jobbing' and 'sparring' relationships in professional services. Building on this, it can be suggested that in the 'jobbing' relationship, the client defines the problems for the service firm, more or less thoroughly setting out the solution it wants implementing. The 'sparring' relationship involves much more negotiation as to the nature of the problem, and the service to be provided: the service firm supplies knowledge as to the nature of the problem that confronts the client. The interactions featured in Figure 1.1 reflect the different types of knowledge being brought together to produce the service. The KIBS has to access and understand the client's knowledge of its processes and markets – and perceived difficulties – and combine this with its own understanding of technological or organisational solutions to the problem. This understanding is based on professional training and experience, including that gained from dealing with problems of other clients. Clients are prepared to entrust KIBS with strategic information since this is necessary for achieving the most fitting solution to their problems. This contributes to the KIBS' stock of knowledge about problems and solutions.

Similar approaches to KIBS have been developed by several researchers. For instance, Strambach (2001) sees KIBS as possessing generic knowledge that they adapt or elaborate in the course of problem-solving and integrating different types of knowledge for particular clients. The knowledge created through these problem-solving interactions may be converted by the KIBS into information that can be communicated and routines that can be applied more generally, for instance in new client relationships. Some KIBS may develop new knowledge through research independent of specific client commissions – this is most common for those operating at knowledge frontiers such as biotechnology R&D or corporate accountancy. The first decade of the twenty-first century saw a considerable increase in studies of how KIBS operate.

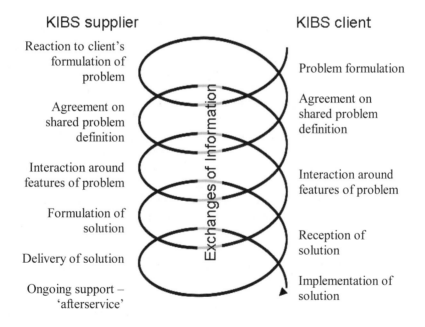

Source: after Miles 2005

Figure 1.1 Interactions between service firms and their clients

However, there has been limited analysis of what happens on the client side of the relationship. Clients will need capabilities to be able to choose among and combine different service suppliers (and to combine or substitute these with in-house skills), and to be able to negotiate the definition of problems and solutions in sparring relationships, and to make use of KIBS inputs. The KISA project focused on this analysis, bringing business service users to the fore.

There have been some studies of how firms select and evaluate business services (including KIBS). Gallouj (1997) outlined four steps they may undertake, beginning with 'search for general information on suppliers'. This may draw on past contacts (both on the service and client side), knowledge within the organisation, assessing the relevance of publications and conference presentations, and so on. Search can be expensive and time-consuming, so clients often take short cuts to locating suppliers. A second step is evaluation of potential suppliers and creating and issuing a call for tender. A list of potential service suppliers is prepared by assessing possible candidates through such criteria as qualifications, nature of the problem, past experience; they are invited to tender for the job (which may be more or less well-defined at this stage). The next step involves evaluation of tenders and short listing candidates who will go on to a final step. The evaluation criteria largely rely on scrutiny of the tenders to assess the candidates understanding of the problem, the approaches to solving it that they propose, and further evidence as to experience and competence (including the specific staff who will work on the problem). Clients typically arrive at a small set of service providers, and in the fourth step they present their proposals, and the client makes a final choice on the basis of a more detailed application of criteria like those employed in earlier steps. Here, more attention will be paid to the precise methodology and proposed solution, project management and control, scope for delivery of results on time, the interaction between KIBS and client that is envisioned, and so on. The client may use signals of quality to reduce uncertainty in their selection and evaluation of the service provider (such signals include certification, reputation, and quality indicators). The client may also require contractual guarantees, and/or contingency clauses (payment by results, penalties for late delivery, and so on) to ensure that the required service is delivered. We would add that 'softer' criteria may come into play – how innovative is the proposed solution? Do we think we could work with these individuals?

Other researchers have looked at the results of KIBS use on clients. Sjøholt (2001) examined transnational consultancy firms and their clients in Norway. He concluded that more sophisticated clients make better use of business services; often they seek to establish long-term 'sparring' relations with their service suppliers. Well-defined and controllable tasks of a more systemic learning nature were generally positively evaluated by the clients. They saw 'less successful' experiences with KIBS sometimes as resulting from their own lack of focus, and often as the fault of the consultants. It was broader, more intangible strategic consultancy assignments that tended to receive more ambiguous assessments in terms of provision of value for money. Sjøholt related the varying experiences to the knowledge transfer mechanisms that had been used. Sometimes inadequate team structures were established (for instance, teams lacking the sort of explicitly trans-disciplinary approach necessitated by contemporary organisational and strategic problems). Chapter 4 in this volume discusses in detail the relationship between mining companies and specialised business services providers.

A similar conclusion, that the character of the relationships had substantial influence on the success of KIBS use (in this case related to innovation processes) was reached by Hislop (2002). In his case studies (four organisations implementing similar technological innovations) the client firms played key roles in shaping their relations with consultancies. The social networks and organisational cultures of the client firm were critical.

In summary, recent research into KIBS is starting to analyse the nature of the interactions between service firms and their clients. We see considerable interest on the part of consultants themselves in demonstrating their value to clients, too; and they may acknowledge and try to account for the variable success of different projects.[5] There is still much that remains unclear concerning the role and importance of these interactions and the skills needed by client firms. What the research into KIBS has clearly established is the position of these organisations as co-producers of knowledge in the modern economy. Other elements in the co-production of knowledge are discussed below.

Other Elements in the Co-production of Knowledge

In addition to KIBS, and one with some similarities to them, RTOs are also involved in the co-production of knowledge. RTOs are (mainly) publicly funded organisations that play a bridging or intermediary role in innovation systems. The term RTO may be applied somewhat differently across countries, reflecting different institutional structures and policy frameworks. But a reasonable definition comes from Hales (2001:1): RTOs are '... organisations with significant core government funding (25 per cent or greater) which supply services to firms individually or collectively in support of scientific and technological innovation and which devote much of their capability (50 per cent or more of their labour) to remaining integrated with the science base.'

For example, within the Australian economy, RTOs can be loosely applied to universities (at least those undertaking R&D, technology transfer and intellectual property roles) and to Commonwealth or State funded bridging institutions, notably: Australian Commonwealth Scientific and Research Organisation (CSIRO); and also Defense Science and Technology Organisation (DSTO), Australia National Nuclear Science and Technology Organisation (ANSTO), and Australian Institute of Marine Science (AIMS).

According to Hales (2002), RTOs are not simply KIBS that happen to be in the public sector: their heritage and often their contractual arrangements, work organization, IP orientation and sense of mission are quite distinctive. But there is certainly evidence that RTOs' activities overlap – and probably increasingly overlap – with those of KIBS (Hales, 2002). In part, this is due to changes in the funding systems of RTOs, as governments have sought to reduce some categories of expenditure and of personnel.

A comprehensive analysis of RTOs and their role in the service economy was undertaken in the six-country European Union (EU) RISE[6] project, completed at the end of the year 2000. The RISE project proposes a new mapping schema for innovation systems, moving away from the institution-based approach of many earlier studies. A function-based approach is developed, in which an innovation system is seen as being embodied in a hybrid economy of tacit and explicit innovation services (Hales, 2001). Under this approach, tangible and intangible scientific and technological services cover both operational and innovation needs of firms. Firms customise the services available to their own needs at specific stages of their innovation processes or of their product life cycles. The providers of these services can then be more or less formal, and the interchanges more or less market-based.

RTOs are important alongside KIBS, but there are other innovation service suppliers. More informal providers of knowledge intensive services include actors from the firms' network: competitors, customers and other organisations from their own industry sector (or from other sectors that share the same or similar problems), contacts made through professional and standards-setting associations, and so on. Provision of inputs to KISA can also come from more organised network sources – for example, through business networks and industry clusters (which may be set up by public agencies or be private initiatives) or industry associations. The ways in which firms integrate these services are important for building and maintaining their innovation capability.

Current innovation studies may overestimate the importance of KIBS and RTOs compared to the use of the more informal transactions from organisations within their 'network space'. For example, the analysis of software firms presented in Chapter 7 indicates that the learning space of these firms includes not only other technology firms and intermediaries of knowledge such as KIBS and RTOs, but also other organisations in their business and social network space can be vital. KISA can take place in any of the engagement activities that the software firm has within other organisations. Such KISA can be then further developed as formal transactions (for example contractual ones) or more informal relationships (for example sharing information); or they may be internal to the firm's innovation process. The KISA associated with external providers of knowledge such as KIBS is most likely to be formal and contractual. This may also be the case for KISA generated with the assistance of an RTO (a university or a research laboratory, or a government department that provides services such as R&D to other organisations). On the other hand, KISA generated in collaboration with a company in geographical proximity, in order to develop a new product or service, may be the result of informal, no-contractual agreements. Such informal, non-commercial KISA can happen at any level of the firm, but they are more likely to appear while interacting with other firms/organisations of the 'network' space of the firm. KIBS and RTOs are within this network space and informal transactions can also occur with them (often with the idea that future contracts may be generated; but also sometimes reflecting personal relationships established during prior interactions, or sympathies and obligations to other members of, say, a geographical cluster).

The chapters presented in this book show the critical importance of these informal relationships for firm innovation. This helps shed light on the complexity of this KISA universe of relationships, how it may be understood, and what role it plays in innovation.

Structure of the Book

The book is divided into three parts. Part I analyses KISA in traditional industries. Part II analyses KISA in service industries; and Part III discusses the strategic and policy implications for skills, employment and management.

I. Traditional industries:

- Chapter 2, the 'Roles of KISA in Aquaculture in Norway' by Heidi Wiig Aslesen, discusses how aquaculture firms maintain and develop productive and innovative capabilities through utilisation of KISA provided by internal and/or external sources. The chapter is based on 25 in-depth firm interviews and a study by Aslesen et al (2002) whereby firms in the sector were divided into four categories according to their knowledge base and ways of organising business activities. The chapter focuses on the use of KISA in building innovation capability in the industry and identifies how different KISAs play varying roles in firms' innovation processes. Importantly the chapter reveals that within the same industry, the types of KISA used both internally and externally, differ greatly. The chapter lists three important policy suggestions targeting KISA to improve innovation capability, competitiveness and efficiency in aquaculture firms: 1) strengthening the internal KISA; 2) stimulate quality of supply of external KISA; and 3) proactive brokering between aquaculture firms and relevant external KISA providers.

- Chapter 3, 'The Role of KISA in Basic Agro-food Processes Innovation: the Case of Orange Packers in Eastern Spain' by José Albors-Garrigos explores the ways in which knowledge intensive activities occur in a small cluster of mature and low-tech industries. The chapter assesses the impact of KISA on the firm's innovation and performance. The author questions whether KISA is correlated with certain characteristics of firms such as size, organisational profile, market focus, and other characteristics. The chapter indicates the impact of the firms' absorption capacity as a co-adjuvant in the KISA effects. Externally provided services for KISA are highlighted for SMEs that have restricted in-house resources. The clustering effect has a significant role in KISA adoption and impact.

- Chapter 4, 'KISA Utilisation in Resource Intensive Industries: the Case of Mining in Australia' by Cristina Martinez-Fernandez discusses the role of mining technology services (MTS) in the transformation of the mining industry into the knowledge economy in Australia. The chapter is largely based on two Australian Research Council studies conducted by the University of Western Sydney. The role played by the MTS firms is significant in fuelling innovation of the mining industry and the dependence on the quality of KISA conducted in collaboration with the mining company. A number of deductions are made: 1) mining companies rely on the expertise and operational capacity of MTS firms operating in mining sites; 2) mining sites constitute hubs of knowledge intensity; 3) the number of MTS companies working in a particular site at any one moment constitutes a complex network of KISA; 4) KISA performed by MTS firms strongly impact innovation and competitiveness of mining firms.

- Chapter 5, 'KISA Role in Tradition Manufacturing Industries: the Case of Ceramics Tiles in Spain' by José Albors-Garrigos, Jose Luis Hervas-Oliver and Patricia Marquez Rodriguez analyses the ways knowledge intensive activities occur in mature industries. The chapter also explores KISA's impact in the firm's performance in correlation with their strategic focus. Multivariable tests were used to map the industry and evaluate the impact of certain activities on performance. The tests revealed the importance of knowledge intensive services as an element of the innovation system. Internal and external service activities, intensive in knowledge, were related to their output in terms of competitive advantages and economic performance.

II. Service industries:

- Chapter 6, 'The Role of KISA in a Public Service: the Case of Entrepreneurial Home-based Care for Elderly in Norway', by Marianne Broch focuses on the rehabilitation and care unit of the city district. The chapter investigates the use of internal and external KISA in innovation processes, the mix and match of such activities and thereby the interactive learning and innovation that takes place. Entrepreneurial home-based care for the elderly shows an organisational culture which encourages employees to look for change and renewal of their activities through KISA. An example of entrepreneurial KISA is taking part in a network that organises interactive learning using mix-and-match knowledge intensive service activities with the different groups. Policy measures are revealed for stimulating networking and cooperation between KISA actors of different public sector organisations and between internal and external KISA providers (public and private). Broch suggests a broader approach to the proactive broker in order to strengthen the role of the public support system in creating functional and permanent networks of firms and public sector organisations.
- Chapter 7, 'KISA Role in Western High-technology Industries: the Case of Software in Australia and Ireland' by Laura E. Martinez-Solano and Cristina Martinez-Fernandez analyses the role of KISA in supporting the innovation process of the software sector and the necessary conditions for their development. The study in Ireland was based on a postal survey among 808 software companies and interviews with senior managers. The study in Australia was conducted through an online survey with follow-up interviews. The chapter identifies that engineering related KISA is considered core for the innovation development of software companies. Although these companies would have preferred to develop KISA internally, they had to obtain at least the most peripheral KISA from external sources. As a result software firms (especially SMEs) would highly benefit from government support to institutionalise their knowledge networks. This would allow them to identify, source and/or develop the various sophisticated KISA needed to compete in the highly innovative and competitive international software market.
- Chapter 8, 'The Use of KISA in the Public Sector' by Ian Miles considers the nature of KISA within public services. The chapter discusses innovative activities of these sectors and on the acquisition of KISA from external sources. Miles notes that these two topics are

closely linked and that this linkage will have considerable bearing on their future. The chapter reveals that the public services have a high reliance on KISA. The KISA approach reveals the need to consider what sorts of knowledge are being employed in these services and how this is organised and managed. It shows the innovation processes in the public sector and the complexity of professional knowledge as representing both opportunities and problems for innovation in these large-scale organisations. The KISA approach highlights the need to investigate how knowledge is mobilised and whether it is integrated or fragmented, diffused or compartmentalised, related to experience and experiment or treated as something static and to be transmitted from above. Public sector KISA is an essential part of the response to today's challenges (environmental sustainability, food/energy security issue and overcoming social exclusion and poverty) and it must be a priority to enable effective operation.

- Chapter 9, 'The New Green Deal and KISA: a Global and Australian Perspective', by Tavis Potts examines two regional case studies in New South Wales (NSW), Australia, that are initiating shifts towards networks of sustainable businesses and explores policy models for boosting green innovation. The chapter discusses how Natural Advantage KISA, which is defined as 'the advantages and benefits that an organisation, community or government can obtain by applying cleaner production and environmentally oriented innovation principles and processes to its operations', can play a significant role in progressing regional development. Green KISA can provide strategies and tools for business development, environmental education and regional innovation delivery that are linked to environmental improvement. The author states that the Natural Advantage concept should not operate in isolation, it should be an integrated strategy that links economic and environmental planning and policies.

- Chapter 10, 'Venture Capitalists as Knowledge Intensive Service Activity Providers' by Samantha Sharpe, examines the use of the KISA framework to evaluate non-financial inputs by venture capitalists to their portfolio firms through the analysis of three case studies. The chapter argues that venture capitalists are not an internal or external source of knowledge for firms, but rather a hybrid of the two. Venture capitalists have intimate knowledge of the internal workings of the portfolio firm and use this knowledge to draw in external resources and knowledge that the portfolio firm needs as non-financial inputs. The chapter reveals the core areas of KISA provision by venture capitalist to their portfolio firm: strategic development services, business planning advice and human resources/recruitment.

III. Strategic Policy Implications

- Chapter 11, 'Implications for Skills, Employment and Management' by Ian Miles and Cristina Martinez-Fernandez, examines the broader implications of the increasing significance of KISA. The chapter discusses the implications in relation to skill requirements and employment generation, and to management strategy, government policy and the responses of educational institutions. The authors consider the nature of KISA occupations and the skills they deploy and report arguments that there are widespread trends towards the broadening of competences needed in these. The chapter reveals that there is a requirement for an adaptable, multi-skilled and highly knowledgeable workforce across the economy, and especially in high-tech industries and knowledge intensive service sectors.

CONCLUSIONS

The KISA approach aims to understand whether and how Knowledge Intensive Service Activities (KISA) is crucial for the innovation development of the firm. This chapter has argued that KISA plays a critical role in the innovation process of firms, as these activities sustain the context where providers of knowledge and expertise interact. These knowledge intensive service activities have received little attention in the literature focusing on R&D and other aspects of firms' innovation.

The importance of the learning space of the firm in the co-production of knowledge, and of KISA as the context where this learning is articulated, raise many questions. For example: what are the best KISA conditions to foster innovation? Are these conditions similar across sectors or do they vary depending on the industry concerned? Firms, KIBS, RTOs and other organisations in the network space of the firm form a knowledge network highly important for the innovation capability of an industry. The analysis of the different KISA in this network provides a rich picture of the amount of knowledge intensity, skills requirements and innovativeness of a particular cluster of firms. At the same time, the analysis of KISA is able to take account of non-commercial inputs to innovation, where informal KISA are involved.

NOTES

1. Indeed, analysis of European data collected in the successive Community Innovation Surveys (CIS) indicates a high correlation between the three – firms and sectors with greater engagement in one type of innovation are also likely to engage in the others.

2. As noted previously, KIBS-type services can also be supplied by firms whose main business activities are not KIBS, and which thus will not be recorded in KIBS sectors. For example, a manufacturing firm may sell testing services in its laboratories to other manufacturers.
3. It may also be worth thinking of some 'creative industries' as working with cultural and aesthetic knowledge, providing support for clients in the form of, for instance, graphic design, media representations, and so on. While some of these are located with other KIBS in the 'business services' groups of official statistics, others are located with entertainment, cultural and other services – they are thus omitted from most statistical overviews of KIBS.
4. Transport services in general are not very graduate-intensive: which is the case for many other services, such as trade services.
5. Management Consultancies Association (2006, 2010).
6. Research and Technology Organisations in the Service Economy, http://centrim.mis.brighton.ac.uk/research/rise.shtml, accessed 20 July 2006.

REFERENCES

Amin, A. and Cohendet, P. (2004), *Architectures of Knowledge – Firms, Capabilities and Communities*, Oxford: Oxford University Press.

Australian Expert Group in Industry Studies (AEGIS) (2003), *Selling Solutions, Emerging Patterns of Product – Service Linkage in the Australian Economy*, Report prepared for the Australian Business Foundation.

Chesbrough, H.W. (2003a), 'The Era of Open Innovation', *Sloan Management Review*, **44** (3), pp. 35–41.

Chesbrough, H. (2003b), 'Open Innovation: How Companies Actually do it', *Harvard Business Review*, **81** (7) July, pp. 12–14

Chesbrough, H., Vanhaverbeke, W. and West, J. (eds) (2006), *Open Innovation: Researching a New Paradigm*, Oxford: Oxford University Press.

Den Hertog, P. (2000), 'Knowledge-intensive Business Services as Co-producers of Innovation', *International Journal of Innovation Management*, **4** (4), pp. 491–528.

Fagerberg, J., Mowery, D. and Nelson, R. (eds.) (2004), *The Oxford Handbook of Innovation*, Oxford: Oxford University Press.

Gallouj, C. (1997), 'Asymmetry of Information and the Service Relationship: Selection and Evaluation of the Service Provider', *International Journal of Service Industry Management*, **8** (1), pp. 42–64.

Hales, M. (2000), 'Services Deliveries in an Economy of Competence Supply', *Synthesis Report Work Package 5 of RISE – RTOs in the Service Economy*, University of Brighton: Centrim.

Hales, M. (2001), 'Birds were Dinosaurs Once – the Diversity and Evolution of Research and Technology Organisations', *RISE Final Report*, University of Brighton: Centrim.

Hales, M. (2002), 'Innovation through Services in Australia – the Strategic

Positioning of Publicly Funded Research and Technology Services', *AEGIS (2002) Working Paper No. 1*, Unpublished draft.

Hales, M. (2004), 'Book Review: Amin, A. and P. Cohendet (2004), Architectures of Knowledge – Firms, Capabilities and Communities', *Research Policy*, **33** (4), pp. 1250–1252.

Hauknes, J. (2000), 'Dynamic Innovation Systems: What is the Role of Services?', in M. Boden and I. Miles (eds.) *Services and the Knowledge-based Economy*, London and New York: Continuum.

Hipp, C., Tether, B. and Miles, I. (2000), 'The Incidence and Effects of Innovation in Services: Evidence from Germany', *International Journal of Innovation Management*, December, pp. 417–54.

Hislop, D. (2002), 'The Client Role in Consultancy Relations During the Appropriation of Technological Innovations', *Research Policy*, **31**, pp. 657–71.

Kirschbaum, R. (2005), 'Open Innovation in Practice', *Research-Technology Management*, **48** (4), pp. 24–28.

Laursen, K. and Salter, A.J. (2006), 'Open Innovation: The Role of Openness in Explaining Innovation Performance among UK Manufacturing Firms', *Strategic Management Journal*, **27** (2), pp. 131–150.

Management Consultancies Association (in association with Management Today) (2006), *Ensuring Sustainable Value from Consultants* London: PriceWaterhouseCoopers available at: http://www.wwyltc.com/Ensuring-sustainable-value-from-consultants.pdf (accessed 26 April 2010).

Management Consultancies Association (2010), *The Value of Consulting*, London: Management Consultancies Association available at: http://www.mca.org.uk/value-consulting (accessed 26 April 2010).

Martinez-Fernandez, C. (2004), 'Regional Collaboration Infrastructure – Effects in the Hunter Valley of NSW', *Australian Planner*, **41** (4), pp. 66–73.

Martinez-Fernandez, C. and Martinez-Solano, L. (2006), 'Knowledge Intensive Service Activities (KISA) in Software Innovation' [Special issue], *International Journal of Services Technology and Management*, **7** (2), pp.109–73.

Miles, I. (1999), 'Services in National Innovation Systems: From Traditional Services to Knowledge Intensive Business Services', in G. Schienstock and O. Kuusi (eds.), *Transformation Towards a Learning Economy: The Challenge to the Finnish Innovation System*, Helsinki: Sitra.

Miles. I. (2005), 'Knowledge-intensive Services and Innovation', in J. Bryson and P. Daniels (eds.) *The Handbook of Service Industries*, Cheltenham, UK and Northampton, MA, USA: Edward Elgar, pp. 277–940.

Miles, I. and Boden, M. (2000), 'Services, Knowledge and Intellectual Property', in B. Andersen, J. Howells, R. Hull, I. Miles and J. Roberts (eds.) *Knowledge and Innovation in the New Service Economy*, Cheltenham, UK and Northampton, MA, USA: Edward Elgar, pp. 159–77.

Miles, I., Kastrinos, N., Bilderbeek, R., den Hertog, P., with Flanagan, K., Huntink, W. and Bouman, M. (1995), 'Knowledge-intensive Business Services: Their Role as Users, Carriers and Sources of Innovation', *Report to the EC DG XIII Luxembourg: Sprint EIMS Programme*.

Muller, E. and Zenker, A. (2001), 'Business Services as Actors of Knowledge Transformation: the Role of KIBS in Regional and National Innovation Systems', *Research Policy*, **30** (9), pp. 1501–16.

Murphy, M. and Vickery, G. (1999), *Strategic Business Services*, Paris: OECD.

Nonaka, I. and Takeuchi, H. (1995), *The Knowledge-creating Company: How Japanese Companies Create the Dynamics of Innovation*, New York: Oxford University Press.

Noya, A. (2009), *The Changing Boundaries of Social Enterprises*, OECD Publishing: Paris.

Organisation for Economic Co-operation and Development (OECD) (2002), *Progress Report on the TIP Case Study in Innovation in Knowledge Intensive Service Activities (KISA)*, 10–11 December, Paris: OECD.

Perkmann, M. and Walsh, K. (2007), 'University Industry Relationships and Open Innovation: Towards a Research Agenda', *International Journal of Management Reviews*, **9** (4), pp. 259–280.

Sjøholt, P. (2001), 'Transfer of Managerial Knowledge by Business Related Services', *Department of Geography, University of Bergen, Norway, Working Paper Number 247–2001. Presented at RESER Conference New Information Technology and Service Activities*, October, Grenoble.

Soosay, C.A. (2003), 'Continuous Innovation in Logistics Services: an Empirical Study of Distribution Centres', PhD Thesis, Sydney: UWS.

Strambach, S. (2001), 'Innovation Processes and the Role of Knowledge-intensive Business Services (KIBS)', in K. Koschatzky, M. Kulicke and A. Zenker (eds.) *Innovation Networks – Concepts and Challenges in the European Perspective. Technology, Innovation and Policy*, Heidelberg/New York: Physica-Verlag, **14**, pp. S53–S68.

Sundbo, J. and Gallouj, F. (2000), 'Innovation as a Loosely Couple System in Services', in J.S. Metcalfe and I. Miles (eds.) *Innovation Systems in the Service Economy*, Dordrecht: Kluwer.

Tether, B.S. and Swann, G.M.P. (2003), 'Services, Innovation and the Science Base: an Investigation into the UK's "System of Innovation" using Evidence from the UK's Third Community Innovation Survey', *Presented at International Workshop on Innovation in Europe: Empirical Studies on Innovation Surveys and Economic Performance*, January, Rome: Institute of Socio-Economic Studies on Innovation and Research Policy, National

Research Council, ISPRI-CNR and University of Urbino, Faculty of Economics.

Tether, B.S., Miles, I., Blind, K., Hipp, C., de Liso, N. and Cainelli, G. (2001),'Innovation in Services – An Analysis of CIS-2 data on Innovation in the Service Sector', *A Report for the European Commission (under CIS-Contact 98/184)*, A version of this report is available as CRIC Working Paper No. 10.

Tidd, J. and Hull, F. (2002), 'Organizing for Service Innovation: Best-practice or Configurations?', *SPRU Electronic Working Papers Series*, Brighton/New York: SPRU/Fordham University, Graduate Business School, No. 77.

Tordoir, P.P. (1996), *The Professional Knowledge Economy: The Management and Integration of Professional Services in Business Organizations*, Dordrecht: Kluwer Academic.

van der Meer, H. (2007), 'Open Innovation – The Dutch Treat: Challenges in Thinking in Business Models', *Creativity and Innovation Management*, **16** (2), pp. 192–202.

West, J. and Gallagher, S. (2006), 'Challenges of Open Innovation: the Paradox of Firm Investment in Open-source Software', *R&D Management*, **36** (3), pp. 319–331.

West, J. and Lakhani, K. (2008), 'Getting Clear about the Role of Communications in Open Innovation', *Industry and Innovation*, **15** (3), May.

Wong, P.K. and He, Z.L. (2002), 'Determinants of Innovation: The Impacts of Client Linkages and Strategic Orientations', *CET Working Paper, Centre for Entrepreneurship,* Kent Ridge Singapore: National University of Singapore.

PART ONE

Traditional Industries

2 Roles of KISA in Aquaculture in Norway[1]

Heidi Wiig Aslesen

The main focus of this chapter is on knowledge intensive service activities (KISA) in the aquaculture industry in Norway. One of the main objectives of the study is to provide insights into how aquaculture firms maintain and develop productive and innovative capabilities through utilisation of KISA, provided by internal and/or external sources. The main research questions are: What internal and external competencies do firms use in innovation, and how are these competencies used to build the firm-specific knowledge and skill base needed to facilitate learning and innovation processes? The main finding is that the use of knowledge intensive service activities and their role in innovation differs according to firms' knowledge base and type of organisation. A general finding is that many of the aquaculture firms' internal knowledge intensive services are at the minimum. The dynamics and quality of interaction between competence suppliers and receivers (the aquaculture firms) seem to be important. Many of the interviewed firms have a focus on minimising fixed cost, internal KISA are often very slim, making it hard to have the appropriate knowledge management practices to maintain new knowledge in the organisation – if external KISA are used in the first place. As such, the ability of external KISA to influence aquaculture firms' knowledge generating processes might vary enormously. The study concludes with three general policy suggestions on how to develop KISA in order to build innovation capability of firms in the aquaculture industry.

INTRODUCTION

Knowledge intensive services are seen to have an increased importance for learning and innovation activity in a more knowledge-based economy. Firms have increasing need for knowledge intensive services (Daniels and Bryson, 2002). These services can come from many sources and can be transmitted to firms in many ways. Firms' ability to interpret, absorb and use knowledge inputs is of importance to firms' ability to innovate and grow.

The main focus in this chapter is on KISA in the aquaculture industry in Norway. Studies of KISA are seen as relevant in order to gain a deeper understanding of the role of knowledge intensive services in innovation processes in general.

One of the main objectives of this chapter is to provide insights into how aquaculture firms maintain and develop productive and innovative capabilities through utilisation of KISA. The main research questions is: What internal and external competencies do firms use when innovating, and how are these competencies used to build the firm-specific knowledge and skill base needed to facilitate learning and innovation processes? Further, the aim of this chapter is to analyse the use of KISA among different types of aquaculture firms.

The chapter is organised as follows; the next section will give a brief introduction to the aquaculture industry in Norway and its economic role. Thereafter the analysis of use of KISA for innovation in aquaculture will be presented, using a typology of aquaculture firms in order to present the analysis. The last sections present the policy suggestions based on the findings of KISA in aquaculture, followed by a short summary.

AQUACULTURE IN NORWAY

Aquaculture is the farming of aquatic organisms including fish, and Norway is one of the world's main farmers of aquacultured Atlantic salmon and trout, which will be the focus of this chapter.

Aquaculture implies some sort of intervention in the rearing process to enhance production, such as regular stocking, feeding, protection from predators, and so on; the management of an aquaculture system is a balance of many elements. Aquaculture is often viewed as a low tech activity, and indeed, in many countries fish farming is carried out with very few resources. However, large global commercial players have developed well functioning sectoral innovation systems (Aslesen, 2009) where all parts of the value chain are highly knowledge intensive and integrated. In modern aquaculture, development is now a joint effort between farmers, investment concerns, equipment manufacturers, service suppliers, scientists and government (FAO, 2009:158).

The aquaculture industry in Norway employed approximately 4870 persons in 2008, having had a 37 per cent increase the last ten years. Even though the number of employees working with salmon and trout in Norway is relatively low, the aquaculture industry's contribution to gross domestic product (GDP) was in 2007 USD 3 billion. Apart from the direct effect of the industry on

Norwegian employment and growth, the sector has an indirect effect on other industries as it is dependent on several input factors such as feed, vaccination, technical equipment and so on, in order to operate: Every person year in the aquaculture industry creates 1.7 person years in other industries (Sandberg et al, 2009). The sector is especially important for employment and economic activity in the more peripheral parts of Norway.

The total sale of farmed fish in Norway has risen dramatically the last years, and the production has more than doubled the last ten years. The production cost per kilogram of Atlantic salmon and trout has steadily decreased from 1991 until 2009, starting at USD 7.3 in 2008-value in 1991, being USD 2.3 in 2008-value in 2007. This suggests an impressive gain of efficiency in the period, suggesting the adoption of new technologies and learning within the aquaculture during the years. The cost of production declined steadily up until the year 2000, where reduction in production costs slowed because the most obvious sources of farm-level cost reduction had been exhausted (Tveterås and Kvaløy, 2004:11). In 2009, processing and distribution to customers were particular target areas for further cost reduction in the value chain.

The industry is very export-oriented and very cyclical, its export ratios varying across the year and between years. Only oil and gas, and 'other means of transport', have more variation in exports (Sandberg et al 2005). Norwegian exports amounted to USD 6.3 billion in 2008, setting a new seafood export record for the fourth year running. Fish from the salmon family are exported from Norway to 98 countries. France is the largest market, which in 2008 bought Norwegian salmon and trout for USD 0.52 billion, accounting for 17 per cent of total sales of Atlantic salmon (The Norwegian Seafood Export Council, 2008), followed by Poland, Russia and Denmark.

Norwegian fish farmers have become more internationalised over the past few years, investing in fish farms in other countries, especially Scotland, The Faroe Islands, USA, and Chile. Norwegian farmers are now operating within important, external markets, often with Norwegian nationals placed in key positions in the new company. Aquaculture of salmonids in other countries has to varying degrees relied on Norwegian expertise and technology. Olafsen et al (2006) have estimated that the export value of marine expertise such as deliverables from 'Suppliers', 'Research, Development and Educational institutions' and 'Other knowledge-intensive services' amounted to USD 0.62 billion in 2005, representing 10 per cent of total marine export value. According to Olafsen et al (2006) this segment could increase its share of marine exports to 25 per cent by 2025.

THE ROLE OF KISA IN AQUACULTURE

The analysis of KISA in the aquaculture industry is based on 25 in-depth firm interviews. Based on the study by Aslesen et al (2002) firms in the sector were divided into four different categories, according to their knowledge base and ways of organising business activity. This categorisation has been used in order to understand KISA strategies. The dimension with regard to knowledge base were chosen since by understanding the structure of the knowledge base one might understand the types of interactive learning processes that firms are able to take part in and determine whether there are recognisable patterns of interaction that evolve as a consequence of this. The aquaculture firms' knowledge bases are either synthetic (practical and experienced based) or analytical (innovation based on use of new scientific or technological knowledge) (Asheim and Gertler, 2005). The other dimension relates to the organization of the firms: whether it is unstructured (few formal structures) or more functionally divided organisation. This analytical grip gives four different types of firms in the aquaculture industry in Norway (see Table 2.1): 'The family firm', 'the coastal enterprise', 'the research-based entrepreneur' and 'the science-based process industry'. This categorization will be used to discuss the findings from the explorative study of aquaculture firms' use of KISA in innovation according to three main research questions:

1. Why do firms use different KISA and what kind of KISA do they use?
2. When do firms use different KISA?
3. How do firms interact (co-production) with KISA?

Table 2.1 Types of aquaculture firms

Knowledge base Organisation	Practical/learning by doing. Incremental, reactive innovation strategy	Scientific knowledge base. Radical and proactive innovation strategy
Entrepreneurial, ad-hoc	'The family firm'	'The research-based entrepreneur'
Structured management system	'The coastal enterprise'	'Science-based process industry'

Source: adopted from Aslesen et al, 2002; Aslesen, 2004

The three main research questions why, when and how in relation to KISA and innovation where understood as:

1. Why (or why not) are knowledge intensive activities used in firms learning and innovation processes? Do all types of firm use KISA in these processes, and if they do, what types of KISA do they emphasise? The

firms were presented with different possible types of KISA:

- Research KISA;
- Development KISA;
- ICT development KISA;
- Legal KISA;
- Banking and financial KISA;
- Accounting and auditing KISA;
- KISA related to organizational development and strategy;
- KISA related to marketing and sales; and
- KISA related to management and training.

Who are the most important providers of such knowledge intensive services to aquaculture firms? Firms were asked about the following providers:

- Internal KISA: service providers inside the organisation often organised as separate departments or units or sometimes only single persons providing services to the companies different business units;
- KISA from the enterprise level;
- Knowledge Intensive Business Services (KIBS): private sector firms providing knowledge based services to other business and non-business organisations, and the knowledge they provide is strategic, technical and professional advice mainly employing the skills of information gathering, processing, and in particular interpretation of information;
- Research and technology organisations (RTOs): specialised providers that offer service as their core business and are public or semi public organisations;
- Network KISA: actors that are part of a companies' vertical linkages, such as different kinds of suppliers and customers. In this definition, we have also included firms that are part of the network of similar actors, such as competitors. This network is loosely structured around the company.

2. When are these different knowledge intensive services used as part of the aquaculture firms' innovation effort, and when have the firms chosen to either internalise or externalise these knowledge intensive services?

3. How is the mix and match of internal and external KISA used in innovation projects?

The next section presents the results and discussion of the analysis.

MAPPING KISA IN DIFFERENT FIRM TYPES

The why, when and how questions are answered for the four different categories of aquaculture firms presented in Table 2.1. However, these are stylised categories; in practice many firms will possibly be found in the intersection between the categories.

Types and Providers of KISA

'The family firm' is a firm that lacks organisational maturity and professional management. Practical and experience-based knowledge of the workers is the most important input into processes of change in these firms. The KISA issues in these firms are rather: Why do you not use/use so little KISA in your internal learning and innovation processes? The answer is that these firms engage in few innovation projects of a more profound nature. When these firms innovate it is through practical knowledge. These firms relate to few external KISA suppliers as they seldom encompass the internal resources (absorptive capacity) or the time or money to relate to a broad set of KISA actors.

KISA in 'The family firm' are mainly used for development purposes and in relation to daily operation of core activities. When problems arise that the firms cannot solve themselves, these actors will primarily draw on competence from suppliers of feed, equipment (also information and communication technology – ICT) and medication as well as their competitors (similar firms – network KISA). The firm will also take part in development projects with actors in their vertical network and is given valuable KISA of practical and experience-based nature (as opposed to scientific) that will affect the direction of their development activities. The network KISA related to adjustments and incremental development activities (especially technologically related) are a very important external KISA for innovation.

Financial KISA are provided by the banks, very often the local banks. Accounting and auditing are by most of the firms externalised or a combination of internal and external service provision. These kinds of KISA are seen to have little impact on firms' innovation activity per se. Banks and other financial institutions thus constitute an important framework for the innovative activities of the aquaculture firms, and it is an external KISA activity that all types of firms draw on, and in some companies this is in fact the only external professional KISA in operation.

Some companies wanted, as far as possible, to only relate to internal KISA in order to have full control over the running of the enterprise. When external KISA were used, it was explained by the companies' lack of relevant internal competence. One small company expressed concern about the fact that they, on the whole, used one single external KISA supplier, and as such did not know if they obtained 'the best' services. Another company argued that external KISA suppliers made the company somewhat vulnerable, since '…the nature of consultants is to "steal" knowledge for the purpose of selling it to other customers' suggesting scepticism shared by many of the interviewed firms in this category.

'The coastal enterprise' is a large multinational firm with departments worldwide. The firm has a professional middle management, which also possesses to some extent practical experience. Even though this type of firm do have more internal KISA than 'the family firm' it still has a small and effective administration and a lean organisation, meaning that they do not encompass all needed KISA internally. Pressures towards increased efficiency and adjustment to lower prices mean that internal KISA has been regarded as a luxury. One might say that these actors do relate to all different kinds of KISA suppliers, besides those that represent more formalised RTOs. The reason for this is that these firms do not base their activity on formalised codified knowledge, but on more practical and experience-based knowledge. KISA related to development activity, to organisational change and strategy, marketing, and sales are activities that are close to core activity and therefore held at some level.

Development KISA are the most important KISA in relation to innovation in 'the coastal enterprise' and is carried out in much the same manner as within the 'family firm'. As in the case of the 'family firm', the network of suppliers and similar firms in the cluster are the most important external KISA for innovation. Most of the 'the coastal enterprises' interviewed purchase ICT development services from external KISA providers like KIBS in the private market; there are often interactive learning processes going on between the internal and external KISA related to ICT development especially on the production side of fish farming related to feeding and production of fish. The development project is often a collaborative effort between software companies, suppliers of equipment and the aquaculture firm, suggesting that the mix and match of internal and external KISA are important factors in relation to innovation in this area. The software solutions, in combination with the technological equipment, are therefore important in the reorganisation and improvement of the production side of fish farming and therefore have an important role in relation to operational processes within the aquaculture firm.

KISA related to organisational and strategy development is characterised as the most important innovation knowledge the last years by some of the larger actors interviewed. Among 'the family firms' and the 'coastal enterprise' there is little tradition of purchasing services related to 'softer' tasks (management and organisational KISA) in the company. Thus it is interesting to note that many companies believe that they will experience an increasing need for external KISA in these areas in the future: The crises that have taken place are in many ways due to the fact that it has been an infant sector lacking sufficient control over the value chain. Companies are asking for more research activity from external research and development (R&D) actors within the area of 'soft innovations' like organisational and strategic development. KISA related to marketing and sales have a particular focus today, as aquaculture firms have come to realise that a narrow focus on production and volume has failed. Many aquaculture firms have altered their organisations in such a way as to allow the market significant influence over production. In one of the companies interviewed a total reorganisation of the enterprise had taken place in the direction of making marketing and sales the main line of activity within the organisation. The focus was now 'to whom shall we sell and how much', rather than 'producing as much as possible' within the licences held. KISA derived from the market side will then become the most important innovation input.

Many of the firms developed the skills of employees by training services obtained from external expert services, either provided by the enterprise group, by Higher Education Institutions (HEIs) or by KIBS.

'The research-based entrepreneur' is a firm often at the research frontier within their field. Many of these firms have a specialisation in relation to feed or fish health and some of the firms can be categorised as biotechnology firms. 'New' knowledge is the driving force of the firms' investments/business activities, these firms therefore use research KISA, legal and banking KISA. 'The research-based entrepreneur' focus solely on their core activity, which is research linked to parts of the value chain in aquaculture. The focus is on scientific and technological knowledge generation. These firms use external research KISA (directly from research institutes, universities, laboratories and so on) when they do not encompass all the needed facilities or knowledge to carry out the project internally. 'The research-based entrepreneurs' think differently with regard to the purchase of external KISA. Important reasons given were lack of facilities needed to carry out in-house research. Time constraints internally are also mentioned as a reason for drawing on external KISA actors. The different externalisation strategies related to R&D KISA can be through outsourcing, sub-contracting, joint-ventures or strategic alliances. 'The research-based entrepreneurs' need to include external knowledge by RTOs and therefore pursues interactive learning processes with external KISA that leads to innovations of a more radical nature.

Some very competent research-based firms systematically protect their inventions by use of secrecy and more formal intellectual property rights (IPR) protection. In that way legal KISA are important for these actors. The existence of 'research-based entrepreneurs' is very much dependent on the availability of risk capital put into companies with a potential for growth and profitability. Venture capital firms may contribute with both capital and competence to companies; however, few venture funds have had the marine sector as its core area of investment.

Firms that represent the 'science-based process industry' are often part of a large corporate structure with all of the different KISA activities internalised to some degree or found within the enterprise structure (or holding company). These firms integrate KISA from the whole value chain, and have the resources available to privatise and control both formalised knowledge generation and its practical application.

The 'science-based process industry' firms are able to use all different kinds of KISA that can match internal KISA, also research KISA. However these firms are also restricted by the pressure towards reducing operating costs. These firms have reached a maturity, which has made them more conscious in relation to what KISA they should have internally and which they should outsource. The increased complexity, structural changes and the general pace of change in society may force these firms to use external KISA to a larger degree than today. Among other things, the constant demand from public authorities, finance institutions and the market are reasons to buy KISA. They usually have a global search for the best actors to supply them with external KISA.

Critical factors for fostering innovation are to hold a sufficient mass of competent research KISA internally. The research activity must be focused, since R&D activities are specialised and need to be viewed as 'state of the art' within their fields. These firms have an offensive, systematic and long-term innovation strategy, which implies great risks with regard to outcome. With regard to internalising research KISA the companies believe that they themselves knew their own research needs, and that internalization provided more transparency in the research process – one may talk openly to all participants in projects without being limited by confidentiality concerns. There may be some risk involved for a research unit to incorporate an external KISA provider, because the learning acquired by the external KISA provider may benefit a competitor. The risk is greater where the aquaculture firm exerts relative control over an area, but less significant in situations of uncertainty.

These companies may not be as dependent on network KISA or the collective knowledge base of the cluster as the other aquaculture firms. This means that the free and accessible knowledge through network KISA are of less importance and these actors therefore may to a lesser extent participate in informal networks in the cluster. Firms with research activity will thus have incentives to hold on to their knowledge. Legal KISA may play an important role in maintaining the competitive advantage of being the 'first mover' in relation to the development of a product or process. This function is served through obtaining copyright on products or processes, and thereby temporarily obstructing others copying their ideas into which significant developing funds have been allocated.

Mergers and acquisitions, changes in ownership, challenges in relation to the market seem to involve the demand for external KISA provision for these firms. For the 'science-based process industry' it seems relevant to use KIBS that had experience on an international level to produce 'benchmarks' and give assessment of the international situation. The emphasis on KISA with marketing and sales as driving principle is considered to be the locomotive of organisational innovations in many of the companies analysed. It is therefore an example of how different knowledge intensive services activities of relevance to innovation have become intertwined, both KISA related to organisation, strategy, finance as well as in relation to marketing and sales.

Table 2.2 lists in each quadrant the different categories of aquaculture firms and the types of KISA they report through the interviews that they use and who (either externally or internally) provide for each type of KISA.

KISA for Innovation

'The family firm' has a rather limited scope of KISA search, both geographically and functionally. These firms are in search for trustworthy KISA providers which know their industry, and with good quality. From the interviews it seems that many of these companies have had bad experiences with regard to the use of external consultants not familiar with the aquaculture industry. External development KISA, gained through the companies' network of similar firms and suppliers of feed and equipment, are the main and most important KISA for these firms' innovation efforts. The collaborative projects are initiated when a problem arises and decisions are taken swiftly, the knowledge used is mostly practical and experienced based. These firms seldom engage in long-term strategic development projects with KISA suppliers. Today a large number of these 'family firm' are owned by large corporations and many of these functions as professional KISA suppliers to their subsidiaries. They offer services in relation to ICT-systems, judicial advice, financial services and engage in organisational development. This constitutes, for the subsidiaries, a type of external KISA 'imposed' by the mother companies.

None of the respondents representing 'the coastal enterprise' respondents saw external KISA as a driving force for innovation in the firm. Apart from the interactive learning processes gained through development projects with suppliers, customers and similar firms (network KISA) few of the respondents considered that external KISA contribute too much learning that goes into the core activity of the firm. External providers rather supply KISA of relevance to support the firms' innovation efforts by giving direction or type of innovation to engage in through their knowledge from other countries or markets. KISA acquired through global KIBS can be used to benchmarking their own activity with related industries. These firms seem to be more integrated in the national production and innovation system, and therefore potentially might have more knowledge intensive service input into their organisation than 'the family firm'. However, since the 'coastal enterprise' also base their innovation on practical and experience-based knowledge, parts of the knowledge infrastructure is still not integrated in their innovation efforts, possibly challenging the innovation potential for these firms in the long run.

Table 2.2 Types of KISA used and relevant KISA providers by categories of firms

Type of firm	KISAs	Network KISA	KISA Providers
Family [Practical/learning by doing. Incremental, reactive innovation strategy; Entrepreneurial, ad-hoc]	Development KISA and ICT development KISA Banking and financial KISA Accounting and auditing KISA KISA providers KISA from enterprise level	Must have Local KIBS (auditing, finance)	
Research-based entrepreneur [Scientific knowledge base. Radical and proactive innovation strategy; Entrepreneurial, ad-hoc]	Research KISA Legal KISA Banking and financial KISA (venture capitalists) KISA providers	KISA from enterprise level RTOs	
Coastal enterprise [Practical/learning by doing. Incremental, reactive innovation strategy. Structured management System]	Development KISA ICT development KISA Banking and financial KISA KISA related to organisational development and strategy KISA related to marketing and sales KISA related to management and training		Network KISA National/global KIBS (finance, strategy, training)
Science-based process industry [Scientific knowledge base. Radical and proactive innovation strategy. Structured management System]	Research and development KISA Legal KISA KISA related to finance, organisational development and strategy KISA related to marketing and sales KISA related to management and training		RTO's Network KISA National/global KIBS (finance, strategy, training)

The 'research-based entrepreneurs' emphasised that by buying KISA you are able to obtain the most specialised and competitive knowledge and the professional aquaculture companies purchase KISA from those KISA providers that possess the best competence regardless of location. Many of these aquaculture firms are of the opinion that generally speaking the quality of KIBS companies has improved in recent years.

Firms representing the 'Science-based process industry' have actually established relations with the knowledge infrastructure both through mobility of KIS personnel and through long-term project cooperation. The collaboration projects with network KISA are less important for innovation, but can be seen as important source of input for the research activities carried out in these firms. KISA input from network actors can offset new research tasks internally. These firms also often engage in projects linked to the core knowledge of the supplied products and are not dependent on the suppliers' ability to 'translate' scientific knowledge into practical knowledge (as the 'family firm' or the 'coastal enterprise').

Summing up KISA

The main findings from the analysis are that even if firms belong to the same industry, their use of knowledge intensive services and KISA's role towards innovation does differ according to firms' knowledge base and type of organisation. The dynamics of the interaction between KISA providers and aquaculture firms differ according to these dimensions, and policy directed towards improving innovation capabilities by means of KISA must relate to these important differences between firms.

The most common aquaculture firm in Norway is to be found in the intersection between 'the family firm' and 'the coastal enterprise'. For these firms internal KISA are often at a minimum, suggesting that the level of internal competence able to recognise the value of new information, assimilate it and apply it to commercial ends is limited. However more professional enterprises among these types are focusing especially on competence building by active use of external KISA, raising the standard of internal knowledge intensive services. Having low levels of internal knowledge intensive services affects firms ability to absorb new information and knowledge from external actors, it also restricts the 'set of significant others' that such firms can relate to, and therefore what kinds of knowledge intensive services that can go into innovation processes.

There is a general scepticism towards the use of external KISA as a source of innovation – but external providers are being used to a larger degree than earlier, especially in the fields of development activities (also moving towards more scientific knowledge milieus) linked to product and process innovations (often incremental), in relation to ICT projects, in relation to banking and financial assistance and in relation to accounting and auditing. Some of the 'coastal enterprises' have also been engaged in user oriented R&D projects, where there has been knowledge input from scientific milieus as well. The challenges to 'the family firm' and 'the coastal enterprise' is to develop internal KISA so that they can manage the knowledge and the innovation process associated with the external supply of different KISA of relevance to innovation.

'The research-based entrepreneurs' and 'the scientific process industry' engage in innovation projects of more radical nature employing also scientific knowledge intensive services into the process. 'The research-based entrepreneurs' relate to network KISA providers, to other parts of the enterprise group and to RTOs. The most important KISA for innovation is research KISA, legal KISA, banking and financial KISA. The restructuring of the industry has also contributed to an increase of demand of external knowledge intensive activities in relation to buying and selling of companies. Both 'The research-based entrepreneurs' and 'the scientific process industry' are better able to use externally available information than 'the family firm' and 'the coastal enterprise', possibly a result of the level of competence and absorptive capacity of these firms, making them more able to translate significant knowledge into the innovation process.

In general, the focus on 'soft innovation' inputs is starting to gain importance in the aquaculture industry. When the firms themselves start to focus on the need for such knowledge intensive services, it can be expected that the supply and quality of such services directed towards the industry will increase. By exploring the different types of firms, it seems obvious that there are certain prerequisites with regard to internal knowledge base and degree of professional management that must be in place if successful learning process between KISA providers and aquaculture firms is to happen.

POLICY IMPLICATION FOR KISA USAGE OF AQUACULTURE FIRMS

This section will focus on specific policy proposals related to KISA for the different types of firms. The target groups for policy are the providers of knowledge intensive services in general, or KISA inside any kinds of firms. The objective of policy targeting KISA, provided either internally or externally, is to improve the innovation capability, competitiveness and efficiency of private firms and public organisations. The focus on knowledge intensive service activities is not an aim in itself; it is a mean to achieve the objective of more innovation, competitiveness and so on.

Differentiated Policy

'The family firms' need to be motivated to strengthen their innovation capability by focusing on competence building of existing internal KISA with special focus on training of employees. 'Soft innovations' generated by focusing on organisational development/strategy, training and project management are only to a limited degree regarded as useful and the firms seldom have the resources, time, or motivation to focus seriously on 'soft innovations'. These firms also need to expand their external linkages, and it seems to be important to use mediators for that purpose since these firms are small and have a limited search radius. Substantial cultural- and language-related barriers must be overcome in the family firm, if more widespread use of KISA is to be achieved, both internally and externally.

The larger degree of maturity in the organisation and the larger degree of vertical integration into the market has made it necessary for 'the coastal enterprise' to respond to a larger and more integrated set of demands from customers and the market than earlier. Links between knowledge areas are getting stronger; consumer acceptance as well as production costs are influenced by health considerations. To handle such complexities in an industry that expands, there is no escape from developing a broad set of internal KISA and to expand external relations, especially to R&D institutions and public authorities as well as to higher education institutions. Many firms lack the necessary internal KISA and resources to make responses, especially to market signals. This is a hampering factor with regard to innovation. 'The coastal enterprises' have become dependent on their external KISA providers, especially the network KISAs, to be fully able to understand production processes and to be able to control the value chain. Policy of importance to these firms should therefore be directed at stimulating their internal KISA in areas of business development with a special focus on marketing and sales. Efforts should also be directed towards raising more analytical knowledge to gain better understanding of how to use research as a tool for product and process development, and to link this with future market demands. There are few KISA suppliers in the market serving the aquaculture sector alone, according to some of the companies interviewed. Few public programmes are directed towards developing 'soft' innovation of relevance to the industry. Rather programmes seem to have a narrow focus on technological development.

'The research-based entrepreneurs' often lack internal KISA in relation to business strategy and marketing skills (more commercial knowledge). 'The research-based entrepreneur' takes part in capital-intensive and time-consuming projects and the interviews revealed that these firms are in need of long-term and knowledge intensive capital often provided by venture capitalists (KIBS). The firms stated that there were few such actors in Norway. However, the greatest problem in the Norwegian aquaculture sector related to salmon and trout is that there are few research-based entrepreneurs. There is a difficulty in moving people out from RTOs and into the business world. There is a lack of focus on important KISA activities like strategic, technical and professional advice on how to run a business (or to be an entrepreneur) in research institutes and universities. These are KISA activities that need to be developed and supplied towards RTOs in order to see the spin-off of more entrepreneur-based firms that also are able to commercialise their new knowledge.

'Science-based process industries' are uncommon in Norwegian aquaculture today. It appears that the main impetus to create integrated operations in which heterogeneous knowledge and scientific knowledge relevant at all stages in the value chain, from microbiology to marketing, comes from international firms establishing themselves in the aquaculture industry by way of acquisitions. These firms main KISA input comes from R&D efforts, and therefore the most important policy discussion held with these actors were related to public R&D policy. Firstly, confidentiality is impossible in a system where numerous actors are involved in evaluating the content of applications and their fundability. Secondly, existing policy tools were only to a limited degree directed at firms with large internal research KISA. Most of the existing policy tools are directed towards SMEs that are not capable of carrying out internal research themselves or lack external linkages.

What kinds of tools should be directed towards the drivers in the industry? Suggestions from the interviewed firms in relation to the strengthening of internal KISA were to:

1. Provide research departments in private companies with the same funding (basis research funding, strategic program funding and so on) as is available to public and semi-public actors.
2. Direct efforts at strengthening the internal KISA of these companies by allowing them access to literature databases and libraries in the same way as universities.

These companies also state more generally that existing policy initiatives are too bureaucratic.

CONCLUSION

This chapter has presented a study of the Norwegian aquaculture industry and its use of KISA. The focus has been on the use of KISA in building innovation capability in the industry. The chapter has identified how different knowledge intensive service activities play different roles in firms' innovation processes. The chapter has also showed that within the same industry, the types of KISA used both internally and externally, differs greatly. Aquaculture firms differ with regard to innovation strategies and with regard to their use of the production and innovation system, therefore KISA play different roles in firms' learning processes, and the reasons for why, when and how KISA are used differs.

To make relevant policies in relation to firms' innovation strategies and to the use of KISA for innovation, it is necessary to take these differences into consideration. The analysis of KISA in building innovation capability can be used in order to focus public policy to the providers of KISA in general and on KISA inside of firms. Policy can be used to stimulate the supply, demand and the network between actors and activities both internal and external to the firm, and the analysis in this chapter has showed that this needs to be done differently for the different types of firms in the aquaculture industry.

The overall policy suggestions targeting KISA to improve innovation capability, competitiveness and efficiency in aquaculture firms must primarily be related to:

1. Strengthening the internal knowledge intensive service activities in aquaculture firms by mapping actual needs in relation to innovation efforts. The needs refer to 'softer innovation' inputs connected with: general business competence, commercialisation, marketing and sales. The need for internal KISA differs depending on type of firms. Financial restraints appear to be a hampering factor with regard to strengthen internal KISA.

2. Stimulate quality of supply of external KISA. The knowledge base of local KISA providers must be based on scientific knowledge, this requires the actors having the ability to convert this knowledge into practical oriented knowledge that the aquaculture firms can relate to. Since these external KISA providers have the potential to stimulate innovation in firms, it is important that they are up-to-date in their field of action and that they identify KISA needs in relation to innovation in their customer firms.

3. Proactive broking between aquaculture firms and relevant external KISA providers is important. There is a need for networking between aquaculture firms and external KISA especially in the field of general business competence. A general scepticism towards external consultants, with lack of industry specific knowledge, is hampering the potential for mix and

match of internal and external KISA with positive impact on internal learning and innovation.

The implication of these findings is that policy initiatives must be differentiated according to the different types of aquaculture firms in order to improve KISA in the Norwegian aquaculture industry.

NOTE

1. This chapter is based on work reported in Aslesen, 2004 and OECD (2004, 2005, 2006). The description of the KISA approach owes much to work done by Jari Kuusisto from the Finnish Institute for Enterprise Management in the OECD KISA project. The KISA project was one of three case studies in innovation launched by the Working Party on Innovation and Technology Policy in OECD to further develop the national innovation system approach. Kuusisto was the researcher organising the final report from the project. The KISA project originated in AEGIS research centre of the University of Western Sydney (Australia).

REFERENCES

Asheim, B.T. and Gertler, M. (2005), 'The Geography of Innovation: Regional Innovation Systems', in J. Fagerberg, D.C. Mowery, and R.R. Nelson, (eds) *The Oxford Handbook of Innovation.* Oxford University Press, Oxford, pp. 291–317.

Aslesen, H.W. (2004), *Knowledge Intensive Service Activities and Innovation in the Norwegian Aquaculture Industry.* STEP report 05-2004, STEP-Centre for Innovation Research, Oslo.

Aslesen, H.W. (2009), 'The Innovation System of Norwegian Aquacultured Salmonids', in J. Fagerberg, D. Mowery, and B. Verspagen, (ed.) *Innovation, Path Dependency and Policy: The Norwegian Case*, Oxford University Press, Oxford and New York.

Aslesen, H.W., Mariussen, Å., Olafsen, T., Winther, U. and Ørstavik, F. (2002), *Innovasjonssystemet i norsk havbruksnæring*, STEP report 16/2002. STEP, Oslo.

Daniels, P.W. and Bryson, J.R. (2002), 'Manufacturing Services and Servicing Manufacturing: Knowledge-based Cities and Changing Forms of Production', *Urban Studies,* **39** (5–6), pp. 977–991.

Food and Agriculture Organization (FAO) (2009), *The State of World Fisheries and Aquaculture 2008*, FAO Fisheries and Aquaculture Department, Food and Agriculture Organisation of the United Nations, Rome.

Norwegian Seafood Export Council (2008), *Statistical Overview 2008*, Norwegian Seafood Export Council (NSEC), www.seafood.no/binary?id =106774.

Olafsen, T., Sandberg, M.G., Senneset, G., Ellingsen, H., Almås, K., Winther, U. and Svennevig, N. (2006), *Exploitation of Marine Living Resources – Global Opportunities for Norwegian Expertise*, report from a working group appointed by DKNVS and NTVA.

Organisation for Economic Co-operation and Development (OECD) (2004), *Knowledge Intensive Services in Innovation: The Changing Role of KISA in the Innovation System*, Interim report. DSTI/STP/TIP (2004) 8. Working party on Innovation and Technology Policy 7–8 June 2004, OECD, Paris.

Organisation for Economic Co-operation and Development (OECD) (2005), *The Role of Knowledge-intensive Service Activities (KISA) in Innovation: Draft Synthesis Report*, DSTI/STP/TIP (2004) 6. Working party on Innovation and Technology Policy 9-10 June 2005, OECD, Paris.

Organisation for Economic Co-operation and Development (OECD) (2006), *Innovation and Knowledge Intensive Service Activities*, OECD, Paris.

Sandberg, M.G., Olafsen, T., Sætermo, I.A., Vik, L.H. and Nowak, M. (2005), *Betydningen av fiskeri- og havbruksnæringen for Norge – en ringvirkningsanalyse 2004*, Sintef Report.

Sandberg, M.G., Volden, G.H., Aarhus, J.I., Hoffman, M. and Olafsen, T. (2009), *Betydningen av fiskeri- og havbruksnæringen for Norge – en ringvirkningsanalyse 2007*, Sintef Fiskeri og Havbruk Report.

Tveterås, R. and Kvaløy, O. (2004), *Vertical Coordination in the Salmon Supply Chain*, Centre for Research in Economics and Business Administration,Working Paper No. 7/04.

3 The Role of KISA in Basic Agro-food Processes Innovation: the Case of Orange Packers in Eastern Spain[1]

José Albors-Garrigos

The relevance of innovation in services has been outlined by the knowledge-intensive business services (KIBS) concept, which has been empirically and theoretically developed in the context of service innovation. The conceptual and methodology approach of knowledge-intensive service activities (KISA) links the production of knowledge to innovative activities, and has become a relevant focus for the analysis of innovation within a firm. Though relatively new, it has received a great deal of attention from practitioners and academics in the last five years.

This chapter will explore, analyse, and compare the ways in which knowledge intensive activities occur in a small cluster of mature and low-tech industries: orange and lemon selection in Spain. The chapter aims to assess the impact of KISA on the firm's innovation and performance, as well as to analyse whether KISA occurrence is correlated with certain characteristics of firms such as size, organisational profile, market focus, and other characteristics. A model correlating these variables will additionally be proposed and validated.

INTRODUCTION

The introduction to this book dealt in detail with the definitions of KIBS, KIS and KISA. Tether (2003) has analysed innovation dynamics in services and classified them into three sectors: traditional, systemic, and knowledge-based. In this chapter we are concerned with the third sector, because of its relevance to the creation and transfer of knowledge and innovation through its support of innovative activities across a wide range of other business fields. Likewise, we are interested in its interconnecting role among the various clusters (Kuusisto and Meyer, 2003).

The impact of KISA or KIS on the industry has been the subject of numerous papers which take the empirical more than the academic approach. The case of high-tech industries has been highlighted by a number of authors (Shan Hu, et al, 2006). Others have analysed its impact on software services (Martinez-Fernandez and Miles, 2006; Martinez-Fernandez and Krishna, 2006, Williams, 2006; Rajala et al, 2008), or medium-tech industries (Albors et al, 2008), tourism services (Touburn, 2004; Collado, 2005) health services (Kivisaari et al, 2004), aquaculture (Aslesen, 2004), mining (Martinez-Fernandez, 2005), traditional industries (Ebersberger, 2004), and manufacturing (Lee, 2004). In previous research, we have analysed how the level or influence of KISA in medium-tech industries, is related to innovation, competitive advantages, and economic performance outputs, as well as to its customer focus (Albors, et al, 2008). The impact of KIS on international competitiveness has been analyzed by Windrum and Tomlinson (1999). The role of KIS in facilitating small and medium enterprise (SME) employment growth, competitiveness, and innovation has been pointed out by Hauknes (1999). Drejer and Vinding (2005), on the other hand, have analysed the influence of geographical distance in the use of KIS by firms.

KISA need inter-firm relationships. In the case of the firms covered by our research, a firm's relational capabilities are fundamental to achieving competitive advantages and export success. Firms must look beyond their boundaries and tap into the distinctive competencies of external factors such as distributors, competitors, suppliers, and other actors (Ling-Yee, and Ogunmokun, 2001; Mcevily and Marcus, 2005; Mcevily and Zaheer, 1999). Moreover, when firms are clustered, firm-specific characteristics, such as absorption capacity or relational capabilities, interact with the cluster resources and produce a synergic effect (Hervas and Albors, 2008).

Following this line of reasoning, we must consider that linkages with local knowledge institutions constitute one of the key elements for the development of new knowledge by firms. Thus, local entities such as R&D centres or universities can support these tasks (Rosenberg and Nelson, 1994). In addition, empirical evidence shows that the proximity of local universities with firms promotes the exchange of ideas (Lindelöf and Löftsen, 2004) and improves the performance of innovative firms (Hanel and St-Pierre, 2006).

Absorptive capacity is defined as the 'rate or quantity of scientific or technological information that a firm can absorb' (Cohen and Levinthal 1990) and which 'can be acquired, assimilated, transformed and exploited' (Zahra and George, 2002). Previous research supports the idea that absorptive capacity is crucial to the effective exportation of external know-how and in obtaining the benefit from complementarities between internal and external resources such as KISA (Hervas and Albors, 2008). Miles (2005b) has also suggested the interrelation between KIS and the firms' absorptive capacity, and Ducatel (2000) has outlined absorptive capacity in the context of IT use. Despite all these, however, there is still a gap in the literature pertaining to KISA, particularly at the micro-level of firms, which this chapter will try to fill.[2]

Finally, some authors (Humphrey and Schmitz, 2002) have analysed the inclusion of firms in the global value chains and the role of local networking and cluster linkages in their upgrading. The industry's (in our case, the citrus sector's) position in the global value chain and the upgrading implications on the firms (Cadilhon et al, 2003; Gereffi et al, 2005) has also been considered as a competitive contribution of KISA (that is innovation and marketing). In our case, upgrading must be based on reinforcing the local governance of firms by active inter-firm cooperation, as well as active cooperation with local institutions. Moreover, innovative activities through learning by doing and spreading innovation in the cluster are fundamental to the upgrading process.

The global processes related to the citrus value chain involve production and product development, as well as delivery to the final consumers. Value-chain analysis, which includes the whole cycle, provides a tool for mapping the governance drives of the chain and outlines both intra-firm organisation dynamics and relationships between firms (Kaplinsky, 2004). It also points out the need to address the ways in which poorer producers and countries connect with producers and consumers in the global economy.

RESEARCH OBJECTIVES AND QUESTIONS

Research Objectives

This chapter will analyse the role of KISA in low-tech industries linked to the agro-food processes. It will demonstrate how KISA play a fundamental role in these activities and contribute, not only to innovation activities of firms, but also to the firm's performance.

As input variables, the chapter will analyse internal and external knowledge service activities, as well as other variables that may influence the orientation of KISA, such as the organisational aspects, strategic management approach, human capital, education and training of its personnel, and the relations with other firms or with research centres. Output variables such as economic performance, employment growth, and innovation indicators are also taken into account in the model.

Problems and Questions: Development of Hypotheses

The problems this chapter tries to solve are related to the following questions: Are KISA relevant to low-tech industries? Do they have a significant impact on a firm's innovation? Does it make any difference whether KISA are internal or external to the firm? Which activities are more pertinent for firms? Are the organisational aspects of firms critical to the adoption of KISA? How do KISA relate to the firms' capabilities? How are the different contributions to KISA mixed and matched by the firm? Are the activities contributory to the upgrade of the firm's position in the value chain? How do the capabilities of the firms facilitate the influence of KISA?

Table 3.1 sums up and defines the relevant hypotheses that the research will try to answer. Figure 3.1 schematically shows the proposed model. According to this model, internal and external KISA, undertaken by firms in the low-tech manufacturing sectors, whether in combination with manufactured outputs or as stand-alone services, contribute to the firms' innovative and economic employment growth and performance. KISA's contribution is, however, regulated by the firm's absorptive capacity as measured by the level of skills and education of the employees.

Table 3.1 Research hypotheses

Hypothesis	References
H_1 KISA have a positive influence on manufacturing firms' innovative activities, irrespective of their technology orientation	Albors et al., 2008; Aslesen, 2004; Ebersberger, 2004; Lee, 2004; Miles, 2005b; OECD, 2006
H_2 KISA have a positive influence on low-tech firms' employment growth and economic performance	Albors et al., 2008; Aslesen, 2004; Haataja and Okkonen, 2005; Miles et al., 1995; Windrum and Tomlinson, 1999
H_3 Absorption capacity of firms is a mediating factor in KISA influence	Hervas and Albors, 2008; Miles, 2005b; Ducatel, 2000; Cohen and Levinthal, 1990; Zahra and George, 2002

THE VALUE CHAIN OF THE CITRUS INDUSTRY

Citrus Production in Spain

Figure 3.2 shows the evolution of citrus production, exports, and imports in Spain during the period 2001–2008. Citrus fruit growers in Spain are concentrated along the eastern and the southern coastal areas. Valencia in the east produces approximately 60 per cent of Spain's total citrus production and 96 per cent of the Spanish export facilities.[3] Exports are on average 4–5 per cent of the total Spanish production, and tend to be concentrated in the Valencia region. Similarly, import facilities are concentrated in the region owing to the distribution infrastructure available in the area. Imports basically occur in the spring and summer seasons when oranges and lemons are not available in Spain.

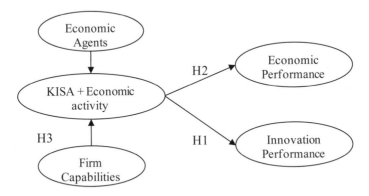

Figure 3.1 KISA and their influence on firms' performance

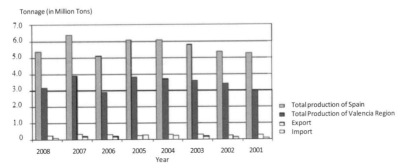

Source: Intercitrus, 2008

Figure 3.2 Evolution of citrus production, exports, and imports in Spain (2001–2008)

An Introduction to the Citrus Industry in Spain

Figure 3.3 sums up the basic steps that form this value chain. The suppliers are either small- or medium-scale farmers working independently or organised as cooperatives, or large producers belonging to groups that have their own export facilities and distribution networks.

The suppliers or farmers grow, pick, and sell the fruits to the selection and packing firms through various types of agreements. Other producers sell their fruits to the processing industry, which transforms them, either into juice, marmalade, or other by-products, depending on the fruit variety. Over the last few years, the international orange juice marketing chain has been marked by different developments, such as the penetration of global beverage brands.

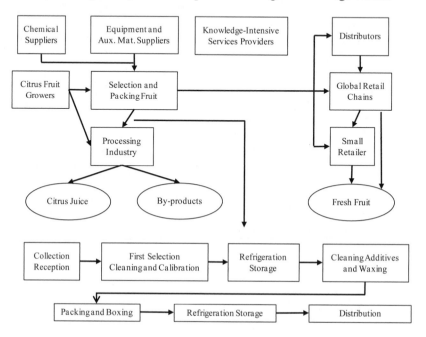

Figure 3.3 The global value chain of the citrus industry: selection and packing subsector process

Some small retailers have their own fruit fields or special agreements with producers. As such, they have the claim to higher-quality products. Recently, the Internet has also facilitated direct distribution from producers to consumers of inorganic chemical-free oranges and lemons. These producers claim that there is a growing market demand for this web-based service.

Distributors and/or agents link the packing firms with the larger global retail chains such as supermarkets, hypermarkets, and other warehouses (Cadilhon, et al, 2003; Gereffi et al, 2005). Some of them have integrated their chains, from the growing fields to the final selling points in Europe or the USA.[4] As citrus products change form and move through various market channels, value is added through labour, capital, and marketing management.

The auxiliary industry is related to input supply businesses that provide fertilizers, chemicals, grove care services, and equipment selection. The latter has lately incorporated more sophisticated hardware such as sensors, electronics, and other hardware, as well as cleaning equipment, waxing, packaging materials, refrigeration and ripening chambers, transportation, and other services and materials. The last phases of the value chain have become critical. Fruits coming from South America and North Africa during the spring and summer seasons in Spain are selected, packed, branded, and exported as indigenous products[5] from Valencia, through the numerous enterprises working in this area.

Our field of study covers a group of packing firms located in the centre of the Valencia Region. This region, where 15 per cent of the Spanish production is concentrated, has a long tradition of citrus exporting. There are approximately 145 firms working in the area. Though it would be difficult to consider them as a cluster, they share the characteristics of local concentration and certain patterns related to customers, suppliers, and others.

These firms tend to hire a high percentage of temporary labour in order to cover their seasonal campaigns because, as mentioned, the fruits are picked according to the campaigns of the various citrus varieties grown in the area. The samples studied covered 122 firms that represent 80 per cent of the firms located in that area.

The average work force of these firms is 60 employees; however, in high seasons they may contract extra manpower, which accounts for 40 per cent of the total. Some firms are managed by the owners, and others hire professional managers. In general, the education profile of the staff is rather low, technically speaking (only 7.1 per cent of the staff has mid- or higher-level degrees). This is a barrier for technology innovation. However, some innovate in terms of processing (30.1 per cent believe their process technology is in the state-of-the-art level). In addition, they hire engineers to oversee this area. Other producers have agreements with research institutes and outsource these tasks. There are two R&D public centres in contact with this cluster: IVIA (Insituto Valenciano de Investigaciones Agronomicas), which is related with agronomical research and IATA (Instituto Agronomico de Tecnologia Alimentaria), which focuses on agro-food research. Overall, practically no firms have their own R&D facilities except for the larger, leading firms.

In general, the size of the firm defines its organisational profile and complexity. Only larger firms have sophisticated organisations with marketing, planning cost control, R&D units, their own distribution channels, and other mechanisms. For this reason, some smaller firms founded a local association, partially supported by the regional government; it owns a dock and a refrigerated warehouse that facilitates export activities, as well as providing health certification. Others have agreements with a local medium-sized trucking company, which has its own European transport structure. As previously mentioned, contacts between firms and suppliers or customers are frequent and are facilitated by local proximity. Nevertheless, and in spite of recommendations to offset their small size, these firms are typically opposed to unified associations such as mergers or joint ventures with competitors.

We have not included the two leading firms in our study because they are not representative of the chosen study subject and would be outliers in the study. Their organisation does shed light on how they have upgraded their position in the value chain and reached their higher hierarchical positions. With a daily production capacity of 2500 tons and a turnover of 100–120 million Euros, they have their own harvesting fields and their activities cover the whole value chain from production (approximately 30 per cent of the total fruit processing), picking, selection, ripening, packaging, and distribution, including a global export network. Their staff could number around 2500 employees, 40 per cent of whom work in the warehouses and packing facilities. Since they have at least 10 production lines, they have incorporated state-of-the-art technology and full automation of their plants and warehouses. Both firms have their own R&D departments where they carry out research on process and product innovation. Furthermore, they have agreements with the two regional R&D centres.

Humphrey and Schmitz (2002) considered that the relationships between buyers (hypermarket chains) and suppliers in citrus packaging firms, with the exception of the largest firms, could be classified as total or quasi-hierarchies, where leading firms directly control the suppliers or completely set the market rules.

RESEARCH AND METHODOLOGY

Field Work

During the first half of 2004, a representative sample of citrus packers in the region was interviewed as part of a regional project supporting SMEs. A total of 122 (84.13 per cent), from a population of 145 firms, agreed to participate in the field work. The contact persons were either the firms' general managers or first line managers. The firms filled in questionnaires and a number of firms (14) were visited personally by the researchers, in order to evaluate the survey more closely. The average size of the staff was 64.75 employees. The size distribution is shown in Figure 3.4. The firms had an average operating experience of 30.8 years.

The survey covered a number of questions. Some questions referred to the firm's organisational characteristics such as size, whether the management was carried out by the owner or a hired professional, the percentage of university graduates among the members of the staff, the firms' employment growth measured by employment, R&D, and internal or external innovative activities. Other questions were included dealing with the number of dedicated full-time staff, local and external commercial contacts as a measure of the firm's network extension and depth, percentage of temporary staff members, number of brandings for product commercialization, marketing external services, grade of innovative equipment such as visual classification, continuous staff training, and other related items.

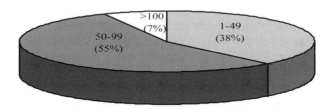

Figure 3.4 Staff size profile of the firms

Variables and Descriptive Results of Field Work

Performance measurement variables

V_1 (Process innovation): Since product innovation is basically carried out by suppliers (citrus growers), innovation in this study is limited to the process.[6] Firms with obsolete process technology and equipment (older than five years) comprise 41.1 per cent, while 36.1 per cent have state-of-the-art technology and equipment. Firms that have acquired recent innovative technology and equipment incorporating some high-tech element such as video-classifying systems accounted for 22.8 per cent.

V_2 (Performance): This variable measures the EBITDA[7] of the firms. Taking the sectoral database profit figures as an average ($x = 3$) and grading this variable from 1 to 5, the sample average was 2.49.

V_3 (Growth): This variable measures the firm's employment variation in the previous five years. Firms that can be classified as stable or had reduced their average workforce accounted for 14.8 per cent, 73.8 per cent had increased their workforce in the range of 1–10 per cent, while 11.5 per cent of the firms had grown over 10 per cent.

V_4 (Export): This indicates the turnover percentage marketed on international markets, the average being 32.5 per cent.

Firm-context variables

V_5 (Size): This refers to firm size measured by staff average number. This is a control variable.

V_6 (Professional management): This variable refers to management style, that is, whether the management of the firm is carried out by the owner or by professional managers. Firms with separate management and ownership accounted for 70.2 per cent.

V_7 (Permanent staff) and V_8 (Temporary staff): These reflect the percentage of permanent employees versus those of seasonal/temporary employees. On the average, 34.59 per cent of the workforce in the firms was permanent and 44.09 per cent, temporary. This is a relevant factor in the sector since most firms work by campaigns because citrus fruits are picked seasonally. It has to be noted though that the tendency is to import citrus from overseas during the growing seasons.

V_9 (Education): This variable represents the staff percentage with mid- or higher-level education. It had a value of 8.32 per cent representing the firm's staff members who had university education.

V_{10} (Training): This variable represents whether the firm carries out technical training courses such as selection, waxing, cleaning, operating the equipment, and other courses in a permanent mode. These courses are generally promoted at no cost by government bodies such as the local agro-food offices. The firms who conduct training for their employees accounted for 58.9 per cent.

V_{11} (Years): This refers to the number of years that the firm has been operating in the market, as well as the KISA carried out internally or contracted externally by the firm.

V_{12} (Accountancy): This represents not only standard accountancy activities services but also other procedures such as tax reporting, standards and norms and particular legal advice, as well as personnel management such as social security registration and payments. Firms who have outsourced accountancy activities provided a value of 29.5 per cent. As had been pointed out by academics (Martinez-Fernandez,2006; Miles, 2003), accountancy services, in spite of what could be expected, play a relevant role in organising knowledge towards influencing strategy and interconnecting firms utilising the same accountancy firm.

V_{13} (International Standards Organization (ISO): This covers activities associated with the International Standards quality certification maintenance which is carried out externally for most firms. Firms that have been registered with ISO 9002 (quality certification) accounted for 32.8 per cent.

V_{14} (Brand): This variable represents branding management, that is, whether firms manage their own brandings with which they commercialise their products. Branding is a key element in positioning the firm in the value chain. Large firms have strong brandings. Branding activity is carried out internally in most cases as seen in the 25.6 per cent value of the total number of firms who market their brandings.

V_{15} (Marketing): This variable is linked to the previous variable. Here, we measure if the firms carry out marketing activities in support of their branding, such as designing and printing brochures describing the product specifications, and designing and printing product packaging. These activities are normally outsourced to external marketing firms. This is a less frequent service and is related to the product's added value. The reply is positive in 24.6 per cent of the cases.

V_{16} (Firm agreements): Eighteen percent of the firms have signed formal agreements with other firms: citrus suppliers or cooperatives, competitors for common campaigns, competitors serving common customers, and other similar situations.[8]

V_{17} (Internal contacts): As pointed out earlier, the firms' internal networking has been measured by the normal, continuous, and formal (written) contacts that firms maintain with local firms in such areas as equipment, chemical, or product suppliers, as well as customers. All the sample firms maintain local contacts: the average number of internal firm contacts is 98.47. This variable can be a measure of the cluster effect of the group.

V_{18} (External contacts): This variable refers to the firms' external networking and had been measured by the normal, continuous, and formal (written) contacts, which firms have with external firms at the national and international levels. These external firms include equipment manufacturers or distribution customers. All the sample firms maintain external contacts, with the average number of firm external contacts being 25.59.

V_{19} (R&D&I): The variable relates to R&D and innovative activities in the last three years.

V_{20} (Internal R&D): This variable represents the internal R&D and innovative activities.

V_{21} (R&D&I employment): This measures the intensity of R&D and innovative activities as evidenced by the respondent identifying at least one employee carrying out R&D and innovative activities.

V_{22} (R&D&I agreements): Finally, this variable measures R&D and innovation agreements with RTC organisations.

The R&D and innovation (R&D&I) variables, they were defined *ex ante* the field study, and were reconsidered *ex post*.[9] Recent studies carried out in Europe point out the fact that R&D is not the only method of innovating. Other methods include technology adoption, incremental changes, imitation, and combining existing knowledge to form new ways (Arundel et al, 2008). Most of these methods require creative effort from the firm's management and employees and will consequently help to develop the firm's in-house innovative capabilities. These capabilities are likely to lead to productivity improvements, improved competitiveness, and to new or improved products and processes that can have wider impacts on the economy. For these reasons, the activities of firms that innovate without performing R&D are now of interest to policy makers (European Commission, 2009). Nevertheless, the same study shows that non-R&D innovators are relatively more dependent than R&D-performing firms. The dependence is shown through the diffusion of knowledge from other firms, particularly through the knowledge embodied in the acquired products and processes and how these non-R&D innovators fail to benefit from the innovation policies (Eurostat, 2009).

In theory, and in relation to R&D or innovation variables, the results were as follows: 21.3 per cent of the firms have carried out some innovative activity in the last three years; 16.4 per cent of the firms could name an employee carrying out R&D or innovative activities; and finally, 8.2 per cent of the firms in the sample had some agreement with a local research institute. It can be concluded that generally, such internal KISA were externally supported in 40 per cent of the cases.

V_{23} (Association): This variable represents the status of the firms; whether active or inactive members of an industry association. Most of them are partners of a cooperative, which manages a refrigerated port warehouse; 45.9 per cent of the firms belonged to an industry association.

Table 3.2 summarizes and describes the variables, their theoretical base, and their range values.

Multivariate Analysis: Empirical Results and Discussion

In order to perform a multivariate analysis, and in order to select and identify the significant independent variables, a factor analysis was carried out as a first measure. The results of the analysis are shown in Table 3.3. A rotation was obtained after eight iterations and the factor analysis detected four components, which could explain 85.20 per cent of the sample variance. These components were associated to the variables in the following way: $C_1 = f(V_{12}; V_{14}; V_{15}; V_{19}; V_{20}; V_{22})$; $C_2 = f(V_5; V_9; V_7)$; $C_3 = f(V_{17}; V_{18})$; and $C_4 = f(V_{11})$. C_1 is associated with KISA such as branding development and marketing management, company agreements, accountancy, total R&D variables, and R&D agreements. C_2 is associated with firms' size, percentage of permanent staff, and education profile of staff. With the exception of size, this component is also a measure of the firm's absorption capacity. C_3 is related with the intensity of the contact networking of the firm. Finally, C_4 represents the experience of the firm represented by the number of years of operation.

Table 3.2 Survey variables, meaning, range values, and references

Symbol	Variable	Meaning	Values	References
Dependent				
V1	Process innovation	Level of innovation in process	0–2	Hervas and Albors, 2008; Hauknes and Antonelli, 1999
V2	Performance	Profits against sector average	1–5	Hervas and Albors, 2008; Miles, 2005b; Hauknes and Antonelli, 1999
V3	Growth	Employment growth level is last five years	0–2	Hervas and Albors, 2008; Miles, 2005b; Den Hertog, 2000
V4	Export	Turnover % on exports	0–4	Hauknes and Antonelli, 1999
Firm's characteristics				
V5	Size	Total average employment size	Control variable	
V6	Professional Management	Management run by a hired professional from outside	0–1	
V7	Permanent Staff	Permanent employment	%	Zahra and George, 2002; Miles et al, 1995; Hervas and Albors, 2008; Cohen and Levinthal, 1990; Ducatel, 2000
V8	Temporary Staff	Temporary employment		
V9	Education	% of employees with university degree		
V10	Training	Regular training for staff	0–1	
V11	Years	Number of years the firm has been operating in the market	Control variable	
KISA				
V12	Accountancy	Accountancy external services	0–1	Martinez-Fernandez, 2006; Miles, 2003
V13	ISO	Quality, the firms certified by an outside ISO 9000 agent	0–1	Miles et al 1995; Hervas and Albors, 2008
V14	Brand	Has its own brands	0-1	Cadilhon et al, 2003; Martinez-Fernandez, 2006; Miles, 2003
V15	Marketing	Marketing services outsourced	0–1	
V16	Firm agreements	Cooperation agreements with other firms	0—1	
V17	Local contacts	Suppliers and customer contacts, local	Continuous	Kaplinsky, 2004; Hervas and Albors, 2008

Table 3.2 (cont.)

Symbol	Variable	Meaning	Values	References
V18	External contacts	Suppliers and customer contacts, international		
V19	R&D&I	Existence of R&D and innovative activities internally	0–1	Lee, 2004; Cadilhon et al 2003; Martinez-Fernandez, 2006; Miles, 2003
V20	Internal R&D&I	Carries out R&D and innovative activities internally	0–1	
V21	R&D&I employment	Full time staff in R&D and innovative activities	0–1	
V22	R&D&I agreements	Formal agreements with technology centres	0–1	
V23	Association	Membership in association	0–1	Humphrey and Schmitz, 2002; Martinez-Fernandez, 2006; Miles, 2003; Ling-yee and Ogunmokun, 2001; Mcevily and Marcus, 2005; Mcevily and Zaher, 1999; Lindelöf and Löftsen, 2004; Hanel and St-Pierre, 2006

Table 3.3 Rotated component matrix

	Component			
Variables	*1*	*2*	*3*	*4*
V_{14} (Brand)	0.9342			
V_{15} (Marketing)	0.9342			
V_9 (Education)		0.9085		
V_{17} (Internal contacts)			0.9065	
V_{18} (External contacts)			0.8840	
V_{19} (R&D&I)	0.9360			
V_{21} (R&D&I employment)	0.8771			
V_{22} (R&D&I agreements)	0.8716			
V_{16} (Firm agreements)	0.7033			
V_{20} (Internal R&D&I)	0.9531			
V_5 (Size)		0.9341		
V_{11} (Years)				0.9347
V_{12} (Accountancy)	0.7011			
V_7 (Permanent employees)		0.9457		

In the second step, we utilised the KISA variables pointed out by Component $C_1 = f (V_{12}; V_{14}; V_{15}; V_{19}; V_{20}; V_{22})$ (α Cronbach = 0.823). These results point out that the most relevant variables associated with KISA with the highest statistical weights are: branding development and marketing management, accountancy services, total R&D&I variables, and R&D&I agreements. The effect of accountancy has been outlined in accordance with the academic literature (OECD, 2006), while the effect of marketing and branding development makes sense from the context of value chain upgrading (Humphrey and Schmitz, 2002). Finally, the effect of R&D&I variables is inherent to the innovation and knowledge intensity of the activity.

In order to expand our analysis of the effect of KISA, we have applied a cluster analysis and regression exercises in order to justify the proposed model (see Table 3.4). A cluster analysis with this new variable (C_1) allowed the classification of the sample in three groups with 4, 36, and 82 members.

The analysis of the mean differences for the value of the different variables in each cluster shows that variables such as V_2 (Performance), V_4 (Export), V_6 (Professional management), V_7 (Permanent staff), V_9, (Education), V_1 (Process innovation), and V_{23} (Association) have statistically significant and different mean values. Moreover, the groups (numbers 1 and 2) with higher KISA values have higher positive replies for these variables.

Table 3.4 Number of cases in each cluster

	Number	Firms	Final Cluster Centres
Cluster	1	4	18.10
	2	36	9.89
	3	82	2.07
Valid		122	

Note: ANOVA for KISA, F= 231,672 with p<0.0001

On the other hand, variables V_3 (Growth), V_5 (Size), and V_{11} (Years) with the latter two being the control variables, do not reveal any statistical mean differences among all cluster groups.

Next, a correlation analysis was performed. This showed a significant correlation between KISA and the output variables such as process innovation (V_1), firm performance (V_2), and level of export intensity (V_4). KISA are correlated with the absorptive capacity variables such as firms' permanent employees (V_7) and education (V_9). No correlation appeared between KISA and the control variable growth (V_3) or the professional management (V_6).

Hence, the multivariate analysis has shown that the outstanding KISA are: branding development and marketing management, accountancy services, R&D and innovative activities (internal), as well as R&D&I agreements (external). Networking activities are relevant, as well as the variables connected with the absorptive capacity of the firms.

KISA appear correlated with the variables reflecting process innovation, firms' performance, and export intensity, as well as the absorptive capacity variables such as the firms' permanent employment and staff education.

Finally, we undertook a regression analysis and a discriminant analysis to identify which dependent variables, in particular, have a stronger influence on the dependent variables: V_2 (Performance), V_4 (Export), or V_1 (Process innovation). The results of this regression analysis show that the independent variables V_{14} (Brand), V_{12} (Accountancy), V_{19} (R&D&I), V_{16} (Firm agreements), and V_{17} (Local contacts) are related with the dependent variable V_2 (Performance). Moreover, the second regression analysis shows that the independent variables V_7 (Permanent staff), V_{12} (Accountancy), and V_{19} (R&D&I) are connected with the dependent variable V_4 (Export).

The results of the discriminant analysis show that the following variables compose the canonical functions that discriminate the process innovation level of the firms. These are V_7 (Permanent staff), V_9 (Education), and V_{16} (Firm agreements).[10]

Figure 3.5 shows the empirical results in relation to the proposed model of KISA interaction and their influence on the firm's performance. The empirical results show that the hypotheses proposed have been validated. H_1, which states that KISA have a relative influence on the firms' innovative activities irrespective of their technology orientation, has been proven to be right in our case (low-tech manufacturing). This has been shown by the cluster and regression analyses. H_2, which proposed that KISA have a relative influence on firms' employment growth and economic performance, has been partially validated because although KISA appear correlated with EBIDTA, this is not the case with the employment growth variable.

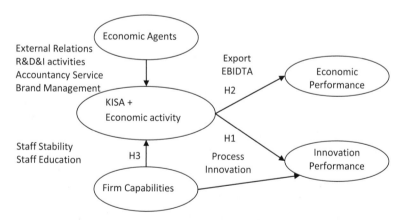

Figure 3.5 Proposed model of KISA interaction and their influence on the firm's performance: empirical results

Finally, H_3, the hypothesis on the influence of firms' absorption capacity, as a moderating influence in the KISA impact, has also been validated. KISA – related variables, such as employees' education and staff stability, have an impact on innovation performance. Meanwhile, it has to be noted that control variables, such as firms' size (measured by the number of employees) and the number of years of operation, are not significant. A third variable, staff employment growth, does not appear to be relevant either. This reinforces the idea that staff stability (permanent workforce) is the relevant dimension in this respect. Finally, it has been observed that most KISA are external, as could be explained by the average firm size of the sample.

CONCLUSIONS

The case discussed in this chapter shows the relevance of KISA in the low-tech sectors, as well as in mature industries, where positioning in the value chain connotes improving the performance of firms. Branding and marketing management, as well as distribution control by firms, help to upgrade their position in the value chain, thus reinforcing their competitiveness and performance. The research consequently links KISA to chain governance and opens up new research prospects.

Among the various types of KISA, branding development, marketing management, firm agreements, accountancy, internal R&D, and innovation activities, as well as external R&D&I have a higher statistical relevance in this research. In particular, the regression analysis showed that branding development, external accountancy activities, R&D and innovation activities, inter-firm formal agreements, as well as local internal contacts (a cluster effect) are correlated with the firms' performance as measured by the EBITDA. The firms' performance measured as turnover export percentage is connected with external accountancy activities, R&D and innovation activities, and permanent staff.

A discriminant analysis used for identifying the variables with the most weight in the firm's innovation level concluded with the formulation of a canonical function composed of firms' formal agreements, permanent staff, and level of education of employees. This function was able to predict the innovation level with 92.3 per cent probability.

The research results point to the relevance of KISA for firm innovation performance as measured by the firms' profits, as well as their export performance. An additional conclusion was the evidence of the impact of the firms' absorption capacity as a moderating influencer in the KISA effects.

Because there is no previously published evidence on these themes, the contribution of the chapter lies basically in exploring KISA's role in innovation in the low-tech and mature sectors. This has implications for innovation policy and the policy makers' recommendations to support KISA, especially those activities that contribute to innovation and particularly in the case of SMEs. It could be pointed out as well that KISA are connected with the issues of human capital and knowledge management. KISA are likewise relevant to low-tech and mature sectors where upgrading the firm's positioning in the value chain implies an improvement in the firm's performance.

Externally provided services for KISA play a relevant role in the case of SMEs with restricted in-house resources. The role of industry associations in the sector consisting of SMEs has to be considered as well. The research showed that the KISA variables associated with this dimension are relevant. The clustering effect is also shown to have synergy with KISA adoption and impact.

Finally, from a practitioner's view, the paper sheds light on the reasons involved in KISA adoption, on how KISA relate to the firms' capabilities, and on how these capabilities (or their absence) can be a barrier to KISA adoption.

NOTES

1. An extended version of this paper has been published in Asian Journal of Technology Innovation (2009), 17 (1), 31–55.
2. Nysveen and Pedersen (2007), as well as Yu, et al (2005) open a debate on this subject from an empirical practitioners' perspective.
3. Total production of 6.13 million tons in 2004–2005. (Intercitrus, 2008)
4. The citrus market is actually a globalised market.
5. Partly because growing and fruit picking costs have become very expensive in Spain.
6. Product innovation is more limited to branding, product selection, and packaging.
7. EBITDA is a performance ratio that stands for 'Earnings Before Interest, Taxes, Depreciation, and Amortization'. It is drawn from the earnings and losses firm sheet.
8. This refers to formal agreements with mutual commitment between the signing parties.
9. During the interview stages, it was acknowledged that firms do not distinguish clearly between R&D and innovation. Thus, it was decided to denominate both activities as innovative in a wider sense. Some of them consisted of incorporating ground-breaking innovative equipment and learning to operate it effectively, adapting the software to their needs, and other mechanisms. This refers to formal agreements with mutual commitment between the signing parties. During the interview stages, it was acknowledged that firms do not distinguish clearly between R&D and innovation. Thus, it was decided to denominate both activities as innovative in a wider sense. Some of them consisted of incorporating ground-breaking innovative equipment and learning to operate it effectively, adapting the software to their needs, and other mechanisms.
10. Statistical tables showing the results have been omitted for space and relevance reasons.

REFERENCES

Albors, J., Hervas, J.L., Marquez, P. and Martinez-Fernandez, M.C. (2008), 'Application of KISA Concept to Innovation Dynamics and its Impact on Firms' Performance', *Management Research News*, **31** (6), pp. 404–17.

Alvesson, M. (1993), 'Organizations as Rhetoric: Knowledge-intensive Firms and the Struggle with Ambiguity', *Journal of Management Studies*, **30** (6), pp. 997–1015.

Arundel A., Bordoy, C. and Kanerva, M. (2008), *Neglected Innovators: How do Innovative Firms that do not Perform R&D Innovate? Results of an Analysis of the Innobarometer 2007 Survey No. 215*, The Hague: Netherlands, INNO Metrics Thematic Paper.

Aslesen, H.W. (2004), *Knowledge-intensive Service Activities and Innovation in the Norwegian Aquaculture Industry*, Project Report from the OECD KISA Study, STEP-4, Brussels: Belgium, European Commission.

Cadilhon, J.J., Fearne, A., Hughes, D. and Moustier, P. (2003), *Wholesale Markets and Food Distribution in Europe: New Strategies for Old Functions*, CFCR Discussion Paper 2, London: Imperial College, Centre for Food Chain Research.

Cohen W. and Levinthal, D. (1990), 'Absorptive Capacity: A New Perspective on Learning and Innovation', *Administrative Science Quarterly*, **35** (1), pp. 128–52.

Collado, J.C. (2005), *KISA and Tourism in Spain*, Madrid: CEOE.

Den Hertog, P.D. (2000), 'Knowledge-intensive Business Services as Co-producers of Innovation', *International Journal of Innovation Management*, **4** (4), pp. 491–528.

Drejer, I. and Vinding, A.L. (2005), 'Location and Collaboration: Manufacturing Firms' Use of Knowledge Intensive Services in Product Innovation'. *European Planning Studies* **13** (6), pp. 879–98.

Ducatel, K. (2000), 'Information Technologies in Non-knowledge Services', in S. Metcalfe, and I. Miles, (eds), *Innovation Systems in the Service Economy – Measurement and Case Study Analysis*, Boston/Dordrecht/London: Kluwer.

Ebersberger, B. (2004), *The Use and Appreciation of KISA in Traditional Industries*, Espoo: Finland, VTT Technology.

European Commission (2009), *European Innovation Scoreboard 2008: Comparative Analysis of Innovation Performance*, Brussels: Belgium.

Eurostat (2009), *Statistics in Focus*, Brussels: Belgium, European Commission.

Gereffi, G., Humphrey, J. and Sturgeon, T. (2005), 'The Governance of Global Value Chains', *Review of International Political Economy*, **12** (1), pp. 78–104.

Haataja, M. and Okkonen, J. (2005), *Competitiveness of Knowledge Intensive Services*, Proceedings eBRF eBusiness Research Forum Conference, Tampere, August 20–22 2004.

Hanel, P. and St-Pierre, M. (2006), 'Industry-University Collaboration by Canadian Manufacturing Firms', *Journal of Technology Transfer*, **31** (3), pp. 485–99.

Hauknes, J. and Antonelli, C. (1999), *KIS What is Their Role?*, Paris: OECD.

Hervas, J.L. and Albors, J.G. (2008), 'The Role of the Firm's Internal and Relational Capabilities in Clusters: When Distance and Embeddedness are Not Enough to Explain Innovation', *Journal of Economic Geography*, **9** (2), pp. 263–83.

Humphrey, J. and Schmitz, H. (2002), 'How does Insertion in Global Value Chains Affect Upgrading in Industrial Clusters?' *Regional Studies*, **36** (9), pp. 1017–27.

Intercitrus (2009), *Annual Report 2008*, Interprofesional Citrícola Española, Valencia, Spain.

Kaplinsky, R. (2004), 'Spreading the Gains from Globalization: What Can Be Learned from Value-chain Analysis?', *Problems of Economic Transition*, **47** (2), pp. 74–115.

Kivisaari, S., Saranummi, N. and Vayrynen, E. (2004), *KISA in Healthcare Innovation*, Helsinki: VTT.

Kuusisto, J. and Meyer, M. (2003), 'Insights into Services and Innovation in the Knowledge-intensive Economy', *Technology Review*, **134**, 2003, Helsinki: Tekes.

Lee, K.R. (2004), 'Utilization of Knowledge-intensive Services for the Innovation of Manufacturers in Korea', *Asian Journal of Technology Innovation*, **12** (2), pp. 209–17.

Lindelöf, P. and Löftsen, H. (2004), 'Proximity as a Resource Base for Competitive Advantage: University Industry Links for Technology Transfer', *Journal of Technology Transfer*, **29** (2), pp. 311–26.

Ling-yee, L. and Ogunmokun, G. (2001), 'The Influence of Interfirm Relational Capabilities on Export Advantage and Performance: an Empirical Analysis', *International Business Review*, **10** (4), pp. 399–420.

Martinez-Fernandez, M.C. (2005), *Knowledge-intensive Service Activities (KISA) in Innovation of the Mining Technology Services Sector in Australia*, Sydney: University of Western Sydney.

Martinez-Fernandez, M.C. (2006), 'Introduction', *International Journal Services Technology and Management*, **7** (2), pp. 109–11.

Martinez-Fernandez, M.C. and Krishna, V.V. (2006), 'KISA in Innovation of Australian Software Firms', *International Journal Services Technology and Management*, **7** (2), pp. 126–36.

Martinez-Fernandez, M.C. and Miles, I. (2006), 'Inside the Software Firm:

Co-production of Knowledge and KISA in the Innovation Process', *International Journal Services Technology and Management*, **7** (2), pp. 115–25.

Mcevily, B. and Marcus, A. (2005), 'Embedded Ties and the Acquisition of Competitive Capabilities', *Strategic Management Journal*, **26** (11), pp. 1003–55.

Mcevily, B. and Zaheer, A. (1999), 'Bridging Ties: A Source of Firm Heterogeneity in Competitive Capabilities', *Strategic Management Journal*, **20** (4), pp. 1133–56.

Miles, I., Kastrinos, N., Flanagan, K., Bilderbeek, R., Hertog, B., Huntink, W. and Bou-man, M. (1995), *Knowledge-Intensive Business Services: Users, Carriers and Sources of Innovation*, European Innovation Monitoring System (EIMS), EIMS Publication No. 15.

Miles, I. (2003), *Knowledge-Intensive Services' Suppliers and Clients, Finland: Report to the Ministry of Trade and Industry Finland*, Studies and Reports 15/2003.

Miles, I. (2005a), 'Knowledge-intensive Business Services: Prospects and Policies', *Foresight*, **7** (6), pp. 9–63.

Miles. I. (2005b), 'Knowledge-intensive Services and Innovation', in J. Bryson and P. Daniels (eds), *The Handbook of Service Industries*, pp. 85–99, Cheltenham, UK and Northampton, MA, USA: Edward Elgar.

Nysveen, H. and Pedersen, P.E. (2007), 'Service Innovation Methodologies, What Can We Learn from Service Innovation and New Service Development Research?', *Report No. 1*, TIPVIS-project, Kristiansand.

OECD (2006), *Innovation and Knowledge Intensive Service Activities*, Organisation for Economic Co-operation and Development: Paris.

Rajala, R. Westerlund, M. and Leminen, S. (2008), 'Knowledge-intensive Service Activities in Software Business', *International Journal of Technology Management*, **41** (3-4), pp. 273–90.

Rosenberg, N. and Nelson, R.R. (1994), 'American Universities and Technical Advance in Industry', *Research Policy*, **23**, pp. 325–48.

Shan Hu, T., Chang, Su-Li, Yuan Lin, C. and Tao Chien, H. (2006), 'Evolution of Knowledge-intensive Services in a High-tech Region: The Case of Hsinchu, Taiwan', *European Planning Studies*, **14** (10), pp. 1363–1385.

Tether, B.S. (2003), 'The Sources and Aims of Innovation in Services: Variety Within and Between Sector', *Economics of Innovation and New Technology*, **12** (6), pp. 1051–81.

Touburn, L. (2004), 'KISA in Tourism and Software', *Innovation Dynamics PTY*, Canberra: Canberra Business Centre.

Williams, J. (2006), 'KISA in Innovation of New Zealand Software Firms', *International Journal of Services Technology and Management*, **7** (2), pp.

5–15.

Windrum, P. and Tomlinson, M. (1999), 'Knowledge-intensive Services and International Competitiveness: A Four-country Comparison', *Technology Analysis and Strategic Management*, **11** (3), pp. 391–408.

Yu, Z.C., Fan, Z.P. and Li, D. (2005), 'A Framework and Operation Mechanism for Knowledge Services', *Journal Institute of Electrical and Electronics Engineers*, 78039-9139, pp. 907-11.

Zahra, S.A. and George, G. (2002), 'Absorptive Capacity: A Review, Re-Conceptualization, and Extension', *Academy of Management Review*, **27** (2), pp. 185–203.

4 KISA Utilisation in Resource Intensive Industries: the Case of Mining in Australia

Cristina Martinez-Fernandez

No other industry in Australia has achieved a greater significance in economic development terms as has Mining. The mineral industries have built national infrastructure throughout Australia for more than a century, and Australia's minerals boom has produced generations of mining technology services (MTS) companies. This chapter discusses the role of MTS firms in the transformation of the mining industry into the knowledge economy. Results from a study of Australian MTS and mining firms suggest that innovation results from the interaction of these firms through knowledge intensive service activities (KISA).

INTRODUCTION

In 2004 the Australian Mining Technology Services Action Agenda (MTSAA) group[1] defined the MTS sector as comprising companies, institutions, associations and other organisations which receive a substantial portion of their revenue, directly or indirectly, from mining companies for the provision of goods and services based on specialised technology, intellectual property or knowledge. Such organisations identify themselves principally with the mineral industry and can be considered KIBS providing specialized services to the mining companies. 'Goods and services' include, but are not confined to, equipment, software, consulting and engineering services, and research and development (R&D). 'Mining' includes exploration, mining (extraction), quarrying and coal and mineral processing (including smelting and refining of metals and minerals).[2]

Apart from the MTSAA there are not sector specific policies for MTS firms in Australia, and data on these firms is not specifically collected by the Australian Bureau of Statistics (ABS). There have been limited government reports describing the sector and defining its boundaries but little is known of the innovation dynamics of the sector or the effects that interactive activities between MTS firms and mining firms have in the transformation of the minerals industry. The data discussed in this paper are largely based on two Australian Research Council studies[3] conducted by the University of Western Sydney. The data suggest that the role of these companies in fuelling innovation of the mining industry is rather significant and at the same time dependent on the quality of knowledge intensive service activities conducted in collaboration with the mining company. The chapter is divided in three sections; an overview of the MTS sector, a discussion of the role of knowledge intensive service activities and a concluding section with policy suggestions.

THE MINING TECHNOLOGY SERVICES (MTS) SECTOR IN AUSTRALIA

The MTS sector makes a significant contribution to Australia's economic growth on its own right, contributing AUD 3120 million (USD 2990 million) to Australia's gross domestic product in 2000–01 and expected to increase by 13 per cent per year to AUD 1.9 billion (USD 1.821 billion) in 2005–06. In addition to its strong domestic focus, the sector is expanding export opportunities in the global minerals marketplace. A survey conducted by Australian Bureau of Agriculture and Resources Economics (ABARE) estimates that gross export sales revenue contributes AUD 1110 million (USD 1064 million) in 2003–04 and this revenue is forecasted to increase to AUD 1240 million (USD 1188 million) in 2004–05 (Tedesco et al 2002; Tedesco and Curtotti, 2005). ABARE and Austmine[4] predict strong annual export growth rates to 2005–06, of at least 25 per cent, with Austmine members potentially contributing up to AUD 6 billion (USD 5.75 billion) in export earnings by 2010 (Macfarlane, 2003). Latest data from Austrade indicate the sector (including foreign-owned companies) is worth AUD 2 billion (USD 1.92 billion) a year in sales outside Australia alone. In part this is due to the rapid modernisation of the mining industry in Asia and Latin America demanding sophisticated underground communications, remote-control systems and mine-planning software (BRW, 2006:54). MTS firms export mainly to East and South East Asia regions; the biggest market is Indonesia (AUD 382 million or USD 366.13million) which accounts for 12.3 per cent of Australia's export market. In order of export market share North America, East and South East Asia and Central and South America are the biggest regions for MTS firms (DITR, 2002).

The ABARE 2004 MTS survey (Tedesco and Curtotti, 2005) shows that there is a minimum of 331 companies in Australia. They range from small companies to the largest mining firms employing whole divisions. The majority of the firms (52.7 per cent) are however small and medium enterprises (SMEs) employing 10 people or less; 25.2 per cent employed between 10 and 50 people, and 22 per cent employed over 50 people. The sector is estimated to have 16,800 full-time equivalents employees down from 17,300 employees in 2000–01. The most important occupations in the sector are high knowledge occupations such as engineers (62.1 per cent), geologists and other earth scientists (49.1 per cent) and computer scientist specialists (46.0 per cent). Managers and administrators are considered important or very important by 42.6 per cent of the firms, down from 58.3 per cent in the 2001 survey. The possibility of a skill shortage over the next five to ten years was considered important by 66.8 per cent of the surveyed companies in 2001. Skilled professionals, particularly those with science, engineering and technology qualifications are considered very important factors to increase the sector's competitive edge. There is also a need to ensure that people already in the Australian mining industry are aware of the MTS sector and the skills and experience required by MTS employers, and that information about relevant training programmes and opportunities is accessible (Tedesco et al 2002).

Mining technology service firms' headquarters are predominantly found in business centres and inner city locations. New South Wales, Victoria and Queensland have the highest number of mining technology companies (O'Connor and Kershaw, 1999). The sector has specific geographical features of clustering in the cities of Sydney and Perth, stressing the importance of network connections to corporate headquarters and other Knowledge Intensive Business Service (KIBS) often associated with financial centres, especially in the case of Sydney Central Business District (CBD). Branches of the main MTS firms are found in the big mining towns such as Mt Isa, Kargoorlie-Boulder and Olympic Dam to name a few.

There are no policies and programmes in Australia specifically supporting the MTS sector or the supply or promotion of KISA in the MTS Sector. However, the current MTS Action Agenda provides the development environment for the sector. The Action Agenda is a cooperative dialogue between industry, Government and State Agencies, with the common aim of promoting sustainable economic growth in the sector. The Mining Technology Service Action Agenda was announced on the 6th of June, 2001. The Action Agenda focuses on five areas:

- Response to the globalisation change;
- Technology and research and development coordination;
- Improving industry market share and competitiveness;

- Education and training; and
- Promotion and marketing. (DITR, 2002)

Research and Development (R&D)

According to a report prepared by ABARE on R&D in exploration and mining (Hogan, 2004) industry investment in R&D focused on applied and experimental development. Total expenditure on R&D in the sector was AUD 456 million (USD 437.04 million) in 2000–2001. Government expenditure on R&D was AUD 147 million (USD 140.85 million) in the same period, with a focus on basic and applied research (see Table 4.1).

Table 4.1 Mining sector R&D expenditure

R&D	Industry expenditure (AU $456 m. or US $437.04m.) (%)	Government expenditure (AU $147m. or US $140.85m.) (%)
Basic	5	40
Applied	23	48
Experimental	72	13

Source: Adapted from Hogan (2004)

R&D relevant to mineral exploration is mainly undertaken within individual companies, industry–government partnerships and public organisations. The main organisations are:

- CSIRO; mainly multidisciplinary research and technology development activities relevant to the Australian geological environment;
- Geoscience Australia; provides state/territory geological surveys and basic geoscience information;
- Universities; focus on basic research into geological processes and Australia's geology;
- The cooperative research centres (CRCs); bring together private and public organisations to solve particular problems;
- AMIRA International; a private organisation that engages in collaborative research by minerals companies in consort with public institutions (DITR, 2002).

The ABARE 2002 report indicates that 41 per cent of respondents did not invest in R&D. This result is typical of the many small companies that comprise the MTS sector. Up to 59 per cent of companies did invest in R&D and their total expenditure in 2000–01 was AUD 382 million (USD 365.9 million), or 12 per cent of gross sales revenue. The 2004 survey shows that

36.8 per cent of respondents did not invest in R&D and the majority of firms (23.8 per cent) invested between AUD 1 and AUD 100,000 (USD 0.96 and USD 95,788). ABARE estimated that 15.7 per cent of Australian MTS companies funded external R&D projects relevant to their MTS operations in Australia. R&D tax concessions and access to finance appear to be the most important issues for Australian MTS companies, with 85.6 per cent and 82.7 per cent respectively of all MTS respondents indicating that R&D was fairly to very important. Low rates of commercialization, low retention of intellectual property, access to public research organisations and availability of staff with specialist skills are also important issues for MTS companies. Current estimates for R&D expenditure are AUD 339 million (USD 324.7 million); 7 per cent of gross sales revenue (Tedesco and Curtotti, 2005).

In particular, R&D has been associated with the success of software applications to mining. According to the Department of Industry, Tourism and Resources (DITR, 2003) 60 per cent of the world's mining operations are now utilising software developed by Australian companies, indicating that Australian MTS companies are at the leading edge of technological innovation in the MTS sector. The sector contributed AUD 1.9 billion (USD 1.82 million) in high technology exports in mining services in 1999–2000 (DITR, 2002).

R&D strategies were noted by 58.5 per cent of the companies surveyed in 2001 by ABARE as an important factor for firm competitive advantage in contrast to other factors of higher importance such as management skills, intellectual capital, reliability as a supplier and quality of MTS goods and services (Tedesco et al, 2002). These other factors that firms report as of higher importance for their development are not considered part of R&D activities linked to industry innovation. However the study reported here found that these 'other knowledge intensive service activities' are strongly linked to innovation performance, the development of firm capabilities for innovation and the transformation of the mineral industry into a more knowledge base industry (Martinez-Fernandez, 2010).

Skills for Innovation

A survey conducted among 25 mining technology firms[5] in 2004 (Martinez-Fernandez et al, 2004) shows that over 80 per cent of respondents combined their products and services into packages as a source of differentiation and competitive advantage. There was also a focus on increasing the number and range of these packages. The importance of 'services' had significantly increased since 2001. These services were many times embedded in the product (for example purpose designed training of an underground digger machine). In relation to the Knowledge Intensive Services (KIS) purchased, companies mention 'IT consulting' (engineering software and IT services) as having a significant impact on company competitiveness because software has enabled virtual product typing and design of a product in three dimensions on the computer. Finite elemental analysis can also be done in 3D to allow testing simulations improving time and cost development. Other services purchased such as 'strategic planning services' have the capacity to make the most impact on the bottom line of the company. Out of the 25 companies interviewed, 40 per cent of firms indicated sourcing innovation services from external sources while another 48 per cent indicated that they sourced innovation services in-house. Private provision of KIS was more widely accessed (50 per cent) than any public provider source alone (Universities/TAFE 41 per cent).

The firms noted the 'ability to change' as the most important skill/capability for innovation. Activities leading to change in 80 per cent of the companies are largely formal processes. An example of one of these activities is internal R&D that plays a central role in change for 68 per cent of the companies. Another activity mentioned as having a central role in 'change' is 'marketing' related activities. The majority of firms, 84 per cent, indicated they build their skills through 'collaboration with major clients and multinational corporations (MNCs)'.

This study of MTS firms shows the main barriers to these firms' innovation process were the organisational management resources required, lack of skilled personnel, the high innovation costs and the great economic risk that is associated with the innovation process.

The study also shows that companies relate skills for innovation to other factors in addition to R&D; notably is the significance of marketing related activities and collaboration activities with clients and other firms. A parallel study with software firms and renewable energy firms found the same results at this level (Martinez-Fernandez et al, 2004). Next section discusses the role of these activities.

ROLE OF KNOWLEDGE INTENSIVE SERVICE ACTIVITIES (KISA) IN INNOVATION OF THE MINING INDUSTRY

The empirical study, part of a larger Australian Research Council (ARC) investigation[6] comprised six case studies of Australian firms; four cases were Mining Technology Companies and two were mining companies (Table 4.2 provides a profile of these companies).

The four case study MTS companies provided services to the two case study mining corporations, which allowed for a better analysis of the relationships between the mining company and the service provider and the activities they perform. The location of mining sites in Australia was considered a significant factor affecting KISA in MTS, given the remoteness of many prosperous mining sites, and the impact this might have on the interactions between companies and with other business in the hosting cities. Two remote locations were chosen for the analysis, and discussions were also held with City Councils and Chambers of Commerce in relation to the contribution of mining and MTS companies to urban development. Figure 4.1 shows the provision of services of the case studies. The MTS companies did not have collaboration links with each other; neither did the two mining companies; but the mining sites provided the context where all the four MTS companies provided services. The mining site functions as a networked environment where ideas are applied by MTS firms acting as 'carriers of knowledge' from one site to the next one. The relationships depicted in Figure 4.1 refer to the provision of services from MTS companies to mining companies. The case studies analysis focused on the knowledge intensive service activities performed in these mining sites.

Table 4.2 Profile of case studies

Cases	Owners	State	Life-cycle	No. Employees	Main Product / Service	Market focus	Recent Innovation	Type of Innovation
MTS Companies								
A	Private Aust.	Qld	Prof. Mgt	5	R&D, technical & training	National	Incremental	Service (training)
B	Public Listed Foreign	Qld	Expansion	1000	Engineering & construction project mgt	National & International	Incremental	Processes (project mgt)
C	Private Aust.	NSW	Expansion	25	Geoscience software	National	Radical	Product (GIS software)
D	Private Aust.	Qld	Expansion	90	Consulting software training	National & International	Incremental	Product (forecasting programme)
Mining Companies								
E	Public Listed Foreign	Qld	Expansion	2500	Copper, lead & zinc	International	Radical	Product, process & organisational
F	Public Listed Foreign	SA	Expansion	5000	Copper, uranium, silver & gold	International	Radical	Process

Source: Martinez-Fernandez, 2005:33

Mining sites in Australia are often located in remote locations that are very rich in minerals which allows for a long-term exploitation and the formation of permanent settlements. Hundreds of contractors can be associated to the mine site, having a significant impact in other services business operating in town, such as retail or hospitality. In this respect mining sites are knowledge intensive hubs and innovation intensive environments. The analysis of the case studies has taken into account the activities performed by mining companies and the impact on community development and city planning strategies of this highly knowledge intensive environment. The study found that although the firm innovation ecosystem is very strong and highly innovative, this environment is confined to the mining site. The hosting cities provide other services related to accommodation, hospitality, transportation and retail – but regional absorptive capacity (RAC) (Roper and Love, 2006) is limited. This might be in part due to the high fly-in, fly-out behaviour of the professionals working in the mining site (both employees and service providers); they might stay in the city for only 3–4 days a week while their family home is in a bigger city or near the coast. Therefore, a dual environment can be observed in these cities: a strong firm innovation ecosystem and a weak city/regional innovation system. The connections between the two are unclear. The study did not find any local urban policy or strategy aimed at connecting with the firm innovation ecosystem.

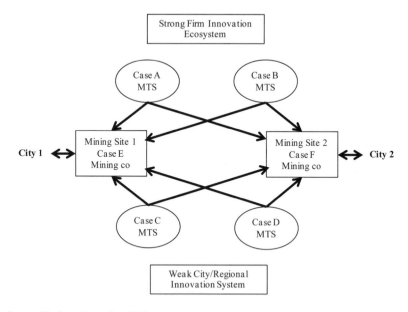

Source: Martinez-Fernandez, 2010

Figure 4.1 Interactivity of companies in mining sites

The mining site is at the centre of the firm's innovation ecosystem with hundreds of specialised activities conducted every day. The study found the following KISA of high or medium importance for both MTS and Mining Companies:

- Exploration and other mining consulting;
- Design & Engineering consulting;
- Technical consulting services;
- Research & Development services;
- IP-related services; and
- Occupational Health and Safety (OH&S).

KISA of high importance for MTS but low importance for mining companies are:

- Marketing services; and
- Industry related training services.

For example, one of the MTS firms gives high importance to R&D, marketing and IP related activities, and medium importance to IT and engineering consultancy and services in generating KISA. The firm created a specialised R&D centre where IT professionals and professionals with mining engineering and geological sciences background are working. As a firm involved in the specialised activity of geosciences and mining exploration many of the inputs to KISA are sourced internally from its R&D centre. Software professionals are mainly involved in developing customised products and processes and designs; professionals in geosciences provide expertise in geophysical interpretation, exploration data integration, imaging, mapping, survey planning and quality control. The firm has developed expertise in developing specialised database services for various clients on closed networks on the Internet. This firm had given high importance to recruitment of professionals with specialised skills to combine and work in interdisciplinary frameworks. The ability and skills of professionals with geological and mining background who can combine and integrate their professional skills with software and IT related activities are the main factors in the criteria for personnel recruitment of this firm.

Interaction with Providers of Expertise for KISA

KISA skills are largely sourced in-house, or from KIBS, or by a combination of both – with the exception of industry development advice which is mainly sourced from industry associations. Only one mining company sourced expertise from universities. Informal networks were also not important as a source of services for KISA which were mainly sourced under formal contracts with MTS firms.

Companies varied in the way they 'interact with external providers' of services for KISA. Thus, these companies, providers of services themselves, also purchase services that then are mixed and matched with their own services. The case study MTS-A would decide on outsourcing on the basis of costs. If it is cost-effective and cheaper to do it internally they will keep it inside. If it is cheaper to outsource that is what the company will do; the best example is with software development skills. The MTS firm prefers to outsource this activity because it cannot afford to develop those services internally and be competitive. For this company sourcing external skills is part of their strategic goals. In terms of evaluation of the services provided, the company has internal processes that allocate responsibilities and they use Key Performance Indicators (KPIs) to put it through management processes and then follow the failures and measure the services through a matrix. The company reviews these processes regularly to make sure they remain competitive.

Professionals have an impact on the innovation absorptive capacity of these companies as they are the ones undertaking KISA. The knowledge is available but the demand is large, as is the number of jobs, where there is much competition to get the best people. Although the company has enough people for the current demand, this is one of the risk issues for the future even if Australia is very self-sufficient in terms of knowledge development.

This MTS company rarely needs to source external services, other than for research or IT purposes. This firm has worked on site with external providers, but these have been 'collaborative exercises' rather than the firm seeking outside advice. Therefore, for this firm, informal networks were important sources of ideas and information. This firm was the smallest of the six case studies, which suggests that informal interactions can be highly important for SMEs. For example, partnerships occur by interacting with other firms in the Innovation Centre where they are located, from word of mouth, or by attending specialised seminars. The firm usually seeks outside advice for some technical aspects associated to their work. The firm will source this from within the Innovation Centre where they are located. For example, IT capability is outsourced because there is not enough expertise in-house. By outsourcing skills there are some risks, such as a potential loss of control and a potential for customers to be headhunted. There are also the difficulties and cost of making commercial arrangements with other companies and possible waste of funds.

One of the mining companies has 'economic reasons for retaining the core knowledge in-house' without the overheads expenses. The firm outsources activities that are needed about 20 per cent of the time as specialists cannot be afforded all the time. The firm believes it is an advantage to have wider expertise available and has confidentiality agreements in place regarding some of its technology so the risks are minimised. The company tries to hold core competences in the organisation and it is part of its philosophy to get things done by a combination of acquisition plus development. If things are not too complicated, they might be able to do them in-house in the future. The firm tries to use the knowledge accumulated by people over the years.

Evaluation is up to the individual project manager. The firm looks at the objectives and how they fit into the overall company goals. As public research organisations such as CSIRO now have to go and ask industry for partnerships, the firm has now some research with Universities and CSIRO.

Another mining company refers to the variety of provision of services in the mine site. They require technical expertise specially in engineering consulting and also on human management on professional development. They also need specific staff for maintenance. In total the firm might have 1000 contractors performing above 300 different KISA on site every day. The firm's largest contractors are in the areas of engineering consulting, training provision and professional development and maintenance. A tender document is usually used first to source the provider. Then there is an interaction with the service provider through a project manager responsible for making the interactions, getting the right people on site, and giving the right information. Unfortunately not all levels of skills are available and sometimes is not possible to attract the best people due to the remoteness of the mine sites. Usually employees stay for 2–3 years only, and exceptionally for a maximum of 15 years; this means a constant drain of knowledge and skills. Part of the contract has KPIs and it is the responsibility of the project manager to follow them up. Some skills such as in Metallurgy are very difficult to obtain, being very technical and with shortages of expertise both in-house and externally. It is difficult to get qualified people, so the firm offers to train people itself in-house instead, through sponsoring university training, apprentices and sometimes sponsoring people from overseas.

For the majority of the case study companies, sourcing external expertise was a cost-related decision where they balanced external sourcing of needed expertise with retention of core knowledge in-house. For mining companies the issue seems also to be linked to the turnaround of personnel and difficulties of finding skilled personnel, and also to the fact that mining sites are knowledge intensive hubs with different complex technologies that require specific and tailored skills. The case studies show very clearly that the interaction processes are intense. The next section discusses how these interactions relate to innovation.

Mix and Match Process and Skills for Innovation

As the client company and the service provider interact through KISA, it was not obvious how firms absorbed ideas and information provided by these activities. Firm MTS-A describes the mix and match of internal–external expertise as a 'process occurring in a daily basis'. This process is driven by 'Project Managers' for certain projects, but the firm is always on the lookout for new inputs and would use them as and when they were suitable, if they were available. Part of the modus operandi of the firm is to develop and maintain long-term relationships with both clients and suppliers/contractors, who became a source of expertise that the firm needs to absorb. The firm does not have a dedicated staff member to deal with all external providers, as their number is not significant. For this company, internal expertise was difficult to replace. When people leave the company, or when their contract is completed, they will often take significant amounts of knowledge and skills with them. However, they also leave a certain amount of knowledge and skills behind them. In some cases the firm has lost people who have left significant 'holes' in their knowledge and skills base. As informal transfer of knowledge is expected and on-going, the firm captures the technical knowledge obtained over the years by writing it up in manual format. Thus, it is readily available for all personnel at a later time, and all archives are freely available to all current employees. Despite the importance of the knowledge generated by the firm, they do not go to any special lengths to protect what they have already garnered from industry. Instead, the firm's business model is based in their ability to produce new material as and when required. R&D of specific technical or training documentation is its most important innovation capability. They also deal significantly with Intellectual Property (IP) – both in what they deliver and in the way it is delivered. Due to the nature of what the firm does as a part of its day-to-day work, it needs to develop in-house skills in marketing their own product and in marketing training as a whole. Their services and products are very difficult to market without a very large budget, and they deal with multinationals from a relatively weak position. One of the managers noted: 'We are a tiny operation compared to the majority of our customers'. Therefore, their innovation processes are largely dependent on their own skills, customized to the client.

MTS-B refers to both internal and external expertise as important for accumulating knowledge. The firm put special emphasis in operating as an 'open book' in the different parts of the company and with the communication flows. For example, conversations with clients are a source of knowledge that is recorded before to formalise a job. The knowledge is recorded in a central system and shared throughout the company. Platforms that the firm uses for integrating and transfer of knowledge are task forces, committees (especially for safety meetings every month), and weekly staff meetings. Formal and informal communications are balanced for learning, and the firm has two managers that keep OH&S knowledge for the group. This firm used to begin work in an informal basis and then progress to a more formal setting involving more people from the company. Informal outings are quite normal with prospective clients. Because the business is so diverse, staff learn from different parts of the company that have different processes leading to different solutions and ways to resolve problems. The firm has two managers looking after knowledge management. Professionals involved in KISA with the client company come from different backgrounds, and their experiences differ a lot, as one of the managers noted:

> People from our company and the client have a combined knowledge that it's not always common ground. We learn from the clients as they maintain the equipment and they want to improve their processes. Sometimes we feel we cannot achieve a common ground, it doesn't happen always. A contract leads to another one and small improvements and designs are made from the interactions. The knowledge also works on the other side; we learn from them while they learn from us. The way the knowledge transfer works is that new ways to do things are implemented for new clients with solutions we have seen in other mining site for other clients. (Martinez-Fernandez, 2005:39)

The quote above points to an interesting point about knowledge facilitating absorptive capacity in both participants of KISA, a process explained by Muller and Zenker (2001) and discussed in Chapter 1.

MTS-C has technological capabilities in developing products and processes and catering to a variety of specialised services; these are mainly dependent on the expertise and skills of its professionals who 'work in interdisciplinary teams' consisting of software, engineering and geoscience backgrounds. As a firm, which is also sustained through an in-house R&D centre, this company has given considerable importance to training which combines professional, technical and marketing skills as the professionals themselves undertake the marketing processes. As the Manager of the firm observed, so-called 'hybrid' teams work on projects of an interdisciplinary nature, mostly interacting with research institutions and government departments in geosciences, mining and exploration. Within these teams the firm has identified certain key professionals whom it terms as 'Product Champions' who coordinate projects and regulate interaction with various clients and customers. These key persons are referred to as 'chip innovator', 'thinker', and 'creator' who are instrumental for absorbing information and knowledge flows and interaction processes for KISA. The firm quite explicitly maintained that such key personnel and their skills cannot be easily obtained externally on a contractual basis. These key personnel are endowed with 'tacit knowledge' and 'competencies' which are person-embodied and are generally developed through processes of 'learning by interaction' or 'learning by doing' over a period of time.

MTS-D mixes and matches expertise and develop skills through project managers. They will continually report to project groups with their experiences. 'Internal rotations and moves and changes of projects' assure integration and transfer of knowledge. There are also internal processes such as 'learning lunches', where someone stands up and presents what they have done through some type of innovation or new way to resolve problems. There is also a 'knowledge coordinator' responsible for keeping a 'dynamic library' of possible solutions so people do not need to reinvent the wheel. People will submit a synopsis of the solution; then other employees can look at it and if they find a better solution through a project they will modify the synopsis for the next person, a type of 'open source' knowledge database. Another mechanism is to have other individuals appointed to the project to act as peer-reviewers for assuring a minimum standard of quality, assuring employees follow the right procedures for documenting the project and so on. This firm has created new ways to manage knowledge that were not there years ago, as one manager reports:

> The reasons for the company to put these mechanisms in place were that they needed to become more efficient in the job; customers wanted quicker jobs and cheaper jobs, there was a frustration internally that we always were reinventing the wheel, so there was a combined requirement that evolved. We also wanted to capitalize in what people have done and not repeat same mistakes twice. (Martinez-Fernandez, 2005:40)

Over the last five years the firm had significant growth in performance for several reasons, one being that a number of structures for knowledge management were put it in place. Through these structures, critical IP is developed internally while support processes are outsourced. The capabilities for innovation in this firm come very much from the relationship with the clients. There is a constant evolutionary process with customers: 'we listen to them, think about what they want, and we can do it now or go away, work on it and then come back'. The most important capability relates to business and management skills. New capabilities needed are in marketing skills, which is also core to the revenue.

Mining company-E indicates that its management of knowledge is specific to the problem; basic knowledge can be integrated but variations of knowledge might be difficult to implement. The company will have natural incremental improvements processes by internal services but specific problems need external solutions that sometimes are radical. The company will then use task forces and working groups. The firm has informal group discussions about new technologies in the group. Knowledge is diffused by letting people know what is happening, and who is playing important roles; but the core of the information is embedded in the group that is managing a particular project. Public relations people inform staff about issues arising from projects. For example, the firm will have written procedures about the operations covering safety and hygiene: it has many procedures for safety reasons at the plant level. The firm also presents technical papers to specialist professional bodies and mining groups. Newsletters, magazines or email are not generally used to disseminate information. The website is also not really used in the same way that universities do for disseminating and attracting new customers. One manager reports: 'Economic factors might force us to do things in a different way but innovation needs the external provision, we need to learn from the effective use of technology that will be around for many years. We have less risk when we take the advice from an external provider' (Martinez-Fernandez, 2005:41).

Mining company-F runs 1 to 2 seminars per month where technical staff meet and listen to an expert. The firm has a 'formal quality documents system' to capture information. Also there are spin-offs from one implemented product to a service. Sometimes the company that provides the software also provides the training so the firm integrates that capability. Sometimes the provider suggests new training or other activity that involves implementation. Depending on the projects in question, the firm will have external experts delivering these services – and not all examples are successful: 'We had an external company to provide the housing for workers, but they didn't understand the culture here and they wanted to profit from the housing and that was a failure. We do this now in-house as we understand better the culture in a remote location' (Martinez-Fernandez, 2005:41).

To disseminate and integrate knowledge this firm has some formal platforms such as project management, seminars, procedures (manuals), and on-going services specific to projects. The firm has project managers with 10 years experience that learn by doing and are responsible for implementation and transfer of knowledge. The strongest capability of the firm refers to their technology: mine design, metallurgy, plant equipment, and mining processes. The firm has a '10-day growth cooper cycle' that is totally managed in-house and that constitutes an innovation that other mines are looking at; it might become a service offered to others in the future. Capabilities for the future are related to maintenance, which is a huge service that has always been provided externally. The aim is to make it in-house because of the on-going cost but attracting staff is the biggest challenge for having this service done in-house.

The case studies suggest that MTS companies do not see themselves as 'users' of services but as providers. The interesting feature here is the activities they develop for the mining company (customers), the way they interact, how they are able to improve in their solution base and how they are able to implement innovation with each job. In doing this, these companies could present similar behaviour as other service providers, such as software or tourism companies. The difference is that the customer itself is an enormous and very dynamic provider of knowledge, as mining companies today held a constellation of services at the mining site. Knowledge interactions are so frequent that the mining site can be considered as a laboratory of continuous learning for the companies working on the site.

The mix and match of internal and external expertise is usually done by project managers, product champions, and knowledge coordinators or by using formal platforms such as seminars and manuals. MTS companies seen to have more innovative solutions when it comes to knowledge management than mining companies despite the fact that mining companies are managing a significant number of contractors every day. This might be due to the fact that MTS companies are highly dependent on the integration of knowledge they learn from each contract, as the application of new solutions is frequently based on their previous experiences. In this way, MTS companies act as transformers of the mining industry by transporting innovations from one mining site to the next one and by providing enhanced solutions based in previous solutions that worked well for other clients. The dependence of mining companies on MTS companies is high when it comes to thinking of better solutions to particular problems. Mining companies rely on MTS firms to provide these solutions or to help them to find the most suitable. MTS companies are then able to implement that solution elsewhere within their confidentiality agreement with the mining company. As a result the whole mining industry, from site to site, benefits and it is transformed through the enhanced technological knowledge flowing through a knowledge-based techno-economic network.

CONCLUSIONS AND POLICY ISSUES

One of the important points arising from this study relates to the significance of KISA to innovation of firms, including an extensive number of activities not traditionally associated to R&D. The survey of mining technology firms and case studies suggest that there are information flows and knowledge flows between different actors in the network space of the firm. KISA are generated within the firm or through interaction processes with customers and external providers in the network space. Results from this study and previous KISA studies of the software and tourism industries (Martinez-Fernandez et al, 2005 a,b) suggest that we need to distinguish between inputs/providers of inputs to KISA and KISA itself as the context of the 'activity'. KISA has both tacit and codified dimensions mediated through professionals and their skills.

The case studies analysis suggests that KISA performed by MTS play a significant role in the transformation of the mining industry in Australia. The following conclusions can be extracted.

First, 'mining companies heavily rely on the expertise and operational capacity of MTS firms operating in mining sites' but is the interaction between client and MTS firms what brings content and quality to the innovation process. This interaction is articulated through KISA which are at the core of the business of mining technology services companies. KISA of high importance for both MTS and Mining Companies are:

- Exploration and other mining consulting;
- Design & Engineering consulting;
- Technical consulting services relevant to industry;
- Research & Development services;
- IP-related services; and
- OH&S.

Services or expert contributions to KISA are largely sourced in-house or by KIBS or by a combination of both with exception of industry development advice which is mainly sourced from industry associations. The process underpinning KISA that is supplied and KISA that is purchased is different and seems to be linked to company competitiveness. Supply of KISA are increasingly happening in the form of 'packages' linking products and services such as maintenance, marketing or management services. Purchase of services is oriented to strengthening the core capabilities of the firm. These include KISA related to IT consulting and Computer Services, Management Consulting and acquisition of new skills or specialist skilled personnel. The purchase of services has a direct relationship with the capabilities firms wish to have in the future. These KISA are not static but subject to changes in the market and to the release of new knowledge as it emerges from R&D efforts and business practices elsewhere.

Secondly, 'mining sites constitute hubs of knowledge intensity' where internal and external experts participate in KISA oriented to prepare innovative solutions tailored to specific problems. The process of KISA development by MTS firms is not dependent exclusively on formal contractual arrangements but on flexible interchanges and interactions across the network of companies in the 'innovation milieu' of the firm. Within this space, those in closer relationship to the 'product' constitute the main 'actors' with regard to sourcing knowledge. These are the sales force front-end staff, customers and clients. KISA collaboration has specially increased among customers and suppliers of the firm. Integration of the different KISA within the company is usually handled by the management team or by a dedicated project manager; it is not a fixed strategy but determined on a project-by-project basis. The mix and match of internal and external expertise is usually done by project managers, product champions, and knowledge coordinators or by using formal platforms such as seminars and manuals.

Thirdly, 'the number of MTS companies working in a particular site at any one moment constitutes a complex network of KISA' that is not usually evaluated, nor does it form part of company's management systems. Hundreds of contractors can be associated with the mine site; they have a significant impact both on the mining company where they operate, and on other KIBS operating in town. In this respect mining sites are innovation intensive ecosystems that often lack the attention to the management of KISA as a value added to the organisational structure.

Fourthly, one of the main conclusions from this study is that KISA performed by MTS firms strongly impact the innovation and competitiveness of mining firms. This impact critically depends on the quality of the interaction between the MTS firm and the mining firm. The frequency and diversity of these KISA are influencing the rapid transformation of the mining industry in the industry knowledge economy into a 'knowledge based techno-economic network'.

Finally, despite mining sites being often found in remote locations, MTS headquarters are predominantly found in business centres and inner city locations. New South Wales, Victoria and Queensland have the highest number of mining technology companies. The sector has specific geographical features of clustering in the cities of Sydney and Perth, stressing the importance of network connections to corporate headquarters and other KIBS often associated with financial centres, especially in the case of Sydney. The study suggests the importance of internationalisation of actors as vital for the innovation process of these companies.

At the same time, and due to the remoteness of mining sites, people, transport infrastructure and logistics plays a major role in the sustained growth of the industry. The study did not found evidences of urban or regional absorptive capacity of the firm innovation ecosystem which appears to be confined within the boundaries of the mining site.

Emerging Policy Themes

The findings suggest the following policy considerations:

- There is a need for governments to promote the awareness of the role of KISA in innovation of traditional industries. Specifically, it is important to focus attention on the different functions of internal and external knowledge intensive services for KISA and their relationships to firm competitiveness. For instance, one function of sourcing external expertise is to keep abreast with international technological innovations and solutions that internal experts might not have been exposed to. Thus, future capabilities might depend on increasing external contributions to KISA;

- Particularly in the mining industry the importance of knowledge management is growing in importance for the sustainability of the industry and government departments should attract attention to the fact that MTS firms have advanced knowledge management systems and practices that can be shared within the mining site environment;

- Significantly the findings of the study suggest that there is a need to see the MTS sector as part of a knowledge based techno-economic network together with mining companies. This network presents clustering features in mining sites and in financial business centres. Thus, policies and programmes oriented to build and develop this network across mining sites and financial business centres would enhance innovation capability of the whole mineral industries;

- Policy programmes could consider promoting or recommending initiatives to enhance KISA that is tailored to both MTS and mining firms as they are part of the same innovation ecosystem and their interactions are indeed of an intense nature;

- There is a need for different government levels in Australia to increase the quality of transport infrastructure and urban logistics for the remote mining areas, as an important part of the MTS sector development. A significant feature of the sector is based on moving people to remote locations that lack the sophisticated network connections and development of more developed urban areas;

- Finally, urban management and planning strategies should be directed to connect the rich innovation systems operating in mining sites with the regional innovation system, which is often comprised of weak connections due to the remote location, the fly-in/fly-out work-pattern of mining professionals, and the high mobility of residents. In particular local SMEs would greatly benefit of greater connection to mining businesses and activity.

NOTES

1. Group set up by the Australian Government, includes business, industry groups and government agencies.
2. MTS Definition, MTSAA implementation committee, May 2004, email communication.

3. ARISE – A000106313 ARC Large Grant and KISA- LP0349167 ARC Linkage Grant.
4. Australian Mineral Industries Association.
5. Includes manufacturers of light and heavy mining machinery.
6. ARC Linkage KISA LP 0349167 studies of the software, Tourism and MTS sectors. http://aegis.uws.edu.au/KISA/main.html

REFERENCES

BRW (Business Review Weekly) (2006), **August** (31) p. 54.

Den Hertog, P. (2000), 'Knowledge-intensive Business Services as Co-producers of Innovation', *International Journal of Innovation Management*, **4** (4), pp. 491–528.

Department of Industry, Tourism and Resources (DITR) (2002), *Mining Technology Services Action Agenda: Background Paper on Issues Affecting the Sector,* DITR: Canberra.

Department of Industry, Tourism and Resources (DITR) (2003), *Mining Technology Services: Australia Leading the World*, Mining Technology Services Action Agenda, Strategic Leaders Group Report to Government, DITR: Canberra.

Gallouj, C. (1997), 'Asymmetry of Information and the Service Relationship: Selection and Evaluation of the Service Provider', *International Journal of Service Industry Management*, **8** (1), pp. 42–64.

Hales, M. (2000), 'Services Deliveries in an Economy of Competence Supply', *Synthesis Report Work Package 5 of RISE – RTOs in the Service Economy*, Brighton: Centrim.

Hauknes, J. (2000), 'Dynamic Innovation Systems: What is the Role of Services?', in M. Boden and I. Miles (eds) *Services and the Knowledge-based Economy*, London and New York: Continuum.

Hogan, L. (2004), *Research and Development in Exploration and Mining Implications for Australia's Gold Industry*, January, ABARE eReport 04.3. Prepared for CSIRO Exploration and Mining, Canberra.

Macfarlane, I. (2003), *Mining Technology Exports to Hit $6 Billion by 2010,* 10 October, Media Release by the Hon. Ian Macfarlane MP, Federal Minister for Industry, Tourism and Resources, Canberra.

Martinez-Fernandez, M.C. (2005), Knowledge Intensive Service Activities (KISA) in Innovation of Mining Technology Services in Australia. Sydney: University of Western Sydney.

Martinez-Fernandez, C. (2010), 'Knowledge Intensive Service Activities in the Success of the Australian Mining Industry', *The Service Industry Journal* **30** (1), pp. 55–70.

Martinez-Fernandez, M.C. and Martinez-Solano, L. (2006), 'Knowledge Intensive Service Activities (KISA) in Software Innovation', *International*

Journal Services Technology and Management, IJSTM Special Issue **7** (2), pp. 109–73.

Martinez-Fernandez, M.C., Soosay, C. and Tremayne, K. (2004), 'The Learning Space of the Service Firm and Elements in the Co-production of Knowledge: Evidence from Australian Service Firms', *International Conference on Knowledge Management (ICKM04) – December 13–15 2004*, Singapore.

Martinez-Fernandez, M.C., Soosay, C., Krishna, V.V., Turpin, T. and Bjorkli, M. (2005a), *Knowledge Intensive Service Activities (KISA) in Innovation of the Software Industry Australia*, University of Western Sydney: Sydney.

Martinez-Fernandez, M.C., Soosay, C., Krishna, V.V., Toner, P., Turpin, T., Bjorkli, M. and Doloswala, K.N. (2005b), *Knowledge Intensive Service Activities (KISA) in Innovation of the Tourism Industry Australia*, Sydney: University of Western Sydney.

Miles, I. (1999), 'Services in National Innovation Systems: From Traditional Services to Knowledge Intensive Business Services', in G. Schienstock and O. Kuusi (eds), *Transformation Towards a Learning Economy: The Challenge to the Finnish Innovation System*, Helsinki: Sitra.

Miles, I. and Boden, M. (2000), 'Services, Knowledge and Intellectual Property', in B. Andersen, J. Howells, R. Hull, I. Miles and J. Roberts (eds), *Knowledge and Innovation in the New Service Economy*, Cheltenham, UK, and Northampton, MA, USA: Edward Elgar.

Miles, I., Kastrinos, N., Bilderbeek, R., Den Hertog, P. with Flanagan, K., Huntink, W. and Bouman, M. (1995), 'Knowledge-intensive Business Services: Their Role as Users, Carriers and Sources of Innovation', *Report to the EC DG XIII Luxembourg: Sprint EIMS Programme*.

Muller, E. and Zenker, A. (2001), 'Business Services as Actors of Knowledge Transformation: The Role of KIBS in Regional and National Innovation Systems', *Research Policy*, **30** (9), pp. 1501–16.

Murphy, M. and Vickery, G. (1999), *Strategic Business Services*, Paris: OECD.

O'Connor K. and Kershaw, L. (1999), *Outsourcing, Producer Services and Shifts in the Geography of the Australian Mining Industry*, http://www.arts.monash.edu.au/ges/who/pdf/mining%20services.pdf [15.05.04].

Organisation for Co-operation and Economic Development (OECD) (2001), *Knowledge Intensive Service Activities in Innovation Systems – Australian Proposal for a Case Study*, DSTI/STP/TIP (2001) 17, Paris: OECD.

Organisation for Co-operation and Economic Development (OECD) (2002), *Progress Report on the TIP Case Study in Innovation in Knowledge Intensive Service Activities (KISA)*, 10–11 December 2002, Paris: OECD.

Organisation for Co-operation and Economic Development (OECD) (2006), *The Role of Knowledge Intensive Activities (KISA) in Innovation*. Paris:

OECD.

Roper, S. and Love, J.H. (2006), 'Innovation and Regional Absorptive Capacity: The Labour Market Dimension' *Annals Regional Sciences*, **40**, pp. 437–47.

Sundbo, J. and Gallouj, F. (2000), 'Innovation as a Loosely Couple System in Services', in J.S. Metcalfe and I. Miles (eds), *Innovation Systems in the Service Economy*, Dordrecht: Kluwer.

Tedesco, L., Copeland, A. and Hogan, L. (2002), *Mining Technology Services in Australia*, ABARE Research Report 02.9, Canberra, June.

Tedesco, L. and Curtotti, R. (2005), *Mining Technology Services: A Review of the Sector in Australia*, ABARE e-Report 05.5, Canberra, April.

5   KISA Role in Traditional Manufacturing Industries: the Case of Ceramic Tiles in Spain

José Albors-Garrigos, Jose Luis Hervas-Oliver and Patricia Marquez Rodriguez

This chapter will explore, analyse and compare the ways in which knowledge intensive activities occur in a mature industry: the ceramic tile sector in Spain. These activities impact the firms' performance in relation to their strategic foci. Through a selection of a dozen variables we applied multivariable tests to map the industry, and evaluate the impact of certain activities on performance. The results suggest that those firms with activities intensive in KISA outperformed the rest. A model is proposed to explain this correlation.

INTRODUCTION

Worldwide ceramic tile production is concentrated in clusters within Spain, Italy, Brazil, India, Mexico and China. Traditionally, up to the mid 1990s European producers were led by Italy (Emilia-Romagna) and Spain (Castellon) whose clusters represented around 70 per cent of the ceramic tile world commerce and more that 40 per cent of the world production (Ascer, 1998). The industry in the leading European territories is formed basically by ceramic tile firms (final production stage), ceramic equipment, and glazing materials suppliers with a high degree of vertical disintegration in both cases, especially in Spain. Both clusters followed a pattern of supplier-driven innovation (in terms of Pavitt's (1984) classification). The majority of the equipment innovations came from the Italian ceramic equipment industry, and similarly, the innovations in the glazing aspect come from the Spanish ceramic glazing industry. Both supplying industries provided innovations and technology to the European first adopters and later to the rest of the value chain worldwide.

Nevertheless, at the present time these European producers jointly represent 47 per cent of the world export share in 2004, following slow growth in the production for Spain (+3.1 per cent) and a decline, for Italy (-6.7 per cent) over the period 2000 to 2004 (ASCER, 2005). On the contrary, new players such as Brazil (+25 per cent), Mexico (+28 per cent) and China (+21.7 per cent) experienced dramatic growth in this period, to the extent that Brazil is closely catching up to Italy in world production figures. Three Brazilian clusters (ceramic districts of Criciuma, Mogi-Guaçu and Santa Gertrudis) and others such as Indonesia, Turkey, and Mexico have experienced a fantastic evolution. China has also overcome the European producers jointly and is also catching up to the figures of international commerce (Table 5.1).

Table 5.1 Production, growth, world production, and export market share

Country	Production (millions of sq. m)	Growth rate accumulated 2000–2004 (%)
China	2200	21.7%
Spain	640	3.1%
Italy	589	-6.7%
Brazil	566	25%
India	270	178%
Indonesia	260	30%
Turkey	216	23%
Mexico	177	28%

Source: Authors, adapted from Ascer (2005), millions of square meters produced

Spain is not only one of the main world producers and number one in the ceramic tile industry in Europe (production of square meters), but the largest world consumer per capita with 8.2 square meters per inhabitant (Ascer, 2005). The cluster of Castellon, which appeared cited in several empirical papers (for example Molina, 2002, Giner and Santa María, 2002) has been recognised as an industrial district phenomenon. Throughout 30 square km approximately there are around 36,000 direct industrial jobs, and more than 300 firms of different industries related to ceramic tile production (ceramic producers, glazing suppliers, clay providers, ceramic machinery suppliers, transport agencies, distributors, among others) are located there. Moreover, different public institutions belonging to the Network of Technological Institutes of the Valencian Community Region (where Castellon belongs); such as the Institute of Ceramic Technology (ITC); and the Association for the Promotion of Ceramics Design (ALICER) are part of the cluster endowment. Educational centres, such as the university Jaume I, offer special courses on ceramic tile production, such as Chemical Engineering in Ceramics, unique in Europe. The Spanish glazing industry, located in Castellon, is the leading world industry, with extended operations in other clusters such as the Italian one and others in Brazil. Even most of the Chinese development has been conducted due to the Spanish glazing industry efforts in China.

Along with Spain, Italy presents one of the strongest ceramic industries in the world. Around 83 per cent of Italy's ceramic tile production is concentrated in the Emilia Romagna region, around Sassuolo, where 30,799 direct jobs (Assopiastrelle, 2002) associated with ceramic tile producers are located, and more than 6000 in the suppliers industries. Similar to Castellon, the Italian region comprises an industrial district where a whole series of public institutions such as the Centre of Ceramics of Bologna (CCB, hereinafter), similar to the ITC. Moreover, private ones such as Assopiastrelle (the trade association of the industry) are located there and interconnecting all industries related to ceramic tile in the region. Italy is the number one ceramic tile exporter in the world, representing a contribution of 26 per cent (Ascer 2005) to international commerce. An important characteristic and strength of Italy's district is the creation of a strong industrial base of machinery for the ceramic tile industry that leads the world market, and expands its innovations to the Italian ceramic tile manufacturers. Spain and Italy together (each country led by their respective clusters, Castellon and Emilia Romagna) represent 47 per cent (ASCER 2005) of the world ceramic tile exports, and 76.8 per cent of European ceramic tile production, with a decrease from 2002 in which represented 90 per cent.

The auxiliary industry has also a different composition on both territories due to the role played in the global value chain. On one hand, the Castellon cluster has a prominent importance in the world-leading glazing industry. However, the Italian cluster was more focused on the ceramic equipment industry. Glazing industry in Castellon is the world leader, accounting with 26 firms which export 60 per cent of the total production valued in 900 million Euros and comprised around 3700 workers in 2004 (ASCER, 2005). In fact, in Italy there are 20 firms located from which the majority are from the Castellon cluster, thus employing 1700 workers, with a turnover around 400 million Euros. Similarly, ceramic machinery equipment from Emilia-Romagna is also the world leader, with a total turnover of 1593.4 million euro in 2004 and exporting 72 per cent of the total production (ACIMAC, 2005). These figures can illustrate what has been corroborated by previous authors (for example Meyer-Stamer et al, 2004) on the idea that upstream, the global value chain main advances are provided by the Spanish glazing industry and the Italian ceramic equipment. In addition, they are also represented in the counterpart clusters. Thus, the clusters are mutually connected, dependent, and reinforced by the suppliers in both industries, to the extent that the majority of the glazing firms in Italy come from Spain and the ceramic equipment producers in Spain come from Italy (Albors, 2002). It should be noted that ceramic equipment producers in Spain are mainly represented (totally or partially) by Italian firms. There are 41 firms listed that are dedicated entirely to the ceramic machinery industry, thus employing around 1400 workers with a turnover of 235 million Euros and 40 per cent of exports over total production (ASCER, 2005).

Institutional endowments were remarkably different in the two territories studied. While the Jaume I University in Castellon offered a unique chemical ceramic engineering degree, which is also connected to the ITC, neither the University of Modena and Reggio Emilia nor the University of Bologna had such a special tertiary degree on ceramics. As a consequence, a substantive difference could be observed in the local universities and also in the R&D institutes located in both clusters. As a matter of fact, the ITC had, in 2004, approximately double the budget for research projects than did the Emilian cluster, while the number of researchers employed full time were 56 in the ITC versus 20 in the CBC (Table 5.2).

In general, both Italian and Spanish clusters are well equipped institutionally. For both have enough public and private mechanisms to provide proper support to the value chain, although interaction and certain institutions like the ITC and their collaboration with the Jaume I University seemed to perform better in Castellon (Meyer-Stamer et al, 2004).

DEVELOPMENT OF HYPOTHESES

The proposed model is based in the relationship between knowledge intensive service activities (KISA) and the firm competencies. Moreover, our focus is based, as it has been already described, on a clustered industry in which firms and institutions are linked due to geographic circumstances. Under this context, KISA occurs at different levels and the absorption of KISA depends on the firm's competitive advantages, learning capability and the whole system may be related to the economic performance.

Firm's Internal Capabilities for KISA Absorption

Scholars belonging to the Resource Based Value mainstream (for example Barney, 1991) argued that organisational capabilities enhance a firm's performance. Moreover innovative firms performed better than those non-innovative (Zaheer and Bell, 2005), considering innovation to be an essential capability.

From this internal perspective, innovation arises from better organisational routines and other core functions moderated by the features of a specific sector (Amit and Schoemaker, 1993). Scholars also linked innovativeness to 'absorptive capacity' (Zaheer and Bell, 2005), defined as the internal organisational features needed to exploit external knowledge (Cohen and Levinthal, 1990). This idea is consistent with the findings of Molina and Martinez (2004), that found firms exploited external resources from R&D institutions or through interactions with suppliers in different ways, partially due to their internal capabilities which limit their use of external ones and the ability to combine these with external ones. As a consequence, the internal capability in a firm influences the absorption and combination of external services with the firm's own capabilities, stressing the learning capacity and positively affecting the performance. Accordingly, we reach the first hypothesis:

Hypothesis 1: 'Firm innovativeness expands the firm's absorptive capability and thus increases the firm's performance'.

Table 5.2 Institutional endowment in the global ceramic tile value chain

Institutions/ Associations	Emilia- Romagna	Castellón	Objectives
Trade associations	Assopias- trelle (ceramic tile) ACIMAC (equipment)	ASCER (ceramic tile), Annfec (glazing) ASEBEC (equipment)	Provide infrastructure for contacts and advice, lobbying, information centres, organisation of fair trades, collective negotiations with government, training courses organisation, joint purchasing, regional marketing, brand building, and so on.
Educational and training centres	University of Bologna and University of Modena, and Reggio Emilia. Cerform	Jaume I University Ceramic Promotion Institute Vocational Training Centre	Provide infrastructure to promote technology and know-how transfer from academia to industry, research and development. Advice and contacts for spin-offs; innovation support, patenting information, training, leading governmental research projects to diffuse knowledge and recommended practices;
R&D institutes	Bologne Ceramic Centre (CCB)	Technological Ceramic Institute (ITC) Technological Design Ceramic Institute (ALICER)	educational support: triple helix
Other institutions	Assocargo (collective logistic centre)	Chambers of Commerce and other institutions -Quality Ceramic Group	Provide governmental and institutional support, information, start-up help, bureaucratic matters, and so on. The Quality Ceramic Club, group of managers promoting excellence and quality in the industry, and trying to reinforce support by regional institutions

Source: Authors; obtained from www.assopiastrelle.com and www.ascer.es

Embedded KISA as External Sources of Innovation Resources

The influence of a superior network position (Gulati et al, 2000; Zaheer and Bell, 2005) has been linked to the role of structural holes (Burt, 1992) in performance (Zaheer and Bell, 2005), proving that a firm bridging structural holes can outperform other non-linked firms (McEvily and Zaheer, 1999) and can improve access to information sharing and trust (Gulati, 1999). Maintaining an active presence in networks leads to the development of absorptive capacity (Stuart, 1998; Zaheer and Bell, 2005) which promotes interorganisational learning through knowledge sharing with other networked firms and institutions (McEvily and Zaheer, 1999). Drawing on these findings, it has been claimed that firms which bridge structural holes have better access to resources (information, knowledge, trust) and adapt better to emerging threats and opportunities (Zaheer and Bell, 2005) in the industry, since knowledge is developed partially through firm interaction (Nahapiet and Ghoshal, 1998). Within the cluster literature the bridging structural holes theory is represented in Johannisson et al's (2002) framework in which the variety of links within a cluster are classified as 'first-order embeddedness' (firm-to-firm relations), 'second-order embeddedness' (firm relations with social and economic institutions) and 'third-order embeddedness' (firms indirectly related through social and economic institutions). These linkage types are based both upon economic (systemic) and social (substantive) embeddedness dimensions. Thus, KISA occurs through these interactions and links which promote the firm's transactions and expand the firm learning capacity to incorporate new resources and capabilities. Accordingly we hypothesise that:

Hypothesis 2: Firms 'which bridge structural holes through KISA enhance their performance'.

The studies discussed above concur that firms acquire resources through both internal and external sources. With the objective of integrating internal and external sources for acquiring competitive capabilities clustered firms will form unique strategic combinations of internal and external resources. While the available cluster endowment is the same for firms located in the cluster, the firms' competitive capabilities will constrain their exploitation of these external resources. Hence, the framework of the 'Organizational Ecology' (Hannan and Freeman, 1977) argues that the scope of analysis in an industry is the 'population of organizations' which adopts similar forms regarding objectives, technologies or markets (Hannan and Freeman, 1977:936). These populations or strategic groups are understood to be 'a group(s) of enterprises that follow similar strategies in terms of key decision variables'

(Porter, 1979:215). In this sense, due to the limitations surrounding cluster endowment, firms are constrained to a certain type of combined internal and external sources for acquiring capabilities, due to the limited range of the cluster's available resources. This actually complements the RBV (Resource Based Value). In fact, there is abundant literature concerning strategic group identification through firms with similar resources and capabilities (Nohria and García-Pont, 1991; Mehra, 1996; Mehra and Floyd, 1998) from the point of view of exclusively own firm resources. Moreover, according to Hervas and Albors (2007), a cluster will feature firms utilising external resources in similar ways. They will vary in, for instance, the use of R&D institutes for testing and laboratory activities, collaboration with other firms in the supply chain management or the pursuance of shared commercial missions into new markets. In conclusion, the authors considered that in the cluster context both similar internal and external combinations of resources are conducted in much the same way within certain groups of firms possessing the same strategic orientation with a shared paradigm and a similar strategic 'reference point' (Fiegembaum and Thomas, 1995). As a consequence, and in support of 'strategic groups' analysis (for example McNamara, Luce and Thompson, 2002; Nohria and García-Pont, 1991) we predicted that within a cluster, strategic heterogeneity (McEvily and Zaheer, 1999; Molina and Martinez, 2004; Lazerson and Lorenzoni, 1999) could exist between groups, while also observing a certain degree of strategic homogeneity as cited in the industrial district literature (Pouder and St. John, 1996:1195), which argued that firms in regions tend to exhibit 'similar resources, cost structures, mental models and competitive behaviour'. Perhaps this homogeneity could be applied to the group level. This implies that within the cluster, it is possible to identify strategic groups of firms, in terms of combining internal and external sources of acquiring resources to underpin skills for competitiveness. In accordance with this, we hypothesise that:

Hypothesis 3: 'Clustered firms are likely to be formed by strategic groups of firms in terms of similar internal and KISA combination to acquire capabilities'.

Furthermore, the association of groups in performance levels is a crucial issue (Mascarenhas and Aaker, 1989) with respect to the study of strategic groups. Levinthal (1995:19) pointed this out when he affirmed that the principal mission of strategic management research centres was the analysis of the diversity of performance between firms. The analysis of the relationship between the profitability of companies and their belonging to strategic groups in an industry has been approached from the theoretical perspective by some authors, such as Dranove, Peteraf and Shanley (1998), to cite some examples, and from the empirical standpoint by others (McNamara, Luce and Thompson, 2002; Lee et al, 2003). While there are other studies reporting no such association (for example Cool and Schendel, 1987), we hypothesise that:

Hypothesis 4: 'Strategic group membership by combination of internal and external KISA are associated to performance level'.

EMPIRICAL STUDY: VARIABLES

Our survey was carried out between March and May of 2004 in 45 firms which agreed to be involved in the study, which was supported by the trade association (ASCER). Individually, the authors visited 40 per cent of the sample firms to interview CEOs (Chief Executive Officers) and other top executives, to gain firsthand knowledge of how firms interpret the questionnaire. Other interviews were held with various professionals in the sector, companies and institutions to know the reality of the industry at first hand. Also, material on the sector was compiled (statistics, articles, press news, databases, sector reports, and so on) to learn more about the industry and the cluster itself. The sample was representative of the cluster population. Its size composition is reflected in Figure 5.1.

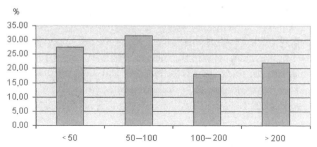

Figure 5.1 Sample size compositions

The peculiarity and potential of the variables used in the study lies in the fact that all of them are specific to the ceramic sector under study as Amit and Schoemaker (1993), and McEvily and Zaheer (1999) recommend. Hence, the metrics are easily comparable and robust to interpretations. In addition, different indicator variables for each block were extracted from the interviews and questionnaires previously planned and depicted from interviews and reviewing the industry. The variables representing knowledge intensive services and competitive aspects were developed and extracted from both internal and external industry resources, as a way to capture firms' knowledge combinations. The following knowledge intensive activities were identified: MKTGKISA (associated with the internal and external marketing functions in the firm); DISTRIBKISA (related to the agreements and services associated with the firm distribution system); DESIGNKISA (related to the internal and external design activities of the firm); PUBLCOMMKISA (referring to the firms PR activities); RTOKISA (refers to the R&D external contractual relationships of the firms); ITKISA (related to the information and communication activities); and PROCEDKISA (quality and environmental certification procedures services). Finally, TRAINING represents the extent and frequency of in-company and external training.

Other variables employed were EDUCATION (reflecting the percentage of employees with a university degree); SIZE (the firm size measured by its payroll); EMPOWERMENT (the degree of delegation management practised in the firm); PRODUCTION (measured in square metres of tiles produced during 2001); and SALES (the 2001 firm turnover measured in Euros). Both variables lead to the unit price variable (UNITPRICE), a potential useful measurement of the market segment served by the firm.

Moreover, KNOWLEDGECUST measured the extent of firm knowledge of the final customer demand. In a production led industry which is being challenged by global competition to evolve rapidly towards a demand led industry this latter variable is related to a critical firm proficiency, thus becoming a customer focused enterprise.

In relation to the economic performance, two indicators have been utilised: ROA (Return on Assets) and ROE (Return on Equity). These are objective, easily found and have been justified by many authors (that is Kaplinsky and Morris, 2001) as an approach to the firm's performance. As a result, Table 5.3 shows the variables utilised in the statistical analysis and justifies its statistical use.

Statistical Analysis

In a first stance, a factor analysis was carried out on the data in order to identify the critical variables, those which were responsible for the maximum sample variance of the observed variables. Three components were identified that accounted for 71.72 per cent of the sample variance.

The three components had the following composition: Component 1 was related to MKTGKISA, DESIGNKISA, PUBLCOMMKISA, DISTRIBKISA, RTOKISA, TRAINING, EDUCATION and KNOWLEDGECUST. This component relates all the relevant KISA activities as a web while the firm competence related to the knowledge of the final customer and its knowledge production capabilities (education level of employees). Component 2 is composed of ROE, representing the output performance; Component 3 is composed of EMPOWERMENT coinciding with the management practices of the firm.

Table 5.3 Survey variable

Variable	Composition	Description	EXT	INT
MKTGKISA α = 0.632	MARKETINGFUNCT	Marketing function and extent in the firm. Likert 1–3		x
	MARKETINGRESEARCH	Marketing Research extent Likert 1–0	x	
DISTRIBKISA α = 0.550	DISTRIBAGREEM	Commercial agreements at sale points for brand exclusivity or other privileges. Lickert 0–3	x	
	REPOSITION	% Market served to direct clients, 0–1		x
	SALEDELEGATIONS	Sales external offices, 0–1	x	
	OWNRETAIL	Existence of own retail chains, Lickert 0–1	x	
DESIGNKISA α = 0.564	DESIGNFUNCTION	Existence of Design Dept. Lickert, 0, 1		
	DESIGNGLAZECOLLAB	Extent of design collaboration with glaze manufacturers, Lickert, 0, 1	x	
	DESIGNOUTS	Extent of design outsourcing, Lickert (0, 1)		x
	DESIGNPERSON	Persons working in the design Dept.	x	
PUBLCOMMKISA α = 0.744	PUBLICITY	Firm Publicity extent, Lickert 0–3	x	
	PUBLICDISTR	Publicity focus towards distributors, Lickert 0–2	x	
	PUBLICFINAL	Publicity focus towards final customer, Lickert 0–2	x	
	EXHIBITION	Number internat. exhibitions attended, Lickert 1–3	x	
	COMMUNMEANS	Extend of public communication policy, 1–5	x	
	EXHIBSTANDLEVEL	Exhibition design and image evaluation, 1–5	x	
RTOKISA α = 0.722	Alicer	Use of R&D Institutions (Alicer); Qualitative Likert 0–2		x
	ITC	Use of R&D Institutions or (ITC); Qualitative Likert 0–3		x
	Socio Alicer	Member of R&D institution, 0–1		x
	WEBSITE	Evaluation of web site functionalities, 1–5		x
PROCEDKISA α = 0.686	ISO14000	Environment certification, 0–1		x

Table 5.3 (cont.)

Variable	Composition	Description	EXT	INT
	ISO9000	ISO quality certification, 0–1		x
	RE	Net Return on Assets (average 1999-03)		
	ROA	Return on Total Assets (average 1999–03)		
	KNOWLEDGE CUSTOMER	Level of customer demand knowledge, Lickert 0–2		
TRAINING	TRAINING	Extent and frequency of in-company training, 0–2		
	EDUCATION	% of university graduates in the firm		
	SIZE	Employment in the firm (number of employees)		
	EMPOWERMENT	Level of team decision making, Lickert 1–3		
	PRODUCTION	Square meters produced (2001)		
	SALES	2003 Turnover in Euros (2001)		

A cluster analysis utilising the k means method with the components developed by the factor analysis classifies the sample in three clusters. Table 5.4 outlines their characteristics. The classifying factors could be represented by the following equation:

- Component 1 = CRITICALKISA + KNOWLEDGE CAPABILITIES (KNOWLEDGECUST; EDUCATION; TRAINING)
- Component 2 = ROE (Performance)
- Component 3 = EMPOWERMENT (Management practices)

From the previous analysis we developed a new composite and additive variable, which we label CRITICALKISA. This variable represents the critical knowledge intensive activities selected by the factor analysis process. Thus, CRITICALKISA = MKTGKISA + DISTRIBKISA + DESIGNKISA + PUBLCOMMKISA + RTOKISA + TRAINING.

A cluster analysis utilising the k means method with this composed variable was able to classify the sample in three clusters composed of 5, 18 and 25 firms and with conglomerates centre values of CRITICALKISA of 58.63, 34.68 and 15.01 respectively.

Are these identified KISA activities correlated with the firm performance? Table 5.4 shows that there is correlation between CRITICALKISA and RE ratio (net return on assets) as well as with the average sales unit price (UNITPRICE), including the export percentage (EXPORT). There is also a correlation with the level of knowledge of customer demand

(KNOWLEDGECUST), but not with management delegation practices (EMPOWERMENT) or with the employees education level (EDUCATION).

Table 5.4 Correlation between critical KISA, management and performance

N = 48	CRITICALKISA			
ROE	Pearson Coeff.	-0.218	Tau *B* Kendall	-0.114
	Sig. (bilateral)	0.141	Sig. (bilateral)	0.259
RE	Pearson Coeff.	0.362[a]	Tau *B* Kendall	0.240[a]
	Sig. (bilateral)	0.012	Sig. (bilateral)	0.018
EMPOWERMENT	Pearson Coeff.	0.054	Tau *B* Kendall	0.066
	Sig. (bilateral)	0.718	Sig. (bilateral)	0.575
EDUCATION	Pearson Coeff.	0.246	Tau *B* Kendall	0.129
	Sig. (bilateral)	0.095	Sig. (bilateral)	0.205
UNITPRICE	Pearson Coeff.	0.272	Tau *B* Kendall	0.213[a]
	Sig. (bilateral)	0.065	Sig. (bilateral)	0.035
EXPORT	Pearson Coeff.	0.334[a]	Tau *B* Kendall	0.261[a]
	Sig. (bilateral)	0.022	Sig. (bilateral)	0.012
KNOWLEDGECUST	Pearson Coeff.	0.711[b]	Tau *B* Kendall	0.482[b]
	Sig. (bilateral)	0.000	Sig. (bilateral)	0.000

Notes:
a Significant correlation @ $p < 0.05$ (bilateral)
b Significant correlation @ $p < 0.01$ (bilateral)

Furthermore, following our analysis, and in order to reflect the firm competitiveness a new composite variable has been developed: COMPETITIVENESS = ROA + UNITPRICE + EXPORT. This variable takes into account ROA, or the ratio of Return on Assets. It also includes the product sales average unit price (obtained by dividing sales figures by the corresponding production figure in square meters) – in a very competitive mature market those firms capable of selling at the highest price segment can be considered competitive in the highest market segment (Albors and Hervas, 2006). Finally, the variable EXPORT has also been included, since those firms having the highest export percentage compete in the most competitive export markets. Flor and Oltra (2005) demonstrated, in the case of the Spanish ceramic tile cluster, the correlation between technology innovation capabilities and the firms' export performance.

The two variables, CRITICALKISA and COMPETITIVENESS are positively correlated (Pearson coefficient = 0.449 for $p < 0.01$, Tau b Kendall coefficient = 0.449 for $p < 0.05$), as expected from the previous correlation analysis. As illustrated in a dispersion chart, representing the values of CRITICALKISA and COMPETITIVENESS on the axes, the sample is distributed normally along the diagonal portion of the chart. Figure 5.2 (a) and (b) shows the dispersion graphs in both cases. When the sample has been classified into clusters according to the factor analysis components (as in

Table 5.4) or according to the CRITICALKISA values, the clusters are distributed along the diagonal line of the chart. However the conglomerates show a sharper differentiation when the composite variable CRITICALKISA is the sole classifying factor.

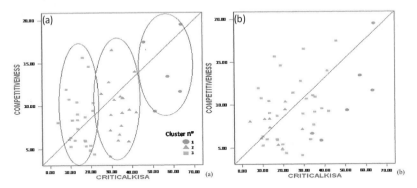

Notes: Sample clustered with factor analysis (b) and CRITICALKISA (a)

Figure 5.2 Dispersion graphs of CRITICALKISA versus competitive variables

Hervas and Albors (2007) working with the same sample, found empirical evidence of the formation of strategic groups in the ceramic cluster, thus linking them to the firm performance levels. Non-parametric approaches were used to test empirical performance differences between groups; this confirmed the existence of heterogeneity in the cluster. The results suggest which strategies were best to achieve top returns. Figure 5.2 shows the results of this analysis. The excellent core cluster of firms, having the higher performance ratios, followed a customer focus, product differentiation strategy and a high R&D activity (cluster 3). The firms composing this cluster overlapped 95 per cent with cluster 1 of Figure 5.2a which utilised the variable CRITICALKISA as the classifying factor.

Discussion

General KISA outcome
The factor analysis identified twenty-two knowledge intensive activities, which can be grouped in seven variables: MKTGKISA, DISTRIBKISA, DESIGNKISA, PUBLCOMMKISA, RTOKISA, ITKISA and TRAINING. These were grouped in a new-composite variable, CRITICALKISA. This variable was found to correlate with certain performance variables such as the net return on assets, the average sales unit price (UNITPRICE), and the

export sales percentage of the firms (EXPORT). On the other hand, CRITICALKISA also correlates with the level of knowledge in the firm and of the customer demand (KNOWLEDGECUST). These service activities are a mix of internal and external activities, in which the majority, are related to the customer end of the ceramic tile value chain (Albors et al, 2008). In particular, these activities are closely related to the firm competences linked to the knowledge of the final customer demands.

Another new composite variable (COMPETITIVENESS) was developed in order to reflect the firm competitiveness (as pointed out before it reflects ROA, the firm price segment as well as its export capabilities); this positively correlates with the knowledge intensive activities composite variable (CRITICALKISA). Furthermore, the results of plotting both variables, CRITICALKISA versus COMPETITIVENESS, as shown in Figure 5.2a/b, exhibit normal distributions, where clusters of firms are grouped in accordance to their level of knowledge intensive activities.

The role of information and communication technologies (ICT) as KISA
In order to investigate the lack of relation of the variable ITKISA to the economic performance outputs, we have also examined the digital accessibility of firms in the sectors of interest. Is their web presence really accessible to users? First, if the web site is easily identifiable, it is also accessible to the users. Speed was considered important, since Internet users are not tolerant of the waiting time required to reach a web site's homepage; if downloading is delayed, potential customers are likely to drift to an alternative site or give up online transactions, at least at that time (Weinberg, 2000). The Informational and Communicational content can include commercial information (that is product descriptions), non-commercial information (for example background of the company) and contact information, allowing the user to evaluate the firm's product and information offers. In addition, Transactional content is used to evaluate if the site counts with the potential of placing orders or conducting online financial transactions. Finally, the Services content explores what the firms offer in terms of service innovations created to facilitate all the processes related to the purchasing, from pre-purchase to after-sales phases.

A sample composed of 44 manufacturers' and 47 distributors' web sites, was utilised during 2005, all of them belonging to the Spanish ceramic tile industry. The evaluation was carried out with different surveys for each group. The manufacturers show relatively good results in terms of navigability and speed, with an average of three languages per page. However, few sites were judged to have sufficient links to external pages. The distributors typically utilise one language per site and practically have no site maps. The manufacturers do not show acceptable results in terms of link frequency use. The information related to the background of manufacturers and distributors is accessible in most cases. This is not the case for other relevant firm information such as departments, news or job opportunities. In relation to the information on products it covers the supply of catalogues as well as the product presentation using decoration settings by manufacturers. However, the information related to technical information, prices, decoration ideas (design), promotions and new products is scarce.

The distributors exhibit their products utilising catalogues or providing links to the manufacturers' web sites. The decoration/design settings are utilised by 36 per cent of the evaluated firms. Sales and new products are not an essential element for them. In general, the transactional content is low for the analysed web sites. Only three manufacturers and three distributors facilitate online orders and just one manufacturer provides information for checking order status. No firm offers online payment options, however, one sole distributor allows other payment forms. Considering the communication content, the analysed firms provide basically e-mail, information for physical contact or a contact form. However, the use of frequently asked questions (FAQs) is almost non-existent as well as after sales procedures or link provision for both groups. Figure 5.3 summarises the survey results for both groups.

Finally, the services content is scarce. Few firms, mainly manufacturers, offer the customer tools for designing their own tiles. Moreover, there are no provisions for collecting customers' ideas or suggestions. The provision of installation guides is the outstanding service offered by 25 per cent of the manufacturers and only one distributor. On the other hand, the service provided by most distributors is limited to some photographs of the store exhibition, and few of them even have options to demand technical advice or budgets through e-mail. The detailed results are shown in Figure 5.4.

Subsequently, a cluster analysis was performed in order to classify the firms according with their results in the exploratory study. This analysis classified the sample in four groups.

In the case of the distributors, the first cluster is formed by firms with web sites that offer limited information in all the dimensions, without any transaction component and with very few services offered through the web. This is the largest group. The second group is composed of firms with higher information content, especially on products, but like the first group without any results in term of transactions, as well as few offered services. The third group is the smallest, and provides more services, but the other components have similar results to the previous groups. Finally, the fourth group, is the only one offering some transaction component to customers as well as a variety of services.

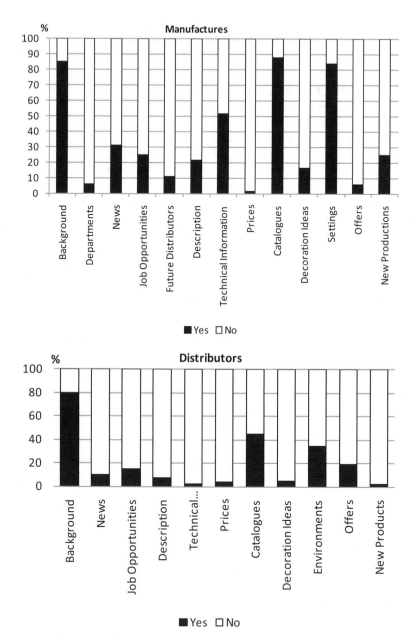

Figure 5.3 Results of firm and product information provided by manufacturers (top) and distributors through web sites (bottom)

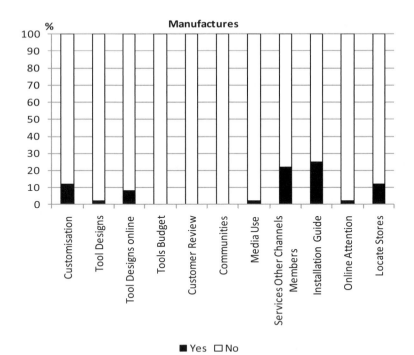

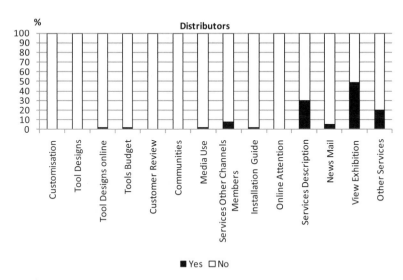

Figure 5.4 Results of services provided by manufacturers (top) and distributors (bottom) through web sites

The manufacturers' cluster analysis also showed four clusters. The first group presents the lowest performance on all the analysed dimensions – and is again the largest group. The second group displays higher performance than the former, especially considering information and communication content. However, the services content is also low, and the transactional content is null. The third group shows the best performance in almost all the dimensions, especially in services content, but still has no transaction through the internet. Finally, the fourth group is similar to the second and third group in terms of firm or product information and communicational content, but is the only group with various attempts to offer customers transactions through the web site.

Thus, the majority of the websites at this time were at the level of 'business cards' providing limited information on the company and its products/services, though with reasonable ease of use (Ross et al, 2000). However, the services content is very limited and the transaction contents are almost non-existent. Therefore, Spanish Ceramic Tile Producers and distributors, in general, are not offering products or services with high knowledge content through their web sites.

These results go some way toward explaining the absence of the variable ITKISA as one of the activities related with the outputs in terms of economic performance. Most firms are simply not using the web in sophisticated ways. A deeper multivariate analysis has demonstrated a positive relationship between net sales and content offered on the web sites in the manufacturers group (Albors et al, 2009). No relationship is observed in distributors' web sites, mainly due to the lack of quality contents. The cluster of excellence in the ceramic tile manufacturers, showed the highest results in information and services content in their web sites, thus confirming the previous conclusions.

FINDINGS AND CONCLUSIONS

The availability of knowledge intensive services is an important element of an innovation system. The surveyed firms need access to technical skills and advice if they are to innovate successfully. They also need access to management services to support innovation and develop their competences. Whether they buy them on the market or develop them in-house depends on their resource capacities. The survey researched the following KISA: employment training, IT services, management consultancy, research and development, marketing services, sales and distribution support, design services, and so on. Most firms accessed most of the listed services externally. The exceptions occur mostly in the case of larger firms, and are related to publicity and communication services. Most of the knowledge service providers were KIBS.

Previous research (Martinez-Fernandez et al, 2004) pointed out that the most important sources of knowledge and ideas for innovation might not be formal service providers, but the people and organisations the firm works with day by day. In addition to the internal sources, there are customers, suppliers, and other firms in the industry which can even be located closely geographically. However, these sources of KISA have not been explored here due to the limitations of the research opportunities. This will be a future subject of research.

The empirical study and consequent statistical analysis supported hypotheses 1 and 2. Variable CRITICALKISA associated with those KISA activities correlated with firm innovative activities and its competitiveness, thus expanding the firm's absorptive capability and thus increasing the firm performance (correlation shown with performance ratios).

The analysis of the ceramic tile cluster in Spain concluded that the internal and external knowledge intensive service activities were related to their output in terms of competitive advantages and economic performance. Overall, the firms studied have been clustered according to their strategic combination of internal and external KISA as sources of competitive advantage forming groups of firms with similar resources and capabilities acquired from internal and external sources in a similar way and being these groups associated with the level of performance. Thus, the results supported hypotheses three and four, showing how KISA acquisition seems to be associated with the firm performance level: a higher degree of KISA acquisition tends to correspond to a higher firm performance. At the same time, the firms located in the groups with higher innovation capacity and KISA acquisition showed higher performance ratios, aligning with the first two hypotheses. Thus, firm's KISA acquisition (CRITICALKISA) is correlated with innovation capability (COMPETITIVENESS). These results imply that internal capabilities and thus absorption capability shaped the KISA acquisition capacity. In other words, the most innovative firms tend to acquire more KISA because their internal capability allowed them to combine and use KISA in their strategies. We would anticipate that similar results will be found in other sectors and locations.

REFERENCES

ACIMAC, (2005), XV Indagine Statistica nazionale sull'industria Italiana delle macchine e attrezzature per ceramica. Italy: Modena.

Albors, J. (2002), 'Networking and Technology Transfer in the Spanish

Ceramic Tiles Cluster. Its Role in the Sector Competitiveness', *The Journal of Technology Transfer*, **27** (3), pp. 263–73.

Albors, J. and Hervas, J.L. (2006), 'The European Tile Ceramic Industry in the XXI Century. Challenges of the Present Decade', *Boletin Sociedad Espanola de Cerámica y Vidrio,* **45** (1), pp. 13–21.

Albors-Garrigos, J., Hervas-Oliver, J.L. and Marquez, P.B. (2008), 'When Technology Innovation is not Enough, New Competitive Paradigms, Revisiting the Spanish Ceramic Tile Sector', *International Journal of Technology Management*, **44** (3/4), pp. 406–26.

Albors-Garrigos, J., Hervas-Oliver, J.L. and Marquez, P.B. (2009), 'Internet and Mature Industries. Its Role in the Creation of Value in the Supply Chain. The Case of Tile Ceramic Manufacturers and Distributors in Spain', *International Journal of Information Management*, **29** (6), pp. 476–82.

Amin, A. and Cohendet, P. (2004), *Architectures of Knowledge – Firms, Capabilities and Communities*, Oxford: Oxford University Press.

Amit, R. and Schoemaker, P. (1993), 'Strategic Assets and Organizational Rent', *Strategic Management Journal*, **14**, pp. 33–46.

ASCER (1998, 2005), *Informes Anuales*, Spain: Castellon.

Assopiastrelle, (2002), *Indagine statistica nazionale Industria italiana delle piastrelle di ceramica*, Italy: Modena.

Barney, J. (1991), 'Firm Resources and Sustained Competitive Advantage', *Journal of Management*, **17** (1), pp. 99–120.

Bogner, W., Mahoney, W. and Thomas, H. (1993), 'The Role of Competitive Groups in Strategy Formulation: a Dynamic Integration on Two Competing Models', *Journal of Management Studies*, **30** (1), pp. 51–67.

Burt, R.S. (1992), *Structured Holes: The Social Structure of Competition*, Cambridge, MA: Harvard University Press.

Cohen, W.M. and Levinthal, D.A. (1990), 'Absorptive Capacity: a New Perspective on Learning and Innovation', *Administrative Science Quarterly* **35** (2), pp. 128–52.

Cool, K. and Schendel, D. (1987), 'Strategic Group Formation and Performance: the Case of the U.S. Pharmaceutical Industry, 1963–82', *Management Science*, **33** (9), pp. 1102–24.

Dranove, D., Peteraf, M. and Shanley, M. (1998), 'Do Strategic Groups Exist? An Economic Framework for Analysis', *Strategic Management Journal*, **19** (2), pp. 1029–44.

Fiegenbaum, A. and Thomas, H. (1995), 'Strategic Groups as Reference Groups: Theory, Modelling and Empirical Examination of Industry and Competitive Strategy', *Strategic Management Journal*, **16**, pp. 461–76.

Flor, M. and Oltra, M.J. (2005), 'The Influence of Firms' Technological Capabilities on Export Performance in Supplier Dominated Industries: the Case of Ceramic Tiles Firms', *R&D Management*, **35** (3), pp. 333–47.

Giner, J.M. and Santa María, M.J. (2002), 'Territorial Systems of Small Firms in Spain: an Analysis of Productive and Organizational Characteristics in Industrial Districts', *Entrepreneurship and Regional Development*, **14** (1), pp. 211–28.

Gulati, R. (1999), 'Network Location and Learning: the Influence of Network Resources and Firm Capabilities on Alliance Formation', *Strategic Management Journal*, **20** (5), pp. 397–420.

Gulati, R., Nohria, N. and Zaheer, A. (2000), 'Strategic Networks', *Strategic Management Journal*, **21** (3), pp. 203–15.

Hannan, M.T. and Freeman, J.H. (1997), 'The Population Ecology of Organizations', *American Journal of Sociology*, **82** (4), pp. 929–64.

Hervas, J.L. and Albors, J. (2007), 'Do the Capabilities of the Cluster Really Matter? Empirical Evidence in a European cluster', *Entrepreneurship and Regional Development*, **19**, 113–126.

Johannisson, B., Ramírez-Pasillas, M. and Karlsson, G. (2002), 'The Institutional Embeddedness of Local Inter-firm Networks: a Leverage for Business Creation', *Entrepreneurship and Regional Development*, **14** (1), pp. 297–315.

Kaplinsky, R. and Morris, M.A. (2001), *Handbook for Value Chain Research*, Institute of Development Studies; UK: University of Sussex.

Lazerson, M.H. and Lorenzoni, G. (1999), 'The Firms that Feed Industrial Districts: a Return to the Italian Source', *Industrial and Corporate Change*, **8** (2), pp. 235–66.

Lee, J., Lee, K. and Rho, S. (2003), 'An Evolutionary Perspective on Strategic Group Emergence: a Genetic Algorithm-based Model', *Strategic Management Journal*, **23** (3), pp. 727–46.

Levinthal, D.A. (1995), 'Strategic Management and the Exploration of Diversity', in C.A. Montgomery, (eds), *Resource-based and Evolutionary Theories of the Firm*, Norwell: Kluwer Academic Publishing.

McNamara, G., Deephouse, D. and Luce, R. (2003), 'Competitive Positioning Within and Cross a Strategic Group Structure: the Performance of Core, Secondary and Solitary Firms', *Strategic Management Journal*, **24** (1), pp. 161–81.

Mcnamara G., Luce, R. and Thompson, G. (2002), 'Examining the Effect of Complexity in Strategic Group Knowledge Structures on Firm Performance', *Strategic Management Journal*, **23** (1), pp. 153–70.

Martinez-Fernandez, M.C., Soosay, C., Bjorkli, M. and Tremayne, K. (2004), *Are Knowledge Intensive Service Activities Enablers of Innovation Processes? A Study of Australian Software Firms*, Sydney: CINET 2004 Conference Proceedings, September.

Mascarenhas, B. and Aaker, D. (1989), 'Mobility Barriers and Strategic Groups', *Strategic Management Journal*, **10** (3), pp. 475–85.

McEvily, B. and Zaheer, A. (1999), 'Bridging Ties: A Source of Firm Heterogeneity in Competitive Capabilities', *Strategic Management Journal*, **20** (4), pp. 1133–56.

Mehra, A. (1996), 'Resource and Market Based Determinants of Performance in the U.S. Banking Industry', *Strategic Management Journal*, **17** (3), pp. 307–22.

Mehra, A. and Floyd, S.W. (1998), 'Product Market Heterogeneity, Resource Limitability and Strategic Group Formation', *Journal of Management*, **24**, pp. 511–31.

Meyer-Stamer, J., Maggi, C. and Seibel, S. (2004), 'Upgrading the Tile Industry of Italy, Spain, and Brazil: Insights from Cluster and Value Chain Analysis', in Schmitz, H. (eds) *Local Enterprises in the Global Economy*, Cheltenham, UK, and Northampton, MA, USA: Edward Elgar, pp. 174–99.

Miles, I., Kastrinos, N., Flanagan, K., Bilderbeek, R., den Hertog, P., Huntink, W. and Bouman, M. (1995), *Knowledge-intensive Business Services: Their Roles as Users, Carriers and Sources of Innovation*, UK: Manchester, PREST University Press.

Molina, X. (2002), 'Industrial Districts and Innovation: the Case of the Spanish Ceramic Tiles Industry', *Entrepreneurship and Regional Development*, **14** (2), pp. 211–28.

Molina, X. and Martinez, T. (2004), 'How Much Difference is There Between Industrial District Firms? A Net Value Creation Approach', *Research Policy*, **33** (3), pp. 473–86.

Nahapiet J. and Ghoshal S. (1998), 'Social Capital, Intellectual Capital, and the Organizational Advantage', *Academy of Management Review*, **23** (2), pp. 242–60.

Nohria, N. and Garcia-Pont, N. (1991), 'Global Strategic Linkages and Industry Structure', *Strategic Management Journal*, **12**, Special Edition, pp. 105–24.

Pavitt, K. (1984), 'Sectoral Patterns of Technical Change: Towards a Taxonomy and a Theory', *Research Policy*, **13**, pp. 343–73.

Porter, M. (1979), 'The Structure within Industries and Companies' Performance', *Review of Economics and Statistics*, **61** (2), pp. 214–27.

Pouder, R. and St. John, C.H. (1996), 'Hot Spots and Blind Spots: Geographical Clusters of Firms and Innovation', *Academy of Management Review*, **21** (1), pp. 1192–1225.

Ross, S., Schreiner, A. and Bjorn-Andersen, N. (2000), *Toward a Framework for Evaluation of Commercial Websites*, Slovenia: Ludvijana, Proceedings 13th International Bled Electronic Commerce Conference.

Stuart, T.E. (1998), 'Network Positions and Propensities to Collaborate: an Investigation of Strategic Alliance Formation in a High-technology

Industry', *Administrative Science Quarterly*, **43**, pp. 668–98.

Weinberg, B. (2000), 'Don't Keep your Internet Customers Waiting too Long at the Virtual Front Door', *Journal of Interactive Marketing*, **14** (1), pp. 6–18.

Zaheer, A. and Bell, G.G. (2005), 'Benefiting from Network Position: Firm Capabilities, Structural Holes and Performance', *Strategic Management Journal*, **26** (9), pp. 809–25.

PART TWO

Service Industries

6 The Role of KISA in a Public Service: the Case of Entrepreneurial Home-based Care for Elderly in Norway

Marianne Broch

This chapter examines how knowledge intensive service activities (KISA) play an important role in a public service in Norway, home-based care for elderly, giving rise to public entrepreneurship and innovation as an important backcloth the general structure of the Norwegian provision of health and social services. In order to provide improved home-based care for the elderly in a city district of Oslo, a combination of organisational and software innovations were developed. The study of KISA in the development, application and adjustment processes of these public sector innovations reveals that internal KISA resources were used in all parts of the innovation project phases, and that new ideas, renewal and innovation activities mostly originate at management level. The reasons for relying heavily on internal KISA in development and innovation processes in public services may include a strong need for relevant systemic competence, as well as limited financial resources available for such activities. External KISA were also used, but on a much more limited scale. One of the important questions arising from the study is how to encourage public sector entrepreneurship in order to improve the services to elderly people living at home. The study highlights two important factors influencing entrepreneurial activities in the public sector: the behaviour of management and the organisational culture. Encouraging public sector entrepreneurship requires a specific strategy of the public sector organisation, one that focuses on change and renewal, and on taking part in interactive learning processes in networks with other public organisations.

HOME-BASED CARE FOR ELDERLY IN NORWAY

The public provision of social and health services for elderly people in Norway has changed significantly the last 20–30 years. Previously the policy was aimed at building nursing homes for the elderly. In the past decades, this strategy has been replaced by a policy targeting the development of home care. The municipalities and city districts are free to choose how to prioritise and organise the home-based health and social services provided for the elderly. This 'freedom' has provided space for innovation.

Home-based care for the elderly[1] in Norway consists mostly of publicly provided health, social and practical services in the residents' own homes. However, some private and other non-public providers are also part of the picture. The first publicly financed system for home-based care in Norway was introduced in the 1950s. At that time the system was planned mainly to relieve the hard-pressed hospitals. It was not until the 1970s that the development of home services for elderly people and other groups developed on a large scale (Christensen and Næss, 1999).

The increase of home-based services in Norway is often associated with a government White Paper (NOU, 1992) recommending that public services to elderly (and physically disabled) people should be provided to a wider extent, in a manner which ensures the users' feeling of being at home. This meant that the services should either be provided in the original homes of the elderly, or else the elderly people could choose to live in small communities of 'care homes' especially designed for elderly or physically impaired people, often in near proximity to other health and social service centres.

Health Care Provision

In contrast to health care provision models in many other Organisation of Economic Co-operation and Development (OECD) countries, where health care services are funded by a mix of social and private insurances, the Norwegian health care system, like other Scandinavian systems, features a predominance of tax-financed public provisions (Rice and Smith, 2002). The Norwegian health care system has succeeded in securing universal coverage and high quality services. But it still faces several challenges, among which are: i) acute capacity shortages, with long waiting lists for hospital admission and lack of physicians and other medical staff; ii) the contrast between the requirements of a cost-efficient health care system on the one hand and the ambition to maintain a full coverage health service in even the most remote parts of the country; and iii) the risk of major increase in expenditure into the future.

The provision of health care has traditionally been in the hands of the public sector, and even today the private provision of health services is at a low level. There are some specialised private hospitals in urban areas and some voluntary health organisations, and significant private provision of ambulatory health care (general practitioners, dentists, physical therapists) has coexisted with the public system throughout the post war period. But most health service provision in Norway is public. The planning, regulation and supervision of the Norwegian health care system is centralised, but the provision of the tasks was transferred to the counties[2] and municipalities during the 1970s and early 1980s. The central supervisory authority, the Norwegian Board of Health, receives instructions from the Ministry of Health and Care Services and is assisted by medical officers who are stationed in the counties. Table 6.1 shows the health care provision in Norway by the various government levels.

Table 6.1 Norwegian health care provision by government level

Government level	Political decision making body	Executing body	
National authorities	Parliament	Ministry of Health and Care Services	Preparing legislation and reforms Approving capacity expansion Budgeting and planning Information management Policy design
		Ministry of Labour and Social Inclusion	National Insurance Administration
			Somatic and mental health institutions
		Regional health authorities (5)	Other specialised medical services (incl. special care for persons with drug and alcohol addictions)
Counties (19)	County councils	County Adm. Authority	Dental care services (in collaboration with the municipalities)
Municipalities (incl. city districts) (431)	Municipal councils	Local administration	Municipal health and social services plan Primary health care Social services/social security administration
	Municipal executive boards Mayors, Sector committees for health and social affairs	Municipal executive boards Health and social services	Nursing homes Care for mentally handicapped persons

Source: Developed on material from Johnsen (2006)

Since 1984 the municipalities have had full responsibility for primary health care. Each municipality must offer services for disease prevention and health provision, diagnosis and treatment of illness, rehabilitation and long-term care. Often this is in 'health centres'. The counties were in charge of the hospitals from 1970 to January 2002, when responsibility for hospitals was transferred back to the national authorities. Norwegian hospitals are now operated as health enterprises, governed by five regional health authorities, and fully owned by the government. Since 1988 the responsibility of running nursing homes was shifted from the counties to the municipalities; and in 1991 the care of mentally retarded people was similarly transferred.

Norwegian municipalities receive grants from central government, and largely fund the primary health care system in Norway. The state-run National Insurance Scheme provides public insurance against individual medical expenses (fees for services) of ambulatory care provided by hospitals and private practitioners (Ministry of Labour and Social Inclusion, 2008). The Norwegian health care system is characterised by extensive coverage, high quality and proven medical competence and the health status of the population is considered to be very good (Johnsen, 2006).

During the 1990s the expenditures on health in Norway grew from 6.4 per cent of gross domestic product (GDP) at the beginning of the decade to a peak of 7.5 per cent in 1999 (OECD, 2002). Due to high petroleum incomes there has been a real growth in the Norwegian economy of more than 30 per cent during the 1990s and total health expenditures grew correspondingly.

Social Care Provision

Social care in Norway includes social welfare services, care for the elderly, disabled and psychiatric patients, and care for alcoholics and drug addicts. During the past 10–15 years Norwegian municipalities acquired increased responsibility for providing health and social care services to these groups. In 2001, cash benefits to elderly people per capita were at an average level compared to the other Nordic countries, as were old-age pensions per pensioner. However, Norway shows by far the highest expenditures (in PPP)[3] on services per person for people aged 65 years and above (NOSOSCO, 2001).

Social Resources and Use

The basic principle of care for the elderly and disabled in Norway is that services and individualised support should be arranged in the home communities of the individual, to enable them to live in their own homes as long as possible. The greatest increase in service provision is in home nursing services, and the combination of home nursing with practical support. There has in fact been a decrease in the number of individuals receiving practical support only. This development is closely related to the objective of keeping particularly elderly people persons in their own home as long as possible, which means that the users of the home-based services tend not to be as healthy and fit as earlier. Also, there has been a general decrease in users of home-based services amongst the 'young' elderly (from 67 to 80 years old), and a marked growth in the group of recipients of 80 years and above (Statistics Norway, 2001).

Considering all receivers of home-based services, men are on average assigned more services than women. This is particularly the case amongst younger users of home-based services. Amongst the older receivers of home-based services the differences are less pronounced, however men tend to receive more services and have a higher need of services than women until the very last period of their lives. Only among people over 90 years of age living at home – a group which is dominated by women – do female users get more help assigned than men.

Employment in the Health and Social Care Sectors

Health and care service provision is work intensive, and the employment in the health and social care sectors constitutes a large part of the total Norwegian workforce. The number of employees in health and social care in general increased considerably during the last 10 years. The total number of employees in 1998 was 383,000; in 2001 it was 417,000 (Statistics Norway, 2003). The health and social work sectors employ a wide spectrum of professions. Labour force statistics[4] distinguish between 'expert professions related to health work' and 'other professions related to health work'. The group of 'expert professions' includes health professionals (other than nurses), nursing and midwifery, and KISA (knowledge intensive service activities) professionals in health work.[5] These KISA professionals include natural science and engineering professions, computing, teaching, business and legal professionals and administrative associate professionals. The group of 'other professions related to health work' includes associate professionals related to nursing and midwifery, personal care and related workers, and a residual group of other professions.[6]

The overall picture is that the number of expert professions in health and social work has increased from around 45,000 to above 51,000 employees in the period 1996 to 2000, rising from 12 to 13.4 per cent of the total employment in the sectors of health and social work. Of this aggregate group of experts the specific KISA professions in health and social care constitute a rather small group of workers. In 1996 KISA professions made up only 0.8

per cent of the total employment in health and social work, by 2000 the share had risen to 1.5 per cent.

KISA IN HOME-BASED SERVICES TO ELDERLY

Innovation as Interactive Learning

Innovation is increasingly viewed as an important activity to stimulate competitiveness of firms and organisations. Innovation activity is seen as a complex, interactive, non-linear learning process. Learning includes the building of new competencies and establishing new skills by individual workers, firms and organisations, and not just a matter of access to new information. This view of the innovation process is based on a broad definition of innovation, so as to include incremental improvements in technology, improved methods or in general new ways of doing things (COM, 1995). This broad definition involves a critique of the linear, sequential model of innovation – which mostly focuses on radical, technological innovations. The broader understanding of innovation means an extension of the range of industries and sectors which are potentially innovative. Traditional, non-research and development-intensive industries and the public sector may be innovative, as well as the more high-tech industries. One of the basic critiques of the linear model is precisely the equation of innovative activities with research and development (R&D), which assigns poor prospects for innovation in traditional industries, service industries and the public sector (Broch and Isaksen, 2004).

The conceptualisation of innovation as interactive learning furthermore emphasises the importance of cooperation in innovation processes as well as a systemic view of innovation. The concept of 'innovation system' (Freeman, 1987; Lundvall, 1992) is based on the idea that the overall innovation performance of an economy to a large extent depends on how firms and organisations manage to utilise the experience and knowledge of other firms and organisations, research institutions, the public sector and so on and mix this with internal capabilities in innovation processes (Gregersen and Johnson, 1997).

Viewing innovation as interactive learning makes us see networking and cooperation as strategically important in promoting the competitiveness of firms and organisations. Cooperation almost always includes interpersonal, human linkages. These linkages are quite different from arms-length, anonymous market transactions. The existence of social institutions facilitates collaboration and the exchange of qualitative information between actors. Thus, 'in networks ... people develop codes of communication, styles of behaviour, trust, methods of cooperation and so on, to facilitate and support interactive learning; (Gregersen and Johnson, 1997:482).

KISA and innovation

The conceptualisation of innovation as interactive learning underscores the importance of KISA. Firms and organisations must build up internal competences and knowledge, and most often mix internal and external knowledge and competences in their learning and innovation processes (Broch and Isaksen, 2004). According to Hales (2001) it is important to distinguish between KISA as functions performed within all firms, and those involving organisations and knowledge intensive services in particular institutional settings. Traditional industry classifications may categorise some service firms as 'knowledge intensive', implying that they perform knowledge intensive service activities, in the same way as knowledge organisations such as research institutes and universities. Such knowledge intensive firms and organisations rely heavily on qualified professionals.

KISA are, however, not bound to the institutional settings of particular knowledge intensive firms or organisations. All firms and organisations, regardless of whether or not they are perceived as knowledge intensive, to a varying degree perform and make use of KISA, which may be provided internally and/or externally to the firm or organisation in question. The role of KISA, then, should not only be considered in terms of the input of qualified professionals, but also in terms of the output of the KISA performed: increased competences in the organisation in question, development of enhanced innovative capabilities and ultimately increased innovation activity of the organisation.

Innovations of the Norwegian health and social care study

The Norwegian case study examined a set of development or innovation projects in the context of home-based care for elderly people in a city district in the capital city, Oslo.[7] The main focus of the study was on the rehabilitation and care unit of the city district. We investigated the use of internal and external KISA in the innovation processes, the mix and match of such activities and the interactive learning and innovation taking place.

Due to the national policy goal of home-based care for elderly people Norwegian municipalities and city districts have experienced increasing demand for such services for elderly people. While there has not been a corresponding growth in state funding of the services, local level governments may prioritise and organise the services according to local needs and preferences. The financial constraints and the 'freedom' of how to organise the home-based services to elderly people have created space for local service innovation.

In order to meet these new challenges, the city district of our case study, was the first city district in Oslo to introduce a so-called 'purchaser-provider' model,[8] in 1999, The basic principle of the purchaser-provider model is to split the organisation of the relevant city district service administration in two: one part has the role of purchaser of services, the other part has the role of service provider (RO, 2004). One of the objectives of introducing the new model was to achieve a more impartial assignment of home-based services for elderly people according to an equality principle. Another objective was to shield the home-based service providers from the storm of demands and requests for services put forward by the elderly users and their relatives. A third objective of introducing the model was to professionalise the case handling of executing the individual assignments, that was required for each user to receive home-based services by the city district.

A few years later, in 2002–2003, the city district reorganised its provision of home-based services for the elderly people by introducing a Rota Scheme and the SmartWalk software. SmartWalk is a computer-based management support application specifically developed by one of the entrepreneurial managers of the rehabilitation and care unit of the city district. SmartWalk provides managers (for example head nurses) with a planning tool to optimise manpower resources needed to provide the required care services.[9] After introducing SmartWalk, management decided to enrol most of its service personnel in a roster, providing more flexibility in the use of the various occupational groups in the rehabilitation and care unit.

The city district also engaged in an innovation project related to the so-called 'achievement-based financing' of services. Here the main focus of the city district was to estimate the prices of the service products they offered to the elderly people living at home. The fundamental principle of achievement-based financing is that the city district receives funding according to the costs connected to the actual service provision of the elderly, rather than a lump-sum budget as was traditionally the case. The innovation process was for all triggered by the introduction of the purchaser-provider model, the challenge of augmenting the provision of services, as well as budget cuts from the city district management related to home-based services. Although some of the innovations developed in the city district are fairly familiar in the private sector, they still must be regarded as public sector innovations because they were totally new to the actors of home-based care in Oslo.

The study of innovation and the use of KISA in home-based services for elderly people in the Norwegian city district indicate that traditionally the actors of the health and social system do not have a very conscious relationship to renewal and innovation activities. The services offered to elderly people at home have traditionally been executed without particular needs of change and innovative thinking. However, more recently, decreasing financial resources for the provision of nursing and care services have created a somewhat more innovation or renewal oriented culture in the sector. Generally there is high willingness to adjust and adapt to changes in framework conditions at all levels of the sector: there continues to be great tolerance for change amongst the actors of the system. One characteristic of the innovation processes we studied in home-based care for elderly people in the city district is, however, the tendency for new ideas, for innovations or renewal activities, to mostly originate at management levels.

Use of KISA in the Innovation Processes of Home-based Care for Elderly

KISA in innovation: purchaser-provider model

Mostly, internal KISAs were seen in the introduction and implementation of the purchaser-provider model. The internal providers include the rehabilitation and care unit management, a planning and economy consultant and the city district manager as well as employees of the new purchaser unit.

The processes of developing, adjusting and implementing the purchaser-provider model involved extensive KISA. Continuous development work has been the strategy and focus of the city district management for many years. This attitude is reflected in the fact that the city district manager, together with a planning and economy consultant, was actually the 'midwives' of the innovative processes being the first city district in Oslo to introduce the purchaser-provider model in 1999. Most of the development and preparation work was undertaken by these pioneers, and the execution, adjustment and implementation of the model was undertaken in cooperation with the management team of the rehabilitation and care unit in the city district.

A totally new purchaser unit had to be established, with new employees – these were actually previous internal personnel, but now combined together in a multidisciplinary group. Additionally the provider units were reorganised according to the 'small integration principle'. Previously the provider units (for example home nurses, home helpers) had been organised in separate pools of employees. In the process of introducing the purchaser-provider model the various pools were merged, put under common management, and divided into joint working groups. The process of introducing the purchaser-provider model thus involved extensive organisational development KISA by the internal management team (the one responsible for home-based services for elderly people in the city district).

One of the most important management KISA in the process of implementing the purchaser-provider model was the 'de-learning' of employees in the system of home-based services for elderly. Previously, the responsibility of defining the needs of the elderly people had been in the hands of the managing trained nurses. The new model restrained the nurses to manage the provision of services according to predefined orders from the purchaser unit only. This change required adjustments and adaptation amongst the providing unit employees, particularly the trained nurses, who felt they were deprived of important tasks in their job. An important KISA of the management was therefore to de-learn and train the employees in their new roles as providers of services and at the same time teach them how to collaborate with the employees of the purchaser unit. The management team of the rehabilitation and care services was very conscious about the need to create a positive collaborating environment, when it was implementing the organisational innovation of the purchaser-provider model. A formal cooperation agreement was developed between the purchaser and the provider units. It was considered particularly important that the personnel of the purchaser unit were familiar with the tasks of the provider units of home-based services for elderly people and have the needed credibility amongst the providers of the services.

The purchaser unit developed information material about the organisational innovation of the city district; this was distributed to the elderly people in the city district. Based on the experiences of interaction with another municipality which had introduced the purchaser-provider model some years earlier[10] the purchaser unit developed information KISA to explain to the service users that their service assignments would be changed, and that they would be approached in a different manner than before. The users were to be approached by the new purchaser unit, which would be responsible for the assignments of the home-based care services to the elderly, rather than the service providers (the head nurses) as previously. The important information exchange between the city district of our study, and the municipality that had more experience in practising the purchaser-provider model, is a good example of interactive learning and mix and match of KISA activities in relation to the introduction of the purchaser-provider model.

As part of introducing the purchaser-provider model, the employees of the newly established purchaser unit took part in a ten day case handling course directed by the training unit of Oslo city. These external KISA training services were very important for the purchaser unit to be able to develop skills needed to implement the purchaser-provider model in a best possible way. Efficient case handling, combined with in-depth knowledge of the range of services in the system of home-based care services for elderly people, forms part of the core competences of a purchaser unit. The training unit provided important KISA to the purchaser unit of the city district particularly related to efficient case handling.

KISA in innovation: rota scheme and SmartWalk

The innovation process of introducing the rota scheme and the development of SmartWalk was rather inward-looking considering the KISA actors involved. The innovation process of introducing the purchaser-provider model involved a general focus on development activities in the management of home-based services for elderly people in the city district. The development of KISA particularly important in the introduction of the rota scheme and SmartWalk was connected to one person in the management team. This key entrepreneurial person was appointed specifically to be responsible for development activities of the home-based service section of the city district.

One of the overall objectives of the provider unit is to increase the amount of direct time spent with the elderly users of the home-based services.[11] The internal development person, with assistance and backing of the management team, was responsible for the development, planning and execution of the various innovation phases of the rota scheme as well as the IT based SmartWalk steering system. SmartWalk integrates the working lists of all employees of home-based services focused on elderly people, and the assignments of the individual elderly users, to obtain the best possible allocation of resources. The working lists and the assignments of the elderly people were integrated in order to optimally perform the home-based services. The innovation itself is not technologically sophisticated, but a rather simple Excel based system combining well-known variables of the system in a new and innovative way, creating an incremental and reengineering innovation.

In these innovation processes the entrepreneurial internal development individual worked closely with development personnel in the Association of Local Government and Regional Authorities (Kommunenes Sentralbund; KS), responsible for a so-called Efficiency Network project[12] in which the city district took active part. There was a close interactive learning process between the KISA entrepreneur and the external advisors and consultants of KS. The employees of KS had in depth competences in KISA areas such as economy and planning of development activities, as well as general systemic competence of the sector of home-based care. These competences were crucial to the successful innovation processes of the city district.

KISA in innovation: achievement-based financing

The process that developed achievement-based financing consisted of many phases, in which both internal and external KISA played important roles. The most important of the many processes which led to the planning and development of an achievement-based financing model in the city district were the cooperation with another innovative municipality that was also introducing the achievement-based financing system,[13] and the participation in the KS Efficiency Network.

The cooperation with the other municipality was very close and active. This municipality had already developed a model for achievement-based financing in relation to a set of public services – which actually initially started up with home-based services for elderly. Its experiences acted as a very important illustration model for the city district of our study. In the close cooperation process between the municipalities, 'our' city district was also interacting with external private sector consultants hired by the other municipality. The knowledge intensive business service (KIBS) firm was deeply involved in the whole development process, contributing general development and project management KISA, as well as providing important in-depth knowledge about accounting and economic modelling (for the other municipality, and thereby indirectly also to 'our' city district).

However, the other municipality's innovation had to be adapted and reengineered to fit the local conditions of the Oslo city district. To be able to continue the cooperation process on equal terms, take a more active part in the project, and be able to adapt and reengineer the lessons into its local settings, the city district needed financial support from the city of Oslo. This financial support was not granted. Yet, despite the lack of specific project financing, the city district did participate in internal project meetings together with the other municipality and the KIBS consultants, as well as in external learning arenas and for where achievement-based financing approaches were discussed. Given the rejection of project financing, the city district brought its development project into the KS Efficiency Network. KS employees contributed significantly to the further development of the ideas of introducing achievement-based financing in the city district of our study – in other words contributed with important external development KISA. In close cooperation with KS employees the management and entrepreneurial development person of the city district engaged in strategic planning for the realisation of its innovative plans for introducing achievement-based financing in the city district.

In 2004 the city district did, after all, obtain financial support from the city of Oslo. It, together with two other Oslo city districts, were defined as pilot city districts to further develop the innovative ideas of achievement-based financing. The tasks of the pilot city districts were to develop a specific model of achievement-based financing adapted to the particular criteria and delegation system of Oslo. This capital city was seen to differ of from the systems of those other Norwegian municipalities which had already introduced achievement-based financing.

Interactive Learning and Collaboration amongst KISA Actors

Altogether the city district used internal KISA resources in all parts of its innovation project phases. Figure 6.1 depicts the KISA actors and activities in the innovation processes. External supply of knowledge intensive service activities was intensively used in the idea and development phases of the projects, however they were used less in the implementation phases of the renewal and innovation processes of this case study.

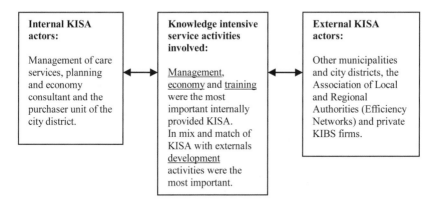

Internal KISA actors:	**Knowledge intensive service activities involved:**	**External KISA actors:**
Management of care services, planning and economy consultant and the purchaser unit of the city district.	Management, economy and training were the most important internally provided KISA. In mix and match of KISA with externals development activities were the most important.	Other municipalities and city districts, the Association of Local and Regional Authorities (Efficiency Networks) and private KIBS firms.

Figure 6.1 KISA actors and activities in innovation processes in home-based services for elderly

The external providers of knowledge intensive services used in relation to innovation processes in the sector of home-based services to elderly people were mostly free of cost. In the innovation processes, the city district cooperated with other public organisations (municipalities, city districts, local authority association) at various levels, in particular. Due to the lack of financial resources, the city district only indirectly cooperated and acquired knowledge through private KIBS consultants[14] (particularly in relation to the development of the achievement-based financing model). There was no use of other (possibly important) external providers of KISA such as for example universities and colleges, research institutes, and other suppliers of various kinds, in this case study.

As pointed out in the introduction to this section, the main focus – when considering innovation processes and the use of internally and externally provided KISA in relation to home-based services for elderly people – is the collaboration relations and interactive learning processes taking place amongst relevant actors. In the production of home-based services for the elderly people, many activities are of crucial importance. But for renewal thinking and innovation processes in the sector, the knowledge intensive service activities and its specific providers are considered to be of particular importance. Much of the discussion above has focused on which KISA, provided either internally or externally to the organisation, were of importance and in what project phases the KISA played a decisive role for innovation. In the next section, the interactive learning processes of producing KISA and thereby internal innovation as well as innovation in cooperation between internal and external KISA actors are discussed in more detail. The main focus will be on reasons or motives for providing KISA either internally or in cooperation with external suppliers.

Motives for Internal KISA Provision

The case study of home-based care for elderly people showed that the most important reasons to provide KISA internally were:

- Strong belief in internal development resources
- Strong systemic and structural competence internally
- Limited financial resources to spend on external KISA

Hence, the case study highlights that there is a strong focus on internal development resources and capabilities in the city district. The innovative processes following the introduction of the purchaser-provider model were clearly initiated and driven by a few entrepreneurial individuals in the management of the rehabilitation and care unit. There may be various motivations for internal entrepreneurship – such as professional status, career path, rewards and change for the sake of change (Perry et al, 1993). The entrepreneurs of this case study were motivated by a genuine interest in the realisation of innovative measures to improve the provision of health and care services for elderly people in the city district. Idealism or dedication to a cause seems to be important factors to explain the drive of these public sector entrepreneurs (Broch et al, 2005).

In the case study, new ideas and entrepreneurial activities seemed mostly to originate at management level, making innovation a top-down activity. Management employees possessed in-depth knowledge about the structural settings and the systemic competence in the area of care for elderly; they converted this into entrepreneurial thinking and action. This specific systemic competence may help explain the rather limited degree to which private sector consultancy firms (KIBS), were used as development or innovation partners in the innovation projects in home-based services for elderly people (and tentatively also in the public sector more generally). The framework conditions of the public sector, and the subsector of home-based services for elderly people more specifically, the culture of the sector, the particular sets of rules and regulations to comply with and how to manoeuvre in the system is a vital competence needed to be able to innovate and implement innovations. External KIBS firms may have strong competences related to innovative processes and knowing how to assist and facilitate private firms to innovate (Miles, 2003). But they may not necessarily hold the relevant systemic competence needed to successfully facilitate innovation processes in public sector organisations. Therefore internal KISA personnel and entrepreneurs in the home-based services for elderly people may be of particular importance to the innovation processes of the public sector.

Another possible explanatory factor for using internal KISA in development and innovation processes is that there are often limited financial resources available to conduct these kinds of activities (unless the project is particularly financed as a 'development' or 'pilot' project with dedicated project funding). Financial restrictions may explain why most of the external KISA suppliers utilised in the innovation processes in home-based services for elderly people comprise of 'public goods suppliers' – other city districts, municipalities and other public organisations such as the Norwegian Association of Local and Regional Authorities (KS). In our case study the interactive learning and collaboration between the city district entrepreneurs and these external KISA suppliers was crucial. This was not only because they possessed the systemic competence of the health and social care sector, but also because they were practically costless for the city district.

The overall attitude of the management of home base services to elderly people thus seemed to be that of relative self-support in terms of new ways of doing things and how to put innovative ideas into practise. However, when there was an evident shortage of internal competence to develop the innovative processes in a desired direction, the management of home-based services to elderly people in the city district of our study was not reluctant to seek competence and knowledge from externals. The use of external KISA are discussed in the next section.

Motives for External KISA Collaboration

Some of the most important reasons for involving external KISA providers related to innovation processes in home-based services for elderly people seem to be:

- Lack of competence in the organisation
- Access to experience and expertise
- External quality checks

The most evident and natural KISA to be performed in a mix and match of service activities between internal and external KISA actors were development KISA. The case study showed that the external sources for innovation, and the most important input of external KISA, came from other municipalities and the Norwegian Association of Local and Regional Authorities (KS). On one hand this cooperation was largely characterised by uncoordinated personal contact between the personnel responsible for the development or innovation processes in the municipalities. Personal, interactive learning played a decisive role for the innovation processes taking place. The employees of the municipalities visited one another and created an environment for mutual learning and knowledge and competence transfer between the public organisations.

On the other hand, since 2002 the city district participated in the formal national Efficiency Network project. This network was a particularly important arena for fruitful cooperation between various municipalities and city districts in the area of nursing and care services.[15] The municipalities and city districts were coordinated in groups to engage in development work of similar kinds. The focus of the networks was benchmarking, good practice and mutual learning. The network was an important learning and development arena for the management of services for elderly people in our city district, and a productive 'greenhouse' for entrepreneurs in the public sector more generally.

This case study bears on questions about how to encourage entrepreneurship in the public sector in order to enhance renewal and innovation activities, and how to organise networking amongst public sector KISA actors to promote interactive learning in order to facilitate innovation – and in the end to create the best possible service solutions (to elderly people living at home in this case). This case study may serve as a good example of how entrepreneurial individuals engaged in KISA were decisive for obtaining successful innovation processes in a public sector organisation.

IMPLICATIONS FOR MANAGEMENT AND POLICY

In our modern and complex society there is an increased focus on innovation and entrepreneurship, because of their perceived impacts on economic growth, change and social development. Entrepreneurs are emphasised as important change agents because of their ability to identify opportunities (needs, wants, problems and challenges), creatively breaking patterns and taking and managing risk, as well as organising and coordinating resources to implement innovative ideas for new, thoughtfully planned ventures (Landström, 2005). Although not as commonly recognised, entrepreneurship is just as important in the public sector as in the private sector. In order to enhance public sector innovation an important question is thereby how to further encourage public sector entrepreneurship.

There are many factors influencing entrepreneurship (or intrapreneuship) in the public sector (Heinonen, 2001). Two factors of particular importance, for influencing entrepreneurial activities amongst employees: i) the behaviour of management; and ii) the organisation culture. The behaviour of management, its vision, commitment, support and management style is of great importance for intrapreneurship and thereby innovation. In our case study, the management itself was entrepreneurial and provided role models for employees of the whole system of providing services for the elderly people at home. The behaviour of management is tightly connected to the second influential factor – the organisational culture, its strategy and structure. These also highly influence intrapreneurship. In our case study the organisational culture encouraged change and renewal activities. One of the most entrepreneurial actors was in fact appointed in a special position with particular focus on KISA and innovation. Thus, the entrepreneurial role was institutionalised in the organisation in a particular development (KISA) position.

Encouraging entrepreneurship, KISA and innovation requires a specific strategy of the public sector organisation. An important part of the organisational strategy of the city district of our case study was to take active part in the Efficiency Network administered by the Association of Local Government and Regional Authorities (KS). As a policy measure the Efficiency Networks seem like a particularly fruitful way of organising interactive learning and mix and match of knowledge intensive service activities of the organisations taking part in the networks. The participating organisations (municipalities and city districts) select one particular activity or service area in which they want to focus and seek to change and renew. In close interaction the actors, with the assistance of the KS employees, engage in processes which in relation to the case study city district developed into a series of innovations.

In general policy measures stimulating networking and cooperation between KISA actors of different public sector organisations, as well as between internal and external KISA providers (public and private) seem particularly important. In this connection policy measures involving proactive brokers of various kinds appear to be a positive and important dimension to encourage KISA and innovation. In the Efficiency Networks the KS employees acted as proactive intermediaries between the municipalities and city districts taking part in the networks.

A broader approach to the proactive broker idea is to strengthen the role of the public support system in creating functional and permanent networks of firms and public sector organisations at various levels. A broader-scoped KISA network programme could be developed, where the objective should be to bring together various types of firms and organisations – small, medium and large, public and private, engaged in different types of KISA. Traditionally

R&D KISA activities have received most attention in the public support system. However, in the network programme other KISA such as management, marketing, design, organisational development, training and recruitment and so on, are proposed to be the main focus of attention. The emphasis should be on the exchange of experiences related to the range of KISA represented in the participating organisations. The network could focus on how to cooperate and learn from one another by communicating good KISA practises in various settings. One possibility would be to seek already existing value networks or clusters to develop these learning arenas further in the particularly important area of KISA in order to strengthen the innovation capability of these firms and organisations.

NOTES

1. The term 'elderly' is defined as pensioners 67 years and above.
2. Since 1974 the 19 counties in Norway have been grouped into five so-called 'health regions' headed by regional health committees.
3. PPP (purchasing power parity) shows the ratio of the prices in national currencies of the same good or service in different countries (OECD).
4. The data used in the case of Norway is from the Labour Force Survey 2001 collected by Statistics Norway (Statistics Norway, 2003). NIFU STEP obtained the data on KISA professionals directly from the Labour Force Survey database, and hence the data is not published. Considerable error sources are connected to this unpublished data, and should therefore be treated as tentative only. The Labour Force Survey uses the International Standard Classification of Occupations – ISCO-88. The data are based on 2-digit data (NACE 85), including health (NACE 851) and social work (NACE 853), a much larger category of employees than in home-based services for elderly people (not specified in NACE). International Standard Classification of Occupations – ISCO-88.
5. In the OECD KISA project KISA professions in health and social work were defined to include the following ISCO categories: 123, 211, 212, 213, 214, 221, 235, 241, 221, 235, 241, 242, 311, 312, 342 and 343.
6. ISCO 513.
7. Due to a reorganisation of the Oslo city districts the city district of Manglerud in 2004 was enlarged and named Østensjø. The city of Oslo has a particular governance structure compared to other major cities in Norway. The capital has a city county district structure and a parliamentary system. Many decision making processes are directed through the aggregate city of Oslo. The city has a double governance system. The administrative governance system is at the superior level managed by the town hall administration. The town hall and the local city county district administrations perform divided and complementary tasks. The supplementary division of tasks is also prevalent at political level. The city council of Oslo is responsible for certain tasks at aggregate level as the local city ward councils have certain responsibilities in the various city county districts.
8. The purchaser part allocates services to eligible clients (the elderly) based on request and applications. In this, the services are specified (that is what kind and how much) in requests (orders) to a provider unit, that is a contractual relationship is established. Afterwards, the purchaser controls if and how the service has been performed (quality assurance), and pays the provider for services rendered. Traditionally, the provider role was bundled into the organisation of the district administration. Introduction of the purchaser-provider model enabled the administration to 'un-bundle' itself, thus opening for market competition in service provision.

9. SmartWalk links lists of service personnel (home nurses and home helpers) to lists of clients and lists specifying exactly what kind of services the elderly people should be given.
10. The municipality of Bærum.
11. The idea of increasing the amount of direct time spent in the homes of the services users was based in perceived good practice in other innovative municipalities. The ideal time distribution was pre-set to be 60 percent direct user time and 40 per cent indirect user time for home nurses and 70–30 for home helpers.
12. The Efficiency Network project was financed by the Ministry of Local Government and Regional Development and the Association of Local and Regional Authorities (KS).
13. The municipality of Kristiansand.
14. KIBS (Knowledge Intensive Business Services) firms.
15. The efficiency network included a wide spectre of fields or themes in which the municipalities or city districts could choose to cooperate including: education, nursing and care services, child care, child welfare, building affairs and social services. The network in which Manglerud took part consisted of three other Oslo city districts and the particular focus of the network was efficiency improvement, quality development and the degree of service coverage in the city districts participating.

REFERENCES

Broch, M. and Isaksen, A. (2004), *Knowledge Intensive Service Activities and Innovation in the Norwegian Software Industry – Part Project Report from the OECD KISA Study*, Oslo: STEP report 03-2004.

Broch, M., Godø, H. and Røste, R. (2005), 'Entrepreneurship in Innovation of Home-based Care for Elderly People in Norway – a Case Study', *Administration – Journal of the Institute of Public Administration of Ireland*, **53** (3), 66–79.

Christensen, K. and Næss, S. (1999), *Kunnskapsstatus om de offentlige omsorgstjenestene* (Knowledge status of the public care services), Bergen: Senter for samfunnsforskning (SEFOS), University of Bergen.

COM (1995), *Green Paper on Innovation*, Bulletin of the European Union, Supplement 5/95, Luxemburg: EU Commission.

Freeman, C. (1987), *Technology Policy and Economic Performance: Lessons from Japan*, London: Pinter Publishing.

Gregersen, B. and Johnson, B. (1997), 'Learning Economies, Innovation Systems and European Integration', *Regional Studies*, **31**, 479–90.

Hales, M. (2001), 'Birds Were Dinosaurs Once – The Diversity and Evolution of Research and Technology Organisations', in RICE – *RTOs in the Service Economy Final Report*, Brighton: CENTRIM, University of Brighton.

Heinonen, J. (2001), 'Entrepreneurship in Public Sector Organisations', *Conference Proceedings of RENT XV in Turku, Finland, 22–23 November 2001*, 223–35.

Johnsen, J.R. (2006), *Health Systems in Transition: Norway,* Copenhagen: WHO Regional Office for Europe on behalf of the European Observatory on Health Systems and Policies.

Landström, H. (2005), *Pioneers in Entrepreneurship and Small Business Research*, NY: Springer Science and Business Media.

Lundvall, B-Å. (1992), *National Systems of Innovation: Towards a Theory of Innovation and Interactive Learning*, London: Pinter Publishing.

Miles, I. (2003), *Knowledge Intensive Services' Suppliers and Clients*, Finland: Ministry of Trade and Industry Finland, Studies and Reports 15/2003.

Ministry of Labour and Social Inclusion (2008), *The Norwegian Social Insurance Scheme 2008*, Oslo: Ministry of Labour and Social Inclusion, A-0008 E.

NOSOSCO (2001), *Social Protection in the Nordic Countries 2001 – Scope, Expenditure and Financing*, Copenhagen: The Nordic Social Statistical Committee.

NOU (1992), *Trygghet – Verdighet – Omsorg,* (Security – Dignity – Care), Oslo: Offentlige publikasjoner.

OECD (Organisation for Economic Co-operation and Development) (2002), *OECD Health Data 2002: a Comparative Analysis of 30 Countries*, Paris: OECD.

Perry, J., Kraemer, K., Dunkle, D. and King, J. (1993), 'Motivations to innovate in public organizations', in B. Bozeman, (ed.), *Public Management, the State of the Art*, San Francisco, CA: Jossey-Bass Public Administration Series.

Rice, N. and Smith, P. (2002), 'Strategic Resource Allocation and Funding Decisions', in E. Mossialos, A. Dixon, J. Figueras and J. Kutzin (eds), *Funding Health Care: Options for Europe*, Buckingham: Open University Press.

RO (2004), *Bestiller–utførermodell i pleie- og omsorgstjenesten – en kartlegging av kommuner og bydeler (Purchaser-provider models in nurse- and care services – a mapping in municipalities and quarters)*, Stjørdal, Norway: RO – Ressurssenteret for omstillinger i kommunen.

Statistics Norway (2001), *Pleie- og omsorgsstatistikk 1994–2000 (Nursing and Care Statistics 1994–2000)*, Official Statistics of Norway C696, Oslo-Kongsvinger: Statistics Norway.

Statistics Norway (2002), *Helsestatistikk 1992–2000 (Health Statistics 1992–2000)*. Official Statistics of Norway C 705, Oslo-Kongsvinger: Statistics Norway.

Statistics Norway (2003), *Arbeidskraftundersøkelsen 2001 (Labor Force Survey 2001)*, Official Statistics of Norway C 748, Oslo-Kongsvinger: Statistics of Norway.

7 KISA Role in Western High-technology Industries: the Case of Software in Australia and Ireland

Laura E. Martinez-Solano and Cristina Martinez-Fernandez

The aim of this chapter is to present an analysis of the role of knowledge intensive service activities (KISA) in supporting the innovation process of the software sector, and to explore the necessary conditions for their development. The chapter discusses the software industry in Australia and Ireland in relation to the following research questions: what are the main characteristics of the innovation processes of the national software sector? what is the role of KISA in the innovation process of software firms? and what are the major policy recommendations to improve the position of KISA in the innovation process of the national software sector? Commonalities are found between these analyses from two remarkably different economies, which allow us to generalise some features of KISA for other nations. Ireland is the world's major software exporter, whilst Australia has developed a very successful specialised software sector. The Irish study was mainly based on a postal survey among 808 software companies (with a 40.1 per cent response rate) and interviews with the senior managers of 16 of these firms. The Australian study was conducted through an online survey with follow-up interviews with 54 respondents to the survey and 41 subsequent in-depth interviews. The key findings of both a technical and policy-analytical nature from each case study and inter-country comparisons should assist policy making and management of software firms.[1 and 2]

INTRODUCTION

Our two country case studies, conducted in Ireland and Australia, examine how KISA participate in the innovation process of the national software sector. Therefore, the chapter draws on the analysis of innovation processes undertaken by Irish and Australian software firms; how software businesses innovate, and what roles KISA play in the innovation process. The key findings of both a technical and policy-analytical nature from each case study and inter-country comparisons are expected to assist policy decision making.

Analysis of National Innovation Systems has rarely considered how firms who are seeking to innovate go about this, in terms of using their own expertise and more specifically 'mixing and matching' it. The main research questions investigated are:

- What are the main characteristics of the innovation processes of the national software sector?
- What is the role of KISA in the innovation process of software firms?
    - What are the core and non-core KISA needed for the development of the innovation process of the software sector?
    - What internal and external KISA are used by software firms?
    - What sources are more frequently used for KISA? How does KISA relate to firm innovation processes?
    - How are different internal and external KISA combined by the firm?
    - What are the major challenges to the innovation process in the software sector?
- What are the major policy recommendations to improve the position of KISA in the innovation process of the national software sector?

Although the objectives and research questions are the same for both case studies, our research methodologies differed, mainly because of limitations of resources, data availability and preference for specific research tools (that is online questionnaires, postal surveys, and so on).

The Irish study was mainly based on the results of a postal survey among 808 software firms (with a 40.1 per cent response rate) and interviews with the senior managers of 16 of these firms. The postal questionnaire version of the survey contained ten multiple-option questions, and the semi-structured questionnaire for the interviews included 36 open questions. In both cases, the (semi-structured) questionnaires covered the following four main sections: 'Industry Background', 'Innovation Process', 'Service of Innovation' and 'Barriers to Innovation'. The questionnaires were developed by combining and adapting the questionnaire designed by the Australian Expert Group in Industry Studies (AEGIS) leading the OECD KISA project (OECD, 2006) and questionnaires used by Martinez-Solano and Phelps (2003). The list of 808 companies was obtained by updating[3] an original list compiled in March 2003 from primary and secondary sources (Enterprise Ireland and the Industrial Development Agency (IDA) Ireland). 125 out of 808 sample software firms were located in the Atlantic Technology Corridor (ATC) (the Counties of Galway, Limerick and Clare), and the other 683 in the South East Coast (SEC) (the Counties of Dublin, Wicklow, Waterford, Wexford and Cork). The ATC and the SEC (particularly in the greater Dublin area) regions are the primary employment centres for the software industry in Ireland (Crone, 2002). After three mail-outs (at monthly intervals from April 2003), the number of respondents (274 – 40.1 per cent)[4] represents 30.4 per cent of the estimated entire population of the Irish software sector at the national level (900 firms).[5]

The Australian case study was undertaken in two steps; an online survey, and semi-structured interviews. Firstly, invitations for the online survey were sent out to companies through nine software industry associations covering all Australian states. The survey questionnaire included questions concerning:

- Background data on firms such as size, ownership, principal products;
- Information on the development of their most important innovative product (MIP) and the capabilities associated with that development;
- Use of services provided internally by specialist divisions in the firm;
- Use of services provided externally by government and private sector agencies;
- Minimal internal capabilities required to receive external expertise;
- Challenges to the innovation process.

The Australian study conducted an online survey with follow-up interviews, with 54 respondents to the survey, and 41 subsequent in-depth interviews. The semi-structured interviews covered all aspects of KISA in firms with different levels of capability. Interviews took respondents through each major service mixing, matching and integrating processes in relation to product or service innovation. Additionally, two software firms were further interviewed in more detail about the decision to seek, receive and integrate internal or external inputs to KISA of different kinds and from different sources. The aim of these interviews was to understand the nature of KISA and the complex web of factors affecting the co-production of knowledge within the firm. The selection of two specialised software firms for the Australian case study was based on several parameters, which are identified as:

- Market focus;
- Size;
- Ownership;
- Annual Turnover;
- Phase of Company Life Cycle;

- Innovation/Industry awards received;
- State location;
- Innovation Processes.

All case studies answer the research questions discussed in the following sections.

WHAT ARE THE MAIN CHARACTERISTICS OF THE INNOVATION PROCESSES OF THE NATIONAL SOFTWARE SECTOR?

As background, this section briefly presents the characteristics of the innovation processes of the software sector in Australia and Ireland. It shows the importance of these innovation processes in both economies, and therefore, the importance of studying the role of KISA in supporting innovation in software sectors. Thus we provide information about employment, number of companies, size of the companies, revenue, exports and the nature of investment. We consider the different technological activities carried out by the software firms in each country. Both studies show the type of radical innovation processes (creation of new products, creation of new process, design) and incremental innovation processes (adaptation of products and adaptation of processes) conducted in the Irish and Australian software sectors, as further explained below.

The Irish Software Sector

The importance of the software sector for Irish national economic growth has been increasingly recognised in recent years (EC, 2000; ETCI, 2002). According to the literature (Sweeney and Tansey, 1998; OECD, 2002), sustainable economic growth is only attained through the process of innovation. Innovation is the competitive advantage of a nation and companies achieve and sustain it (Porter, 1990) and policy makers will benefit from understanding the conditions that are conducive to innovation in the software sector (HEA, 2002; NDP, 2001).

In the Irish case study, it was found that the information and communication technology (ICT) sector comprises more than 1000 organisations of varying scale, from indigenous hardware start-ups to the world's largest software companies. The ICT industry directly employs 100,000 people; 55,000 of them are employed by overseas ICT companies; including IBM, Intel, Hewlett Packard, Dell and Microsoft operating in Ireland. In 2002, exports in this sector exceeded EUR 28 billion – one-third of

Irish exports (ICTSCC, 2003; IDA, 2003). Since the 1980s, most leading US software vendors, including Microsoft, Oracle and Symantec, have based their European operation centres in and around Dublin, and a thriving indigenous software development industry has developed. In total, there are more than 900 international and indigenous software companies located in Ireland, employing over 25,000 people and generating a combined turnover of over EUR 7.6 billion (HotOrigin, 2003).

According to the OECD *Information Technology Outlook* 2000, Ireland was the largest exporter of software goods in the world (IDA, 2003). The indigenous industry is characterised by a large number of relatively small firms with a strong export orientation (CSO, 2002, FORFAS, 2002). It comprises approximately 600 companies, about 250 of which have significant levels of overseas sales, principally to the US and EU. In 2002, their exports amounted to EUR 1.5 billion, an increase of more than 5 per cent over the previous year. The indigenous sector employs more than 11,000 people and generates revenues of EUR 1.27 billion. In total, the software sector in Ireland is responsible for nearly 8 per cent of Ireland's gross domestic product (GDP) and nearly 10 per cent of its exports (HotOrigin, 2001). Also, the results of a postal survey to 808 software firms (with a 40.1 per cent response rate) show that 73.7 per cent of the respondents are fully Irish-owned, while the remaining firms have some form of foreign investment. While 86.1 per cent are micro and small firms, 10.2 per cent are medium and only 1.5 per cent are large firms.[6]

A PWC report (1999) categorized the firms according to core (systems software, programming languages and tools, data management/data mining) and non-core (software services and bespoke development, applications software, localisation services) software technologies. The core technology category is considered to be of the highest value to the Irish Software Industry: it provides the potential to build firms that are internationally competitive in terms of their global positioning, market share and growth (Crone, 2002). The number of companies participating in the core technology sectors is significantly lower than that in the non-core technology sectors. Within the core technologies category, 21.9 per cent of respondents develop systems software, while 6.2 per cent engage in data management and data mining, and 4 per cent of respondents develop programming languages and tools. More firms engage in non-core technologies. Fifty per cent of companies develop applications software, 26.3 per cent offer bespoke software development and services and just 3.3 per cent engage in localisation activities.

Differences between the indigenous and foreign companies were also observed (Dicken, 2003; Dunning, 1995). Foreign companies participate more than Irish-owned firms do in core software technologies. A high percentage of foreign firms specialise in systems software technology (40 per cent) but none of them sell the other two core technologies, whereas just 17.8 per cent of the Irish-owned firms offer systems software technology, 7.9 per cent data management and 4.5 per cent programming languages. In general, the Irish-owned firms are more heavily involved in non-core technology sectors than the foreign firm are within the non-core category. Fifty-one per cent of Irish-owned firms offer applications software, but also 25.7 per cent sell bespoke software, 21.3 per cent software services, and 3 per cent localisation software. Meanwhile, one-third (33.3 per cent) of foreign firms operate in the application software sector and 26.7 per cent in the bespoke software.

Additionally, the survey indicates that the majority of the Irish software firms conduct their innovation processes (new product, new process, design and redesign, adaptation of product, adaptation of process) in-house, and within Ireland. In the case of new product development and the design and re-design of products, 83 per cent and 77 per cent of the firms respectively, use their in-house facilities. Also one-third of respondents use external sources for process development (30 per cent), adaptation of product (30 per cent) and adaptation of process (38 per cent).

The Australian Software Sector

As revealed in the Irish case, the Australian case study also shows that the software industry is a dynamic component of rapidly changing ICT market structure as a result of technical innovation, new entry, alliances, mergers and acquisitions, and fierce competition (OECD, 2003). The Australian Bureau of Statistics (ABS) publishes data on ICT, and includes software production and services in the category 'ICT Specialists: Computer Services' (ABS, 2004). The ICT industry comprises 24,000 firms employing a quarter of a million people and contributes about EUR 35.57 billion to the Australian economy, about 6.3 per cent of GDP. It is estimated that there are about 8 to 10 thousand specialist software firms in Australia in this industry, and, at minimum, 1654 software companies registered on the self-reporting software Kompass database in 2002. The majority of ICT firms are composed of very small companies, with 80 per cent employing only 1–4 people. Only 1 per cent of the companies employ more than 100 people (ABS, 2004). This pattern may well be reflected in the software sector within the industry. In addition, considerable software development occurs across the economy not for sale by firms for internal use.

In 2002, Software Engineering Australia data indicated that the majority of the companies surveyed are application developers with incremental innovation processes and funding originating from internal sources. Customers were regarded as the main partners for innovation. Sources of knowledge mostly included internal expertise. Furthermore, firms in the study indicated that their core capabilities were comprised of research and development, competent skills and knowledge and IP development. Companies in this section have a high knowledge intensity occupation level. In 2002, about half of all ICT workers (52 per cent) were computing professionals, a grouping which covers system managers, designers, programmers and auditors, software designers, and applications and analyst programmers. Growth in ICT employment was strongest for computing professionals and technicians (it increased by 43 per cent in 2002).

Over the last few years since 1996, Australian ICT industry (both in hardware and products and software services) has become increasingly dependent on foreign sources. The available data and information is for the period between 1996 and 2001. The export of ICT goods and services displayed around a 6.4 per cent annual growth over the 1991–2001 decade. From around EUR 2.8 billion in 1995–96, the ICT export revenue increased to EUR 4.19 billion in 2001 (EUR 2.44 billion ICT goods and EUR 1.75 billion services). The ICT services export increased by 65 per cent in this period. Even though the export market is relatively small compared to several countries in the world, the point to be noted is that more than 90 per cent of the export market is oriented to North America and Europe, indicating the very high level of operation. Note that the export figures do not indicate the extent of ICT components (services and goods) that are embedded in a range of manufactured exports (Martinez-Fernandez et al, 2005).

On the imports side, imports have risen by EUR 9.12 million annually between 1995–96 and 2001 to reach EUR 12.14 billion. IT goods (computers, computer peripherals, printers and so on) constituted EUR 6.53 billion, communications hardware EUR 3.581 billion and ICT services accounted for EUR 2.03 billion. From the overall perspective of international trade in ICT, the negative trade balance in a way also indicates the dependent nature of Australian ICT industry. The deficit which stood at EUR 4.63 billion in 1996–97 increased to EUR 7.93 billion in 2000–01 and to EUR 10.1 in 2002–03 according to a release by Australian Computer Society Media (Martinez-Fernandez et al, 2005).

The Australian Bureau of Statistics (2002) report indicated that in 1999, Australia had 75,000 people employed in ICT Services and Computer Related Activities. This constituted 0.84 per cent of Australia's total employment in 1999. Other data – from Software Engineering Australia (2002) – suggested that the Australian software and services sector has a total workforce of approximately 61,000: 31 per cent of the total ICT industry in 2002. Together with employment and in-house training on the job, the growth and success of innovation in the ICT industry is to a large extent dependent on the supply of human resources trained in vocational and higher educational institutions. The overall figures indicate that there has been over a 100 per cent increase in ICT professionals over the decade 1992 to 2002 (Martinez-Fernandez and Krishna, 2006). In Australia, ICT workers – both in software and hardware – require high technology skills, particularly since about 90 per cent of EUR 4.3 billion (2000–01) ICT export market is oriented towards the industrially advanced countries of North America and Europe.

After giving an overview of the importance and characteristics of these innovative software sectors within the Australian and Irish economies, the following section explains the role of KISA in the innovation process of the software firms in these software sectors.

WHAT IS THE ROLE OF KISA IN THE INNOVATION PROCESS OF SOFTWARE FIRMS?

Both case studies agree that activities oriented towards the use and integration of knowledge are important for building and maintaining a firm's innovation capability (Martinez-Fernandez and Miles, 2006; Martinez-Solano, 2006; Broch and Isaken, 2004; Lee et al, 2003). KISA can vary according to the firm's own capabilities, their innovation processes and 'processes of engagement' with external and internal provision of knowledge. Thus, KISA can be different in each firm and may indeed be the ones that differentiate a firm from its competitors. Despite the importance of KISA, their formation and interaction, which affect the firm's capabilities, remains an ad hoc and largely informal process that firms are not totally aware of, but this study tries to clarify.

For this purpose, this section addresses the importance of understanding what the role of KISA is in the innovation process of the software firms, responding to the questions: 'What are the core and non-core KISA needed for the development of the innovation process of the software sector?', 'What internal and external KISA are used by software firms?' and 'How are different internal and external KISA combined by the firm?'

What are the Core and Non-core KISA Needed for the Development of the Innovation Process of the Software Sector?

In the Irish and Australian studies, it was observed that the classification of a KISA as a core or non-core activity for the development of the innovation process of a software firm strongly determines whether this firm will prefer this KISA to be accessed from internal or external sources.

In both Australian and Irish cases, the core KISA for software firms were engineering related KISA; such as product development management, engineering management, testing and customer-support engineering (Abrahamson et al, 2002; Rothman, 1996). The software development units interviewed were highly specialised in developing a particular (engineering) product area. This specialisation allows them to master their technology and increase their competitive advantage (LC, 1996; IPL, 1996). Small software firms (51 per cent of the sample in the Irish case study) are often better described as software 'product development' units, centred on technologists (mainly engineers) or innovators whose main competitive advantage is to create clever solutions to technical problems. Additionally, it was found that strong market competition also makes software firms outsource peripheral KISA principally related to innovation management, international marketing, finance, legal and accounting. The development and combination of these core and peripheral KISA are highly sophisticated and normally takes several years to achieve. Therefore, policy makers concerned with the role of KISA must also understand the most convenient ways to access and integrate internal and external KISA to the firm within the appropriate time period.

What Internal and External KISA are Used by Software Firms?

Internal KISA

The majority of the firms in the two case studies reported that they would prefer to develop all their KISA internally, rather than rely on external inputs. The Irish software firms reported that the motives for internalising KISA are to retain control of the company's core technology development and to protect internal knowledge from rival firms. However, the companies do externalise KISA in order to obtain technology that is not available internally, but is needed to ensure competitiveness. They access external inputs to KISA to focus on performing core KISA in-house, and outsource those at the periphery to specialised firms. Other firms may just lack the resources to internally develop some peripheral – but also core – KISA. These external KISA can enable the company to create, complement, improve or support their own internal KISA. The Australian software firms also noted some determinants for sourcing KISA internally such as, cost factors, unreliability/bad experiences encountered when sourcing externally, time constraints, and maintenance of relations with customers.

It was found that only the larger firms can develop most of the required KISA internally to highly competitive levels. Meanwhile, the findings show that a considerable number of the smaller software firms (with less than 50 employees) do not have enough employees to internally develop all these needed sophisticated KISA. Then, these small firms develop some core KISA in-house, and source the other KISA from specialised (private, public or academic) entities.

In the case of Ireland, the sample is divided by nature of investment, since it has considerable foreign direct investment (FDI) principally from the USA. Irish-owned firms access the KISA primarily within their Irish base. Foreign-owned companies rely to a greater degree on their internal units abroad for these professional services (see also Taylor, 1986; Vernon, 1966). For instance, the foreign-owned companies access marketing services (75 per cent), engineering consultancy (63 per cent) and management consultancy (63 per cent) from the overseas units of their corporations. According to the interviewees in the Irish case study, the foreign-owned software R&D units have closer links with other units located abroad within their multinational corporations (MNCs) than with the units located in the Irish subsidiary. The reason for this is that these software development units mainly produce products for the global or regional market and the necessary KISA are not always available in their Irish subsidiary. For instance, the management and marketing decisions concerning their global-market products are conducted at their headquarters, which are usually located abroad. Also, this development unit (formed mainly by engineers) has to work closely and frequently with the other engineering departments of the corporation.

External KISA
External contributions to KISA can be sourced from public, private (that is Knowledge Intensive Business Services (KIBS)), academic and hybrid (that is Research and Technology Organisations (RTOs)) sectors. The private sector is the most accessed external KISA source. In the Australian study, it was observed that organisations are more likely to meet their commercial objectives and maximise their success if the direct management is not so much oriented towards controlling inputs but more focused on the finished output, with attention directed towards the vision of the final 'product' or 'service'. The study of software firms revealed that reasons why firms seek external contributions to KISA, include:

- Lack of in-house expertise;
- Free resources to allow the company to focus on its core business;
- Maintain flexibility, responsiveness;
- Accelerate process improvement/re-engineering benefits;
- Access external software capabilities or technologies;
- Avoid technology obsolescence;
- Reduce and control operating costs;
- Reduce cycle times;
- Improve customer service;
- Avoid extensive capital outlay.

The results of these case studies are consistent with the literature on knowledge acquisition (Tidd and Trewhella, 1997:362; Granstrand et al, 1992) that says '...it is often more convenient to source... [KISA]... externally, rather than to incur the risk, cost and time-scale related to in-house development... The rate of technology change, together with the ... complex nature of... [KISA]... means that few organizations can afford to maintain in-house expertise [and KISA] in every potentially relevant area...' (Tidd and Trewhella, 1997:362).

In the Irish case study, it was observed that the surveyed firms most commonly access the universities and Public Sector Research (PSRs) institutions for R&D services, engineering consultancy and development advice and yet these only represent 8.8 per cent, 4.7 per cent and 2.6 per cent, respectively, of respondents. When the Irish analysis is divided by nature of investment and company size, there is no significant difference observed in these activities, except in the case of R&D services. Here 23.3 per cent of foreign firms access universities and PSRs compared to 7.4 per cent of Irish firms. However, only 2 out of 16 of the interviewed companies who were involved in R&D programmes with the universities reported that they had internalised the outcomes of these R&D programmes. This could be due to the fact that many of these programmes have only been in existence for a few years.

The Australian firms surveyed said that they sourced expertise from the private sector more than from other public institutions or industry organisations for services related to staff recruitment and legal and Intellectual Property (IP) related consulting. Moreover, strategic development is usually sourced from the private sector in combination with in-house provision. The role of industry associations does not seem to be greatly significant for the provision of expertise, apart from the (significant) areas of engineering consultancy, IT development advice and IT training services. The Australian case study shows that the role of RTOs[7] – providers such as government laboratories, universities or technology-transfer agencies – is also important to the development of the software innovation system, even though the surveyed firms did not use these organisations to a large extent. In relation to the role of RTOs in KISA, these public sector organisations are able to produce best practices and services that also contribute to external sources for KISA (for example CSIRO[8] knowledge services). In turn, these services may also set examples for industries or private firms to follow. Secondly, the public sector may have more resources and expertise to conduct such activities. Thirdly, they have the capability to invest in infrastructure and technology while private firms may not.

Government participation as an external KISA provider
The Australian government played a role in providing services to software firms. Some Australian firms sought the advice of state government agencies when developing their software. Other firms participated in the COMET[9] programme which provides access to marketing research, business development advice and other services related to the organisational management of KISA. The public sector appears to play an important role in encouraging innovation within the software industry as more than 40 per cent of the firms interviewed accessed government grants.

The Irish case study found that a crucial input to KISA provided by the government is the funding of the innovation processes of firms. Almost half (47 per cent) of the analysed firms obtain government grants for their innovation process – 48 per cent of Irish companies and 30 per cent of foreign firms, 44 per cent of micro and 53 per cent of small-sized companies. While the interviewees in the Irish case study consider government grants to be quite substantial, two reasons cited for not taking advantage of government financial support were: the lengthy process involved (mentioned by 22 per cent) and the lack of available information (15 per cent). The interviewees also explain that it is a complex process, in which it is sometimes necessary to contract to a specialised agency in order to obtain government funding. With regard to private funding, 82 per cent of respondents self fund their innovation process, 19 per cent rely on pre-paid (client) funding and 21 per cent use other sources of private funding.

Location of external KISA
When considering the geographical source of external inputs to KISA, national level sources emerged as those most widely accessed by Irish respondents. Irish-owned firms access the majority of their external KISA nationally. When foreign-owned companies externally access KISA inputs, they commonly rely on international sources more than regional or national sources. The international market is a much more important external source than the local market for accessing high-technology-based KISA such as R&D services (43 per cent), development advice (43 per cent), technical consultancy (40 per cent) and marketing (37 per cent).

Australia is a much larger country, and the Australian software companies display different behaviour to Irish firms in this respect. The software firms that participated in the Australian survey, interviews and case studies mainly used Knowledge Intensive Business Services (KIBS)[9] as knowledge service providers; these companies seek expertise from local providers to a greater extent than from national or international sources (Miles et al, 1994). Following the Muller and Zenker (2001) analysis of the role of business services as actors in knowledge transformation in regional innovation systems, these software firms are both exposed to and strengthened by the local innovation system in which they are embedded.

How are Different Internal and External KISA combined by the Firm?

Analysts argue that the ability of firms to innovate rests on their ability to learn. This learning is not only confined within the company's own walls but sourced through learning from others in the system of innovation (Hales, 2001:52). Thus, this adds to an understanding of the importance of both encouraging the development of selected KISA internally to the firm and facilitating the availability of other needed KISA from external sources. This analysis identifies some of the main factors considered to combine internal and external KISA. For this purpose, we first consider: 'Selection of external KISA' and the turn to 'Integration of internal and external KISA'.

Selection of external KISA

The firms in the Australian case study were asked to elaborate on the selection of their KISA-input providers. Some firms agreed that the selection of an outsourcing partner requires careful consideration. They needed to make an informed choice regarding outsourcing providers. Since there are information asymmetries in the market, which can lead to suboptimal information, they relied on different methods to select and source the right services. This strategic sourcing of providers was used by the firms in order to effect a significant improvement in overall business performance. The firms identify service providers based on their reputations in the industry, recommendations from industry partners, networks, associations or even advice from consultancy firms and government departments.

The majority of Australian firms interviewed tended to base their assessment and selection on three main factors: the price of the service, the performance standards associated with the service and the evaluation of the service upon completion. Most of all, the software firms determined whether the price of the activity was competitive in terms of the expected results, and looked for some form of guarantee or follow-up or maintenance services. Some software-specialising companies in the Australian case study performed a cost–benefit analysis in deciding to which partner they would outsource services. This cost–benefit analysis assesses the relevance of the specialised services in relation to the firm's strategy and if these services refer to a core capability. Very few firms indicated that they look for performance in line (or exceeding, in a few circumstances) with industry standards or benchmarks, which is understandable as this is a very complex area in the software industry. Most firms looked for services or performance consistent with the business or software requirements. Other Australian firms evaluated performance on the basis of previous experience with other service providers. It was agreed that an evaluation should be conducted upon completion of the activity: this would determine the provider's effectiveness and worthiness of continued service provision. Hence, in each instance, they were looking for a superior service to what they had previously experienced. This indicates a strategy to pursue continuous or incremental innovation, where firms are continuously seeking improved methods and activities.

In engaging external professionals, Australian firms commented on the need to clearly define all the requirements of the service. Initially, they have to identify the importance of the appropriate KISA in order to outsource without losing the competitive advantage of the firm. Then, they have to communicate what is expected from the provider. The vendors have to be short-listed. Some Australian firms felt that the services offered were bundled as a package and saw the necessity to engage in contracts and agreements about the service level and specificity. In addition, they added that negotiations could help to govern the firms' relationship with the selected service provider.

Integration of internal KISA and external KISA

Integration of internal KISA: In the process of obtaining, integrating or producing KISA contributions, new knowledge can be generated in the firms. The capacity of organisations to harness and capitalise on this depends on their strategic management and coordination of resources. The interviews with the managers of the Australian firms investigated the use of various methods for retaining and diffusing knowledge or intellectual capital within the firm. Almost two-fifths of firms interviewed used brief documents or memos as a convenient method of systemising information and diffusing knowledge across the organisation. Other Australian firms indicated that information is collated into full reports or stored in a database for future retrieval. Some Australian organisations adopted International Standards Organisation (ISO) 9001 guidelines, requiring them to document all components of the process so that they can be catalogued, stored and become a resource for future projects. About a third of the Australian firms affirmed that tacit knowledge sometimes relies on informal methods for transmission to, and assimilation by, employees. Social events, informal communication and meetings are considered reliable methods of information diffusion. Some examples include after-work drinks, lunch meetings, and company outings.

In the Irish case study, it was observed that the integration of internal contributions to KISA occurs when the software development units interact with other units of the corporation, through a hierarchical organisational system that becomes more complex as the company grows (Dicken, 1998). For instance, the Irish product development units interviewed obtain development advice, management consultancy and global marketing services from higher hierarchical levels (HQ), while they work closely with other product development units without hierarchical barriers. These Irish development units may subcontract (to a lower hierarchical level) highly specialised engineering and technical consultancy work internally or externally to that specific Irish unit. ICT technology facilitates the achievement of autonomy and specialisation in the different units of the corporation to perform their functions and participate in the decentralised decision making of the company (Hirschey and Caves, 1981). However, tacit knowledge is still a barrier for the integration of KISA among units located in separate geographical areas (Howells, 1996).

Integration of external KISA and knowledge network formation: One of the findings from both case studies was that software companies try to form knowledge networks with private, public, academic or hybrid organisations (Leydesdorff and Etzkowitz, 1998). Some examples of these networks actors are: equipment suppliers, components suppliers, data programs suppliers, consultancy firms, ICT firms and other software suppliers. It is observed that KISA are not only enacted within formal contract relationships, but also within informal relationships among the 'network space' of the firm.

The case studies findings agree with Leydesdorff and Etzkowitz (1998), who argue about the importance of network institutionalisation to guide, facilitate and empower inter-firm and intra-firm innovation capability. For instance, some Australian organisations enter into a consortium, whilst some partnerships are organised through the relevant industry association. One example is the Australian Information Industry Association (AIIA), which offers assistance in such matters by organising networks, sessions and seminars between MNCs and smaller organisations. The Australian Technology Park was mentioned as offering a business incubator programme, providing consulting advice and administrative support for emerging and promising small companies. Almost one-third of the firms interviewed had some interaction with universities and public sector research organisations. Some of them maintained long-term relations in terms of developing software and establishing the latest development and research in their areas. It was generally agreed by the analysed firms that collaboration with organisations in their network space facilitated innovation in some form or another because knowledge and expertise about their products was greatly improved, contributing to the capabilities of firms.

The external KISA providers were categorised in two groups: subcontractors and collaborators (Casson, 2003). Within the last group, the most successful collaboration is the one between software companies and large customers.

- Subcontractors – Some firms in both case studies do not expect to internalise the skills of the service provider (the main exceptions are training services and specific research and development). When this is the case, they tend to be very specific about the service they subcontract. They said that their suppliers need to have a clear understanding of the service they are looking for. For example, in the case of Ireland, it was found that most of the foreign-owned development units interviewed were part of self-sufficient corporations in terms of the required inputs to KISA. For the few service activities that the product development departments access externally, they tend to obtain the lower-technology-based KISA (for example translation services, technical writing) from indigenous firms and the higher-technology KISA (for example research, development) from other MNCs, which are usually located abroad.
- Collaborators – in other cases, the sampled firms were interested in building long-term relationships with their knowledge partners to facilitate knowledge transfer based on quality, reliability and trust. Since most of the Irish-owned software firms interviewed were of a small size, they are not as self-sufficient as the Irish foreign-owned software units. Therefore, they must look for external sources to obtain or complement internal inputs to KISA. In comparison to the Irish foreign-owned software units, they access more traditional professional-based inputs to KISA from indigenous firms such as marketing, legal and accounting, sales and distribution. They tend to use high-technology-based inputs to KISA (R&D, training) from firms located abroad. Many Irish firms have developed long-term relationships with external suppliers based abroad, since the necessary high-technology skills are not yet available in Ireland.

It was reported that the Australian case is slightly different, since software firms have more opportunity to develop higher technology activities (that is R&D) with local providers. In the context of the dynamic Australian software industry, higher knowledge levels seem to lead to new products and to innovative processes. This is further facilitated by formal institutions such as universities and government research organisations (Gupta et al, 2000), where research activities can support incremental innovation in firms (Mowery, 1983). The process of transforming knowledge into innovative capabilities involves co-transformation of that knowledge onto products and services with new or improved characteristics.

This is borne out by two Australian case studies (Martinez-Fernandez et al, 2005) that illustrate how government programmes targeting ICT are important in establishing an in-house R&D base and in developing important software products to sustain market expansion over time. Secondly, the interaction with and learning from public RTOs and government agencies and programmes plays an important role in the KISA developed by these firms because these RTOs and government agencies are their main customers with whom they have established long-term formal relationships. The Australian study also found a relationship between the size and sector of operation of the firms and the R&D intensity and ability to collaborate and benefit from such agencies and government programmes.

Customer–software firm relation: The case studies agreed that some of the most fruitful collaborations were the ones between software firm and customer. In the case of Australia, for instance, 78 per cent of the firms surveyed indicated that customers were considered the main partners for innovative activities. Both cases show that in these types of relationships, the most common interaction is between small (or micro) firms and larger customers. This type of relationship is seen as most desirable for mutual benefit.

The Irish case study demonstrated that the small software firm can interact with its larger customer to develop its own new products. This case study shows that software companies use some large customers as partners for R&D but also as channels for marketing, technology standardisation, sales and distribution. They use their customer company to test and launch a new product in their customers' market. This relationship involves a deep knowledge interaction which may take months or years to develop, but that can be crucial for the generation of (customer/software company) new product ideas.

In this way, small software firms do not need to invest and risk their own limited resources during the development period of their innovations. Once the new software product has been well tested and accepted by the first customer, the software firm often independently adapts and sells it to other customers, who may belong to different industrial sectors. The small company is able to both remain independent and to sell its software innovation to other industrial sectors. Any potential dependency of the small software firm on the larger customer, which could be expected by the disparity between their sizes, is overcome by the lack of knowledge of the larger customer about the software industry. The technology spillovers from the software firm to other customers can lead to the formation of knowledge networks that benefit the innovation development among different industries with a positive consequence to economic growth (Zanfei, 2000; Cantwell, 1999; Dunning, 1997; Porter, 1990). It is therefore in the vested interest of the government to encourage innovation development of the software industry.

The next section will show the major challenges to this innovation process in the software industries of Australia and Ireland.

What are the Major Challenges to the Innovation Process in the Software Sector?

Barriers to innovation

In the Irish case study, the main challenges to the innovation process that were identified by the surveyed firms as very important were those of an economic nature, such as the lack of appropriate financial sources (52.9 per cent), excessive economic risk (38.3 per cent) and high costs (34.3 per cent). A lack of customer responsiveness (29.6 per cent) and information on markets (27 per cent) were also identified as major challenges by a lower, but still significant, number of respondents. In terms of the nature of investment, 59.4 per cent of Irish-owned companies indicated that the lack of appropriate sources of finance is of great importance (compared to 26.7 per cent of foreign-owned companies). In the Irish study, the lack of qualified personnel is a significant barrier, according to 26.7 per cent of the foreign-owned companies surveyed. Furthermore, most of the MNCs interviewed observed a decrease in the quality of new graduates in the science and technology fields.

The majority of software firms in the Australian study indicated that what hindered successful innovation was a lack of appropriate financial opportunities, knowledge and knowledge workers. Other factors that affected their development efforts were high innovation costs, great economic risk, inadequate market information and a lack of organisational management resources. These barriers have implications for quality and innovation in terms of KISA since firms need adequate resources to acquire, produce or integrate knowledge intensive services by employing the appropriate skilled professionals. All these factors will have some impact on the firm's ability to carry out or increase their KISA and therefore on their ability to innovate. The Australian case studies have further confirmed that tacit and informal components of KISA (which may be person and organisation embodied) play a crucial role both in market expansion and product development activities. These components were also seen to be important for absorbing and assimilating inputs to generate KISA. Also, training to update skills and retain personnel in a situation of rapid technological advances in the ICT industry appears to be problematic and challenging for sustaining both technical and organisational capabilities due to the limited participation of SMEs in training and skills upgrading activities and the difficulties in recruiting people with the right skills. The Australian firms were concerned that outsourcing KISA to foreign countries would have serious implications for the future development of the industry.

IPR mechanisms

In terms of protecting their innovative activities, the survey results of the Irish case study indicate that the firms use a variety of IPR (Intellectual Property Rights) policies. Copyright is the main form of IPR policy used by Irish respondents (53 per cent), while trademarks and patents are used by more than one-third of the analysed firms. The interviews with the Irish MNCs revealed that patents and copyrights are generally held centrally in the US Headquarters. The Irish indigenous companies emphasised that they found patenting a long and complicated process. This may explain why intangible forms of IPR such as secrecy, complexity of design and speed to market are frequently used by surveyed indigenous companies to protect their knowledge with 36.6 per cent of Irish-owned firms using secrecy as compared to 16.7 per cent of foreign-owned companies.

The Australian study discovered challenges in obtaining external knowledge for innovation. Some firms faced refusals to license by other firms. There were also many requirements for entering into cross-licensing agreements with other firms that were considered difficult to fulfil. In addition, ten firms indicated that some external service providers were very protective of the knowledge they possessed and were cautious about sharing it. They refused to transfer the technical know-how in order to protect their capabilities. The analysed firms chose to adopt both formal and informal methods to protect the knowledge they developed in-house. Similarly to the Irish case study, among the formal methods of protection, copyright was systematically relied on by more than half of the firms in the study. Other significant methods were trademarks and patents. The Australian companies systematically used more informal rather than formal methods and these included secrecy, complexity of design and speed to market. It is clear that Intellectual Property (IP) protection is now seen as a prospective means to gain competitive advantage and as a way to safeguard innovations.

Protection of IP in the software industry has changed over time. It now requires more sophisticated and specialised expertise, which is usually not available in-house. Initially, most computer programs were protected by firms as trade secrets and by using contract law. However, as software development and supply developed, copyright and patents increasingly protected innovation in the industry (OECD, 2004). Patenting offers stronger protection than copyright does. Patents do not allow the ideas to be copied or expressed in a different way. The adoption of Open Source software by some companies opens up a new range of IP issues as the pressure from users to make source codes available has considerably increased with the success of Open Source and Linux environments. Patents are therefore becoming increasingly important in the software industry because they offer a stronger protection for the innovation features of products (Huppertz, 2004). At the time of the survey (2003), 30 per cent of the studied firms used Open Source at some stage of product development, but patents were not used to any great extent. There were indications that the adoption of Open Source software in Australia was growing as large firms support its development (Malcolm, 2003).

WHAT ARE THE MAJOR POLICY RECOMMENDATIONS TO IMPROVE THE POSITION OF KISA IN THE INNOVATION PROCESS OF THE SOFTWARE SECTOR?

The results of these case studies suggest five policy areas in which to improve the participation of KISA in the innovation process of the software sector: Design of tailored policies in conjunction with general policies; Improvement of the time-scale and cost of funding applications; Adaptation of software-education-related policies and programmes to the needs of the industry; Design of instruments that encourage more software-industry-oriented research within related university departments; Design of policies and programmes that promote and facilitate access to external KISA through the development and institutionalisation of knowledge networks. These policies are explained below.

Design of Tailored Policies in Conjunction with General Policies

It was found that firms appreciate governmental efforts to make different knowledge intensive services available to promote their business development. Currently, this is done through a variety of policies and programmes such as R&D grants, start-up incubators, training courses, and R&D at universities. For instance, the Australian case study reported that the government programme COMET provides access to marketing research, business development advice, and organisation management. The case of Ireland reports that the government also offers R&D services, R&D grants (through universities) and the services of agencies to penetrate international markets.

Despite these positive efforts, the firms in the software sector need increasingly customised policies. Due to the importance of the software sector in national economic growth, more KISA-related policies and programmes designed specifically for this industry would have a positive impact on the development and competitiveness of the nation. Across both case studies, when external providers were accessed by software firms, private sector providers were used significantly more frequently for KISA than public sector providers and programmes. In many cases, it was found that the public provision of expertise was not relevant to their actual needs, or that the mechanisms to access it were too complex.

Improvement of the Time-scale and Cost of Funding Applications

According to the country cases, one of the most important challenges for innovation within software firms is the lack of adequate financial backing. Some firms reported that although government R&D funding is provided, there are significant transaction costs attached to making applications for funding. One example of this is the need to contract a specialised agency to apply for funding. There is a high risk that the companies who are successful in acquiring funding may not be the most innovative and competitive but, in fact, the most resourceful and well-heeled. Firms are concerned that the bureaucratic process for applications is inadequate for funding technology development on time. While these challenges are not unique to software innovation, policy makers may need to investigate the funding issues – such as time-scale and transaction cost – that are especially disadvantageous.

Adaptation of Software-education-related Policies and Programmes to the Needs of the Industry

The analysed firms considered governmental investment into the promotion of education relevant to software business development as positive. However, the majority of the interviewed companies considered that universities and other 'knowledge-generating' institutions could better target the KISA needs of the software sector. In relation to universities, Irish companies reported that new graduates in computer science should have a higher standard of engineering related knowledge. Some interviewees even suggested that the government could invest in computer science from the earliest stages of an individual's education. In addition, knowing that computer science graduates will likely work for a small software company, they saw advantages in these people acquiring knowledge in other professional fields relevant to the software sector such as international service marketing, including innovation management in services, finance, law and accounting.

Policy makers might usefully investigate the government's role in providing this human capability enhancement to software firm workers. Also, it was considered beneficial for the development of the software sector that professionals with different backgrounds have more opportunity to obtain a diploma or degree related to software development.

Design of Instruments that Encourage more Software-industry-oriented Research within Related University Departments

Software firms in the case studies generally see universities more as educational institutions rather than research centres. Only a small number of

Irish firms (8.8 per cent), compared to 30 per cent of the analysed firms in Australia, use the R&D from universities or public institutions for their commercial purpose. Irish interviewees reported that the university research does not meet the needs of the software sector. It has been argued that universities undertake tasks that go far beyond the needs of the industry (Hales, 2001). Policy makers may wish to investigate ways to promote collaboration between university-based research departments and software firms in order to develop strong software-industry-oriented research programmes within university departments.

Design of Policies and Programmes that Promote and Facilitate Access to External KISA through the Development of Knowledge Networks

The results emphasised the need for governments to facilitate the formation of more formal knowledge networks that will impartially allow software companies to easily identify and access the most suitable KISA providers from public, private or academic sources at national and international levels. Information about these providers such as product service, size, sales, exports, quality standards, subsidiaries, and so on, should ideally be available. More formal and institutionalised knowledge networks would facilitate the sustainable innovation development of the software sector. The cost of searching, selecting and accessing adequate external KISA are much too high for small software firms. Leaving the purchase of knowledge intensive services to the market alone may therefore jeopardise further development of the software industry. Policy makers may wish to investigate the adequacy of the market structure and participation to see whether innovation opportunities are reached at all phases of the innovation system of the software company. A great amount of knowledge acquisition occurs in an informal, non-commercial way through the organisations that are in the proximity of the software firm. Facilitating and promoting knowledge networks may be an efficient way to support this.

CONCLUSIONS

This paper has sought answer the following research questions: What are the main characteristics of the innovation processes of the national software sector? What is the role of KISA in the innovation process of software firms? What are the major policy recommendations to improve the position of KISA in the innovation process of the national software sector? The paper draws on case studies conducted in Ireland and Australia in 2003, using slightly different research methods, conducted under the auspices of the OECD TIP Working Group.

On the first question, as it is expected, the size of the economy defined some key characteristics of the software industry. For instance, the number (1654) of software firms in Australia is almost twice the number (900) of companies in Ireland. Also Irish firms are heavily export-oriented independently from their size because of their origins; meanwhile the Australian firms may have a stronger need to satisfy the vast size of the national market. In fact it was reported that Australia presents a deficit in its ICT sector, while ITC exports count for one third of the total exports of Ireland. Both software sectors are mainly formed by small-size firms involved in accessing, developing and/or providing Knowledge Intensive Service Activities. This study reaffirms the importance of the software sector for the economic development of the nation.

Analysing the role of KISA in the innovation process, it was found that engineering related KISA are considered core for the innovation development of the company. The analysed companies expressed that they would have liked to develop internally all their needed KISA, but since no firm is completely autonomous, they have to obtain at least the most peripheral KISA from external sources. Therefore software firms specially the small-size ones would highly benefit by more government support to institutionalise their knowledge networks, which would allow them to identify, sourcing and/or develop the different sophisticated KISA needed to compete in their high innovative and competitive market. The specific strategy that software firms currently follow when they choose to internalise or externalise KISA indicates the constraints they are under in maintaining the control and ownership of the core knowledge needed to preserve their competitiveness. The integration of these different inputs to KISA remains an ad hoc, largely informal and unplanned process of which firms are not totally aware. The integration of KISA contributions remains a challenge for these firms. The study of software development firms revealed a significant level of ingenuity and ability in the sector.

The main policy recommendations are that we need: the design of more tailored policies in conjunction with general policies; the improvement of time-scale and cost of funding applications; the adaptation of software-education-related policies and programmes to the needs of the software industry in the long-term; the design of instruments that encourage more software-industry-oriented research within related university departments; and the design of policies and programmes that promote and facilitate access to external KISA through the development of knowledge networks.

Finally, it should be mentioned that the results of the present study concerning recommendations and policies originated from the Australian and

Irish studies and may not always be applicable to other countries. The role of KISA may differ according to each nation's needs and conditions. This study presents some of the earliest investigations into this new area of study, and its limitations indicate a need to continue interrogating common concepts. However, because of the high level of comprehensive analysis used in these two case studies, it is expected that they provide a strong platform for future investigations in other countries.

NOTES

1. The Irish case study was mostly conducted in CISC, University of Ireland, Galway. The Irish research team was Laura E. Martinez-Solano, Majella Giblin and Edel Walsh (see Martinez-Solano et al, 2006, Martinez-Solano et al, 2005). L.E. Martinez-Solano Warwick Innovative Manufacturing Research Centre, University of Warwick.
2. The study of Australia was conducted in AEGIS, University of Western Sydney. The Australian research team was M.C. Martinez-Fernandez, Claudine Soosay, Veni Venkata Krishna, Tim Turpin and Merete Bjorkli (see Martinez-Fernandez and Krishna, 2006, Martinez-Fernandez et al, 2005).
3. After sending the questionnaire three times, 125 envelopes were returned as undeliverable and these companies were deemed to be no longer operating and therefore removed from the sample list.
4. The percentage of companies that answered the questionnaire was higher in the ATC (48.5 per cent) than in the SEC (38.5 per cent), which may be due to the fact that the ATC companies were also contacted by telephone before sending them the first two mail shots.
5. Source: (EINID 2000 and 2004).
6. Most of this research was conducted at CISC, University of Ireland, Galway.
7. For a review of the role of RTOs in innovation, see Hales (2001).
8. CSIRO is the Australian public funded research institute.
9. COMET is an Australian Federal Government Program focusing on Commercialisation Emerging Technologies (Martinez-Fernandez and Bjorkli, 2003).
10. See Martinez-Fernandez and Miles (2006) for information on the relationship of KIBS & KISA.

REFERENCES

Abrahamson, P., Salo, O., Ronkainen, J. and Warsta, J. (2002), *Agile Software Development Methods*, Valtion Teknillinen Tutkimuskeskus (VTT) Publications 478, Oulu: University of Oulu.

Australian Bureau of Statistics (ABS) (2002), *2001–2002 Information Technology*, Canberra, ABS.

Australian Bureau of Statistics (ABS) (2004), *Information and Communication Technology, Australia*, Catalogue Number 8126.0, Canberra, ABS.

Broch, M. and Isaksen, A. (2004), 'Knowledge Intensive Service Activities and Innovation in the Norwegian Software Industry', Part Project Report from the Organisation of Economic Co-operation and Development (OECD) Knowledge Intensive Service Activities (KISA) study, STEP-Centre for Innovation Research, unpublished paper, Paris: OECD.

Cantwell, J. (1999), 'From the Early Internationalization of Corporate Technology to Global Technology Sourcing', *Transnational Corporations*, **8** (2), 72–92.

Casson, M. (2003), 'The Entrepreneur: An Economic Theory', Cheltenham, UK and Northampton, MA, USA: Edward Elgar.

Central Statistics Office (CSO) (2002), *Statistical Abstract 2002*, Dublin: CSO.

Crone, M. (2002), 'A Profile of the Irish Software Industry', Consultation paper, Belfast: Northern Ireland Economic Research Centre.

Dicken, P. (1998), *Global Shift, Transforming the World Economy*, 3rd edn, London: Paul Chapman Publishing.

Dicken, P. (2003), *Global Shift, Transforming the World Economy*, 4th edn, London: Sara-George (SAGE) Publications Limited.

Dunning J.H. (1997), 'Some Paradoxes of the Emerging Global Economy: the Multinational Solution', in J.H. Dunning (ed.), *Alliance Capitalism and Global Business*, London: Routledge, pp. 357–72.

Dunning, J.H. (1995), 'Reappraising the Eclectic Paradigm in an Age of Alliance Capitalism', *Journal of International Business Studies*, **26** (3), pterprise Ireland's National Informatics Directorate (EINID) (2000), *Software Industry Statistics from 1991–2000*, Dublin: Enterprise Ireland.

Enterprise Ireland's National Informatics Directorate (EINID) (2004), June. http://www.nsd.ie/htm/ssii/stat/htm

European Commission (EC) (2000), *Innovation Policy in a Knowledge-Based Economy*, A Maastricht Economic and Social Research and Training Centre on Innovation and Technology (MERIT) Study Commissioned by the European Commission, Luxembourg: Enterprise Directorate-General.

European Trend Chart on Innovation (ETCI) (2002), *Country Report*, Ireland: ETCI, October 2001–September 2002. http://www.trendchart.org/Reports/Documents/Ireland_CR_September_2002.pdf

Granstrand, O., E. Bohlin, C. Oskarsson and Sjöberg, N. (1992), 'External Technology Acquisition in Large Multitechnology Corporations', *R&D Management*, 22, pp. 111-33.

Gupta, B., Iyer, L.S. and Aronsen, J.E. (2000), 'Knowledge Management: Practices and Challenges', *Industrial Management and Data Systems*, **100** (1), pp. 17–21.

Hales, M. (2001), *Birds were Dinosaurs Once – The Diversity and Evolution of Research and Technology Organisations*, RISE Final Report, Centre for Research in Innovation Management (Centrim).

Hall, P. (1994), *Innovation, Economics and Evolution*, New York: Harvester-

Wheatsheaf.

Higher Education Authority (HEA) (2002), *Creating and Sustaining the Innovation Society*, Dublin: HEA.

Hirschey, R.C. and Caves, R. (1981), 'Internationalisation of Research and Transfer of Technology by MNEs', *Oxford Bulletin of Economics and Statistics*, **43** (2), pp. 115–130.

HotOrigin (2001), 'Ireland's Emerging Software Cluster: A Hothouse of Future Stars', Dublin: HotOrigin.

HotOrigin (2003), 'Ireland's Software Cluster, Innovation – the Fuel for International Success', Dublin: HotOrigin.

Howells, J. (1996), 'Tacit Knowledge, Innovation and Technology Transfer', *Technology Analysis and Strategic Management*, **8** (2), pp. 91–106.

Huppertz, M-T. (2004), 'The Role of IPR for the Software Industry: a Changing Landscape?', Patents, Innovation and Economic Performance OECD Conference Proceedings, Paris: OECD.

Industrial Development Agency (IDA) (2003), 'Achieve European Competitive Advantage; Guide to Tax and Financial Incentives in Ireland', Dublin: IDA.

Information and Communications Technology Standards Consultative Committee (ICTSCC) (2003), 'Annual Report 2003', Dublin: National Standards Authority of Ireland (NSAI).

Information Processing Limited (IPL) (1996), *Software Testing and Software Development Lifecycles*, Report prepared by IPL, Bath.

Ireland's National Policy Advisory Body for Enterprise and Science (FORFAS) (2002), *Research and Development in the Business Sector 1999*, Dublin: FORFAS.

Laker Consulting (LC) Property Limited (1996), *Software Project Management*, Report prepared by LC PTY Ltd Information Technology Software Solutions.

Lee K., Shim, S., Jeong, B. and Hwang, J. (2003), *Knowledge Intensive Service Activities (KISA) in Korea's Innovation System*, Korea: Science and Technology Policy Institute, 2002 Strategy Research Partnership of Korea Development Institute (KDI).

Leydesdorff, L. and Etzkowitz, H. (1998), 'The Triple Helix as a Model for Innovation Studies', *Science and Public Policy*, **25** (3), pp. 195–203.

Malcolm, J. (2003), 'Problems in Open Source Licensing', Software, April, pp. 69–72.

Martinez-Fernandez, M.C. and Bjorkli, M. (2003), *Firm Behaviour and Knowledge Intensive Service Activities: The Case of the COMET Program in Australia*. AEGIS, University of Western Sydney.

Martinez-Fernandez, M.C. and Krishna, V.V. (2006), 'KISA in Innovation of Australian Software Firms', *International Journal Services Technology and Management* (IJSTM), Special Issue **7** (2), pp. 126–136.

Martinez-Fernandez, M.C. and Miles, I. (2006) 'Inside the Software Firm: Co-production of Knowledge and KISA in the Innovation Process', *International Journal Services Technology and Management* (IJSTM), Special Issue **7** (2), pp. 115–25.

Martinez-Fernandez, M.C., Soosay, C., Krishna, V.V., Turpin, T. and Bjorkli, M. (2005), *Knowledge Intensive Service Activities (KISA) in Innovation of the Software Industry in Australia*, Sydney: University of Western Sydney.

Martinez-Solano, L.E. (2006), 'Role and Significance of KISA in the Innovation of the Software Industry', *International Journal of Services Technology and Management*, **7** (2), 163–72.

Martinez-Solano, L. E. and N. Phelps (2003), 'The Technological Activities of EU MNEs in Mexico', *International Planning Studies*, **8** (1), Feb.

Martinez-Solano, L.E., Giblin, M. and Walshe, E. (2005), 'Knowledge-Intensive Service Activities (KISAs) in the Irish Software Sector', Paris: OECD Directorate for Science, Technology and Industry, Committee for Scientific and Technological Policy, February.

Martinez-Solano, L.E., Giblin, M. and Walshe, E. (2006), 'KISA in Innovation of Irish Software Firms', *International Journal of Services Technology and Management*, **7** (2), 137–45.

Miles, I., Kastrinos, N., Flanagan, K., Bilderbeek, R., den Hertog, P., Huntink, W. and Bourman, M. (1994), *Knowledge-Intensive Business Services: Their Roles as Users, Carriers and Sources of Innovation*, Manchester: Policy Research in Engineering, Science and Technology (PREST).

Mowery, D. (1983), 'The Relationships between Intrafirm and Contractual Forms of Industrial Research in American Manufacturing 1900–1940', *Explorations in Economic History*, **20** (4), pp. 351–74.

Muller, E. and Zenker, A. (2001), 'Business Services as Actors of Knowledge Transformation: the Role of KIBS in Regional and National Innovation Systems', *Research Policy*, **30**, pp. 1501–16.

National Development Plan (NDP) (2001), 'Guide to Funding under the National Development Plan and Community Support Framework 2000–2006', Dublin.

Organisation for Economic Co-operation and Development (OECD) (2000), *Small and Medium Enterprise Outlook*, 2000 edn., Paris: OECD.

Organisation for Economic Co-operation and Development (OECD) (2002), *Dynamising National Innovation Systems*, Paris: OECD.

Organisation for Economic Co-operation and Development (OECD) (2003), *Knowledge Intensive Service Activities in the Software Industry*. Draft Synthesis Report of TIP Innovation Case Studies on KISA: Software Module, Directorate for Science, Technology and Industry/Science and

Technology Policy/Innovation and Technology Policy, **11**, Paris: OECD.

Organisation for Economic Co-operation and Development (OECD) (2004), *Patents, Innovation and Economic Performance OECD Conference Proceedings*, Paris: OECD.

Organisation for Economic Co-operation and Development (OECD) (2006), *Innovation and Knowledge-Intensive Service Activities*, Paris: OECD.

Porter, M.E. (1990), *The Competitive Advantage of Nations*, London: Macmillan Press.

PriceWaterhouseCoopers (PWC) (1999), *Strategic Development of Internationally Traded Service Industries Throughout Ireland*, Software report, Dublin: Enterprise Ireland.

Rothman, J. (1996), *Applying Systems Thinking to the Issues of Software Product Development*, Rothman Consulting Group Incorporation.

Sayer, A. (1992), *Method in Social Science: A Realist Approach*, 2nd edn. London: Routledge.

Software Engineering Australia (2002), *Software Industry Report*, Canberra.

Sweeney, P. and Tansey, P. (1998), *The Celtic Tiger: Ireland's Continuing Economic Miracle*, 2nd ed Dublin: Oak Tree Press.

Taylor, M. (1986), 'The Product-cycle Model: A Critique', *Environment and Planning A*, **18**, pp. 751–61.

Tidd, J. and Trewhella, M.J. (1997), 'Organizational and Technological Antecedents for Knowledge Acquisition and Learning', *R&D Management*, **27** (4), pp. 359–75.

Vernon, R. (1966), 'International Investment and International Trade in the Product Cycle', *The Quarterly Journal of Economics*, **LXXX**, pp. 190–207.

Zanfei, A. (2000), 'Transnational Firms and the Changing Organisation of Innovative Activities', *Cambridge Journal of Economics*, **24**, pp. 515–42.

8   The Use of KISA in the Public Sector

Ian Miles

This chapter discusses the use of Knowledge Intensive Service Activities (KISA) in public sector organisations. Some of these organisations are not only enormous, but are also particularly intensive employers of graduates, and have strikingly complex institutional structures. The dynamics of KISA requirements, and the way in which these are sourced, have many points of convergence with developments in the private sector – but also many points of divergence. However, these dynamics can be influenced very directly by policy decisions, not least those affecting the boundary between public and private service provision. This means that past trends may be of limited use for delineating the future, as policies are rethought, following the economic crisis of recent years.

INTRODUCTION

What is the public sector? A simple definition is: those parts of the economy that are owned and controlled by governments of some level (national, regional or local) – as contrasted to the profit-oriented private sector and the 'third sector' (of charities, not-for-profit organisations, and so on). But this definition includes nationalised industries, that may be under government control in some countries, but that are most often owned and run by private business. For example, in the UK some heavy industries have been in the past owned by the state (coal and steel), and this has even been the case for high-tech car and aerospace firms. Even in the USA, where the private sector runs many industries that are elsewhere public services, we see nationalisation at times of crisis: for example the railroad industry was nationalised during the First World War. It is still quite common for petroleum and telecommunications companies to be state-owned in many regions of the world, though privatisation of such industries has been common in Europe (where the EU has pressed for liberalisation and free markets).

Even in economic activities where the state predominates – and did for most of the twentieth century – there is often some private provision. Thus the large-scale public services like health and education services are, in many countries, also activities where the public sector is available for the mass of the population, but there are opportunities to purchase services from private providers. Such services, and other social and community services, may also be available from third sector organisations, which sometimes specialise in innovative services, or those aimed at groups that public services are not reaching effectively. Public sector activities like policing and defence, and public administration, are less often ones where citizens have 'choice', in the sense that they can choose how to acquire services by allocating their disposable income across service providers. The justifications for this are that these services are prone to market failure or worse, that many citizens may lack resources to access services they clearly need, that there are social benefits from public provision, and so on. 'Choice' is meant to take the form of political choice, made by votes in the ballot box rather than cash from the wallet.

Even so, governments may choose to employ private firms rather than use their own organisations to design and supply public services, or parts of them. Often these contracted out elements of public services are supposedly peripheral activities – such as cleaning and catering in hospitals and schools. Such peripheral activities may turn out to be rather more core than expected, as in the discovery that poor levels of hospital cleaning are associated with serious threats of hospital-acquired infection, obviating the effects of beneficial hospital treatments! Sometimes less peripheral service elements are contracted out, too. For example, so-called 'contract cities' in the USA pay private firms to supply huge swathes of their public services. There are trends to the 'privatisation of war', with the introduction of private security firms into international affairs – a step beyond long-established mercenary activities. Sometimes it is private citizens or commercial organisations that 'augment' public services provided by the state – and even in the field of policing there are cases of communities employing private security staff to maintain law and order and keep out the riff-raff, for instance.

While public sector organisations will all require KISA at management and organisational levels, some public sector fields are particularly knowledge-intensive. As Chapter 11 documents, for example, education and health services are outstanding for the high share of graduates in their employment (in contrast, public administration is unusually high in terms of the share of middle-level skilled workers: office workers without higher qualifications, corresponding to the classic notion of bureaucracy, while not being themselves powerful bureaucrats). Such services are often what are classically seen as public services. It should be noted, though, that many statistics on such services combine both public and private organisations. Furthermore, there is great diversity in the way in which such services are provided in different countries: for example, whether doctors are state employees, or self-employed people or employees of firms, who are reimbursed from government or a mix of public and private insurance. The arrangements are so diverse that we cannot hope to detail them here (see OECD, 2009).

Additionally, it is misleading to think of the public sector as solely providing services for the general public, or for the security of the nation. It is common to find government departments (at national and more local levels) who are seeking to benefit industry, including supporting industrial R&D, standards setting, cluster formation, training, and the like.

In this chapter we will consider the nature of KISA within public services, especially insofar as they bear upon the innovative activities of these sectors, and on the acquisition of KISA from external sources. We shall see that these two topics are closely linked, and that this linkage will have considerable bearing on their future.

KISA WITHIN PUBLIC SERVICES

Varieties of Public Service KISA

Public services are diverse: brain surgery and dustbin emptying are largely conducted as public services, in many countries. There is an internationally standardised classification of public services (the Classification of the Functions of Government, COFOG), and this can be used in various ways, though most of the publications seem to focus on comparing different government expenditures. Table 8.1 sets out the three-digit COFOG classification.

These categories are widely used to classify government expenditures, though data on public sector employment may also be classified in such terms. A case of the latter is provided by Statistics Denmark,[1] which reports that in the first quarter of 2010 some 29 per cent of the employed population were employed by the public sector. By far the largest proportion of these workers (34 per cent) were in division 6 (Social Protection); Divisions 9 (Education) and 7 (Health) follow with 21.3 per cent and 23.1 per cent of the public sector workforce respectively. Division 1 (General Public Services) was substantially lower (7.6 per cent), with Divisions 3, 4 and 8 all around 3 per cent, and the remainder at less than 1 per cent each. Just as public expenditure and overall public employment levels, and the structure of public expenditure, vary from country to country, so we can expect the specific figures of employment to vary a great deal across countries – even countries with similar levels of income and socioeconomic structure. But health, education and social services are leading in public sector activities across the industrial world. Thus, more generally, but with a less detailed breakdown of sectors, Cedefop (2008:91) reports that across the EU 25 countries in 2006, some 9.5 per cent of employment was in health and social work; some 6.9 per cent in education, and 6.8 per cent in public administration and defence (a share of the first two categories, at least, will be employed by private and non-profit organisations).

Table 8.1 The COFOG classification of public services, three digit level

01. GENERAL PUBLIC SERVICES – 01.1 Executive and legislative organs; financial and fiscal affairs; external affairs; 01.2 Foreign economic aid; 01.3 General services; 01.4 Basic research; 01.5 Research and development; 01.5 General public services n.e.c.
02. DEFENCE – 02.1 Military and civil defence; 02.2 Foreign military aid; 02.3 Research and development; 02.4 Defence affairs and services n.e.c.
03. PUBLIC ORDER AND SAFETY – 03.1 Police and fire protection; 03.2 Law courts; 03.3 Prisons; 03.4 Research and development; 03.5 Public order and safety affairs and services n.e.c.
04. EDUCATION – 04.1 Pre-primary and primary education; 04.2 Secondary education; 04.3 Tertiary education; 04.4 Education not definable by level; 04.5 Subsidiary services to education; 04.6 Research and development; 04.7 Education affairs and services n.e.c.
05. HEALTH – 05.1 Hospital services; 05.2 Out-patient services; 05.3 Public health services; 05.4 Prescribed medical products, equipment and appliances; 05.5 Research and development; 05.6 Health affairs and services n.e.c.
06. SOCIAL PROTECTION – 06.1 Sickness; 06.2 Disability; 06.3 Old age; 06.4 Survivors; 06.5 Family and children; 06.6 Unemployment; 06.7 Housing and social exclusion; 06.8 Research and development; 06.9 Social protection affairs and services n.e.c.
07. RECREATION, CULTURE AND RELIGION – 07.1 Recreational services; 07.2 Cultural services; 07.3 Broadcasting and publishing services; 07.4 Religious and other community services; 07.5 Research and development; 07.6 Recreational, cultural and religious affairs and services n.e.c.
08. HOUSING AND COMMUNITY AMENITIES – 08.1 Housing and community development; 08.2 Water supply; 08.3 Street lighting; 08.4 Research and development; 08.5 Housing and community amenity affairs and services n.e.c.
09. ENVIRONMENT PROTECTION – 09.1 Refuse collection, treatment and disposal; 09.2 Sewage systems and waste water treatment; 09.3 Pollution abatement; 09.4 Nature conservation; 09.5 Research and development; 09.6 Environment protection affairs and services n.e.c.
10. GENERAL ECONOMIC AFFAIRS – 10.1 General economic and commercial affairs; 10.2 General labour affairs; 10.3 Research and development; 10.4 General economic affairs and services n.e.c.
11. SECTORAL ECONOMIC AFFAIRS – 11.1 Fuel and energy; 11.2 Agriculture; forestry; fishing and hunting; 11.3 Mining and mineral resources other than mineral fuels; manufacturing; construction; 11.4 Transport; 11.5 Communication; 11.6 Distributive trades, storage and warehousing; hotels and restaurants; tourism; 11.7 Multipurpose development projects; 11.8 Research and development; 11.9 Sectoral economic affairs and services n.e.c
12. EXPENDITURES NOT CLASSIFIED BY DIVISION – 12.1 Public debt transactions; 12.2 Transfers of a general character between different levels of government; 12.3 Other expenditures not classified by division

Source: OECD (1997)

Tepe (2009) analysed trends in public sector employment over 17 OECD countries between 1995 and 2005. Since wages (and pensions) for public employees are very important elements of government expenditure – almost a quarter of government expenditure and 11 per cent of gross domestic product (GDP) in 2005 in the 17 countries – downsizing of public employment and the containment of personnel costs is a core public policy issue. Tepe confirmed earlier studies indicating that, after a long period of substantial growth, the size of the public workforce was decreased round the end of the twentieth century and beginning of the twenty-first. Disaggregating employment into public administration, education and health sector employment (the latter being largest) he found that there was very little change in the level of employment in public administration, while the health and education sector has experienced employment reform and job loss over these 10 years. Most countries had been able to contain public personnel expenditure, in absolute terms. Public administration has, by and large, been less subject to downsizing and outsourcing than the main public services, where we can expect to see considerable change in the organisation of KISA over recent years.

All public services involve KISA, their managerial and related functions. But some – like education and health – require KISA in the process of delivery of their key public services, because they are dealing with complex problems and a wide variety of citizen circumstances. To a large extent, what they deliver to end-users are knowledge intensive services (KIS). Much specialised knowledge is required in some of these services, most notably in the wide variety of medical specialisms.

As if this diversity of specialised knowledge was not complicated enough, there is a key feature of large-scale services to deal with. The public services are intended to reach very large numbers of people, often to cover the whole population of a country (not to mention people in transit or on vacation, and citizens who are currently abroad). Some of the services can be accomplished via electronic or even postal communication. However many require face-to-face interaction. Thus schools, colleges, surgeries, hospitals, and many other public service institutions, have to be replicated in numerous locations across the territory of the nation. Some of these are organisations that provide essentially similar sets of basic services, though they may vary dramatically in size. Some are providing more specialised services, typically for a wider geographical area – or at least a wider population base (thus a large city may have some specialised schools and clinics, while a rural area of the same size may only have the more generalist institutions). This all makes for a complex organisation hierarchy, with the complexity only increased by the activity of different levels of government and by structural changes that follow shifts in government policy.

One important consequence of this is that public services managers are often working in large organisations (for example a sizeable University or hospital, that often spans many buildings – perhaps in more than one location, and that may employ thousands of people processing tens of thousands of people at any one time). Even if the particular operating unit is smaller, it will typically be embedded within a large national or regional organisation, with multiple levels of management, with bureaucratic rules (often introduced in efforts to ensure social justice in public services), and with numerous lines of contact with other units and organisations. Management in such organisations may be fairly divorced from the KISA and associated knowledge employed in service production and delivery top end-users. In some organisations managers are drawn from the KISA practitioners, but in others they are professional managers with little experience of the specific KISA provided to end-users.

At the time of writing, England's National Health Service (NHS) is being subject to another series of huge reforms, whose long-term implications are a matter of deep controversy (some commentators argue that the financial crisis has provided an excuse for the Conservative Party to embark upon a long-cherished programme of privatisation of public services). One of the changes that is being explored, and which seems to meet with fairly wide public approval, is the introduction of 'doctor-managers' – medical specialists who spend a proportion of their time undertaking strategic management functions, and receiving the KISA training that can enable them to do so effectively. Other changes mean abolishing a layer of decision making and giving general practitioners (family doctors) more scope to make decisions about allocation of funds for patient care, which may introduce a greater degree of market competition into health services. Some commentators (for example Milne, 2010) view this as prefiguring 'the end of the NHS'.

The NHS is at present one of the largest employing organisations in the world, with well over a million employees. It has thus had to go to some lengths to manage the KISA and other occupations it employs. Its documentation of occupational categories and statistics provides insight into the diversity of KISA roles and the inherent complexity of organisation of such a large-scale public service. Overall the NHS works with over 1200 separate job titles (NHS, 2010). Let us just focus on staff employed in Hospital and Community Health Services, putting the parallel data on General Practice to one side (Table 8.2). In September 2009, these services are recorded as employing a little over 100,000 'medical and dental' staff – effectively people with doctor-level qualifications – and almost 1.2 million 'non-medical' staff. But practically half of this latter category, 562,747 employees, are professionally qualified clinical staff (Qualified nursing, midwifery and health visiting staff – with almost 400,000 employees, this is by far the largest part of this group; Qualified scientific, therapeutic and technical staff; Allied health professions; Qualified healthcare scientists; Other qualified scientific, therapeutic and technical staff; and Qualified ambulance service staff). Also 377,617 employees, are recorded as providing support to clinical staff (over 300,000 providing support to doctors and nursing staff). Another 236,103 provide NHS infrastructure support – this includes Central functions (about half of this figure); Hotel, property and estates staff; and Managers and senior managers (about a fifth of the infrastructure support).

Table 8.2 Staff numbers in main occupational groups in England's National Health Service, Hospital and Community Health Services, September 2009

Medical and dental staff	**All Specialties**	**102,961**
Speciality Groups	Accident & emergency	4,962
	Anaesthetics	11,330
	Clinical oncology	1,107
	Dental group	2,791
	General medicine group	27,425
	Obstetrics & gynaecology	5,440
	Paediatric group	7,753
	Pathology group	4,252
	PHM & CHS group	3,529
	Psychiatry group	9,934
	Radiology group	3,580
	Surgical group	20,858
Non-medical staff	**All non-medical staff**	**1,176,831**
Professionally qualified clinical staff (total = 562,747)	Qualified nursing, midwifery & health visiting staff	395,229
	Qualified scientific, therapeutic & technical staff	149,596
	Allied health professions	73,953
	Qualified healthcare scientists	32,378
	Other qualified scientific, therapeutic and technical staff	43,265
	Qualified ambulance service staff	17,922
Support to clinical staff (total = 377,617)	Support to doctors & nursing staff	303,424
	Support to ST&T staff	59,831
	Support to ambulance service staff	14,362
NHS infrastructure support (total = 236,103)	Central functions	115,818
	Hotel, property & estates staff	75,624
	Managers & senior managers	44,661
Other staff or those with unknown classification		364

Source: Tables from the NHS Information Centre for Health and Social Care (2009).

The details on medical staff are presented in terms of twelve speciality groups (and ten grades within these, but this level of detail is too much to go into here). Around a quarter of these are general medicine, with large numbers specialising in surgery, followed by smaller numbers specialised in anaesthetics, psychiatry and paediatrics.

Furthermore, the types of knowledge that should be deployed to function well in occupations have been codified by the NHS, in its *Knowledge and Skills Framework* (NHS, 2005). This identifies some 30 'dimensions', which are broad functions required in NHS services. There are 6 core dimensions, involving skills and knowledge needed to some extent in all NHS posts. These involve capabilities related to: Communication; Personal and people development; Health, safety and security; Service improvement; Quality; and Equality and diversity. The other 24 dimensions are more specific, applying only to some of the NHS posts. These are grouped into a number of themes (Health and wellbeing – 10 dimensions; Estates and facilities – 3 dimensions; Information and knowledge – 3 dimensions; and General – 8 dimensions). For each dimension, there are 4 levels, essentially increasingly sophisticated capabilities, and attached to each of these are indicators that describe how knowledge and skills should be applied at that level. Together, the dimensions describe the capabilities required for each of the many occupations within the NHS. The higher levels on each dimension are essentially KISA, the lower are more routine and less-skilled activities. In this respect this system, and these indicators, resemble a version of the USA's O*NET system, tailored to this large health service organisation (the O*NET data on public service occupations – see Department of Labor, 2010 – could be mined for descriptions of these roles in the USA, much as Consoli and Hortelano, 2009, have used this source for studying skills and knowledge deployed in business services).

Table 8.3 presents (less detailed) occupational data for schools in England only (other statistics cover the remaining parts of the United Kingdom). Three quarters of a million people are employed in public sector schools, to which we would need to add those responsible for management and evaluation of schools in local authorities, central government, examination bodies (setting and marking school exams), and the regulatory agency, Office for Standards in Education (OFSTED), whose statistics on school performance are widely disseminated and discussed (not least by parents seeking to ensure the quality of their children's education). The data do not cover all nurseries, or purely private education; and of course the public education system also includes the extensive further and higher education sectors (that engage further high-level KISA employees).

Teachers are graduates, and they will tend to specialise in particular bodies of knowledge, in addition to possessing general teaching skills. Major areas of the curriculum have very large numbers of teachers associated with them, and some schools specialise in areas such as sciences, languages or performing arts. The core list of secondary school subjects – some 16 subjects – is supplemented by a range of optional and vocational subjects.

But many of the teaching support staff also engage in KISA, at least for good portions of their working life. Looking just at those schools maintained by local authorities, there were 432,800 teachers (full-time equivalents – FTEs) employed in January 2009; and the total number of support staff (FTE) was 338,900 for every four teachers there were almost three support workers. More than half of these were teaching assistants (over 180,000 FTE – often acting as associate professionals and, for example, working with smaller groups in classroom settings), with the remainder being administrative staff (over 71,000 FTE – many providing clerical services, but with a range of other functions), technicians (over 24,000 FTE – for example, audiovisual, ICT and laboratory support) and a sizeable number of 'other support staff' (almost 62,000 FTE).

Table 8.3 Staff numbers in main occupational groups in England's schools, January 2009

	Occupational Group	**FTE Employees (,000)**
Nursery and primary schools	All regular teachers	198.5
	Total Support Staff	181.4
	- Teaching assistants	118.3
	- Other support staff	63.2
	Total Workforce	380.0
Secondary	All regular teachers	212.6
	Total Support Staff	123.1
	- Teaching assistants	39.3
	- Other support staff	83.8
	Total Workforce	335.6
Special Schools (for example for children with disabilities)	All regular teachers	14.9
	Total Support Staff	30.3
	- Teaching assistants	21.3
	- Other support staff	9.0
	Total Workforce	45.2
Pupil Referral Units and other non-school education	All regular teachers	6.8
	Total Support Staff	4.1
	- Teaching assistants	2.7
	- Other support staff	1.4
	Total Workforce	10.9
Total maintained sector	All regular teachers	432.8
	Total Support Staff	338.9
	- Teaching assistants	181.6
	- Other support staff	157.3
	Total Workforce	771.7
City Technology Colleges (CTCs) and academies	All regular teachers	9.9
	Total Support Staff	7.0
	- Teaching assistants	2.1
	- Other support staff	4.9
	Total Workforce	16.9
LA maintained schools, CTCs and academies	All regular teachers	442.7
	Total Support Staff	345.9
	- Teaching assistants	183.7
	- Other support staff	162.2
	Total Workforce	788.6

Source: Department for Education (2010) Table 1

The data provided give us further information on several other features of the working arrangements, and issues such as pupil-teacher ratios (16.5 for nursery schools, 21.4 for primary schools, 15.9 for secondary schools, and 6.2 for special schools). While the local authority maintained system dominates public education at present, policy changes instituted in 2010 may lead to many more schools becoming 'academies', responsible much more for their own strategic directions. Some commentators welcome this as a shift of power to the grassroots, some as opening the door to privatisation of the school system.

Schools and hospital are of course very different, and within each group there are several different types of organisation – and many establishments, dispersed around the country. Management structures vary considerably, across sectors and countries. So do modes of channelling funding to these organisations – and ways in which they spend money, in their purchasing decisions. As large employers of highly professional staff, they face similar issues around employee capacity to resist imposed changes, to generate their own working routines and/or innovations, and to define what mixture of public good and professional interest to pursue. These issues too will vary in how they evolve across sectors and countries, depending upon such issues as workforce unionisation and politicisation, social attitudes as to these services and professions, and more.

The Service Encounter

There are many public services that are provided to end-users, and many styles of service delivery by which this is accomplished. A single end-user, in the course of a protracted interaction with a public service agency, may be in reception of a succession of numerous services (think of a school pupil or University student, an inhabitant of a care home, or one of many other roles as a consumer of public services). Often the services – especially the more knowledge intensive ones – are delivered on a face-to-face basis, with service provider and end-user being collocated and working together (to a greater or lesser extent) in the service production (the anaesthetised patient in a surgical operation is near one extreme of this coproduction, the student making a presentation in a seminar is near the other; but some less knowledge intensive services – for example, street cleaning – may require little involvement of the citizens). Sometimes the service is provided on a one-to-one basis (doctor and patient, tutor and graduate student...); often there are multiple end-users being served at once (for example the conventional classroom), and often there are multiple public service employees present (for example in an operating theatre). But in practically all these cases, we see the (relatively expensive) time of the (relatively highly) qualified service worker being spent interacting with the end-user.

Often what is taking place is a process of customising a fairly familiar service – the teacher delivering a routine lecture to a class, tailoring a few elements to the reactions of the students, is a case in point (it is interesting to note that it may not be apparent to the outside observer that this is a routine or familiar exposition, as opposed to a completely new one which the teacher has just spent many hours preparing). Again, there are cases where the service provider is mainly in the business of customising the service by combining together familiar 'modules' that are assigned to the specific end-user as the result of specialist understanding. This may describe, for instance, how a doctor will often be functioning when a patient presents him or her with a set of symptoms; if a diagnosis is immediately apparent, then a standard treatment routine may be applied (though often doctors will need to modify these considerably to fit what they know about the patient's living circumstances, other health conditions and medication, and so on). In other cases, what is required is highly specialised, as when complex surgical procedures are carried out in highly uncertain conditions; and the service content may be extremely novel, as when a discussion with a graduate student involves developing new understandings on both sides. In Scott's words – and by 'clinicians' he refers to a wide range of professionals, not just health workers – 'the more experienced clinicians do not simply apply mechanically their textbook remedies, but rather more or less creatively adapt their generalized principles to the specific problems confronted. In doing so, in a case-by-case incremental fashion, clinical professionals, like carriers, participate in the creative process of proposing new distinctions, measures and methods in a "bottom-up" incremental fashion' (Scott, 2008:228).[2]

Probably the most common KIS encounters will involve relatively high levels of customisation or specialisation. This is speculative, but is supported by the high levels of 'problem-solving' and 'complex tasks' reported by public service workers in the European Working Conditions Survey (see Chapter 11). One complicating issue is the protracted nature of public service provision, such that many end-users engage in a succession of service encounters with the supplier or the public sector organisation more generally. They undertake what the service marketing community often describe as a 'service journey', and is referred to in health circles as a 'pathway'. Depending on the nature of the service, we might expect decreasing complexity and increasing routinisation of interactions (for example where a patient is subject to long-term monitoring) – or quite the reverse (for example where a patient's health is slowly deteriorating). In any case, the professional KIS worker is liable to be exercising a fairly high degree of autonomy in their work, and is required to exercise a fairly high degree of flexibility where it comes to meeting and coping with changing and often unpredictable end-user demands.

More variability concerns the outcomes of the service. First of all, many KIS provision processes in the public sector are not monitored in any detail; they are the responsibility of the professional worker, whose specialist judgement is deemed sufficient to ensure that correct procedures are followed and quality service provision achieved. There are economic and social reasons for this: already costly labour time is being contributed by the professional, so introducing intensive supervision or observation would be adding even more costs to an expensive process. Furthermore, professional workers are resistant to being inspected or interfered with, which they see as questioning their judgement and reducing their autonomy. The move to a more litigious society, where public services can be sued for not meeting expectations, together with concerns about the potential for abuse within service relationships and the desire to enhance service efficiency, has meant that many KIS are subject to auditing – meaning that 'paper trails' have to be established recording the encounters between end-users and service providers.

Second, the ultimate outcome of the service encounter may be difficult to assess. Some outcomes may be immediately apparent to many observers (for example that an accident victim's life has been saved), though often time is taken for the outcome to be visible, and many aspects of the outcome may be known only to the end-users themselves. Public sector organisations may set themselves specific performance indicators with which to assess outcomes (numbers of patients discharged within a given time period, numbers of students achieving particular examination results). These indicators may affect management priorities and public expenditure decisions (what is allocated to 'good' or 'failing' schools, for example). As noted earlier, they may be influential for the decisions and views of the general public (for example school 'league tables'), which implies that 'informed consumers' of public services are themselves undertaking a measure of KISA in selecting among service units. The indicators may also be employed by other service providers (as when doctors have a choice as to which hospital they should refer their patients to).

But such indicators are notoriously likely to be influenced by numerous factors in addition to the quality and efficiency of service provision (end-users who have poorer health or education to begin with, will require more and possibly different service inputs if they are to achieve an outcome as remotely as good as do the more privileged). And they are often criticised as leading to a narrowing of the understanding of what the service is providing (patient's long-term prospects may be enhanced by a longer period of hospital care rather than be dispatched to fend for themselves; a 'well-rounded education' may be sacrificed in order to maximise scores on a specific set of examinations). So it could be concluded that there are KISA skills required for the interpretation of such data, just as there are for their production.

The use of such indicators and targets is a key element of what has become known as the new public management (NPM). NPM, or at least some parts of its agenda, has been very widely introduced in the public services of many countries over the past few decades.[3] The label refers to a set of practices, and the philosophy behind them, that are supposedly aimed at improving the efficiency and effectiveness of public services, in large part by subjecting them to similar disciplines as are seen to govern private business.[4] There are several other elements to this; the hiring of managers versed in private business, finding ways of rewarding staff in relation to their efforts and achievements (for example performance-related pay); the elicitation of more customer feedback, introduction of methods providing for more customer choice and for 'marketisation' within the service (so service providers compete with one another, in servicing other parts of the public sector as well as end-users); outsourcing of peripheral and even core functions to the private sector, and so on. The emulation of private business may extend to encouraging public sector organisations to find ways to protect and profit from their innovations and intellectual property. In relation to KISA, NPM can be seen as putting in place a layer of reporting and monitoring that can be seen as a form of Knowledge Management.

Knowledge Management and KISA Management

As far as the managerial and administrative KISA professions are concerned, this layer of reporting and monitoring is Knowledge Management. It is Knowledge Management that tells them about how their organisations are functioning (in terms of some key indicators, if not in terms of others, or of underlying processes). This Knowledge Management enables them to manage the work of other KISA professions.

For those professions that are more directly concerned with providing services to end-users, however, these systems are of more limited value. They may organise data ('manage knowledge') on performance, but they do not reflect the core knowledge of these service providers. Here, knowledge is gained through combinations of formal education, on-the-job learning, and a variety of interactions with other professionals. Knowledge Management consists of these formal training systems, practical arrangements for gaining experience and sharing it via mentoring and similar activities. There are other types of information system, however, that can provide data to support KISA providers execute their core functions – for example, such data management systems as electronic patient records and digital X-ray systems in hospitals, and online archives of teaching material and student records in schools.

An important development in health services is the production and application of highly systematic data on specific protocols, practices and techniques. A substantial literature on 'health technology' assessment and clinical trials has accumulated over the past decades – marked by journals such as *Health Technology Assessment*, the *International Journal of Healthcare Technology and Management* and the *International Journal of Technology Assessment in Health Care*. In the UK, the National Institute for Health and Clinical Excellence (NICE) is a public sector organisation that makes recommendations to the NHS on new and existing medicines, treatments and procedures, and on the treatment and care of people with specific diseases and conditions. It uses health technology assessments, independent committees and experts, to provide guidance on the value-for-money of specific treatments, and as well as (sometimes controversially) recommending the use or non-use of a particular treatment by the NHS, provides "NHS Evidence", which it describes as 'a Google-style device that allows NHS staff to search the Internet for up-to-date evidence of effectiveness and examples of best practice in relation to health and social care.'[5] This represents a form of knowledge management about techniques and approaches in service delivery.

Much of the work of KISA professional service providers, however, remains hard to grasp within such formal systems. This is precisely because it involves a variety of service activities conducted over lengthy periods of time and varying across service encounters. Automated data capture remains limited. Tools for transforming the rich content of the service interaction into standardised codified information are still a distant prospect.[6] Instead of information systems, more conventional supervision and mentoring – having staff observing or working together in service production – are employed. The ways and extent to which this is implemented varies across KISA and service organisations. Most typically, opinions/experiences are recorded on individual practice and performance, rather than on the underlying knowledge and its application.

This has several results in practice. One is that there is considerable scope for arguments about the judgements reached as to individual capabilities, and it can be very difficult to determine in any objective way just who should be promoted or demoted (cases of professional misconduct are often very hard fought). Another is that it is not always clear why performance differs across KISA employees and organisations. We may have relatively coherent indicators of outcomes, and these may even be corrected to give us 'value-added indicators' (how much better this intake of clients has fared compared to intakes of clients of similar background in other organisations). But explaining these performance variations, and determining which elements of practice should be replicated or avoided, is very problematic.

This leads directly to a persistent issue concerning the public services. It is widely argued that these sectors face an innovation deficit – they are said to be less innovative than private firms, and thus failing to deliver sufficient quality and efficiency improvements to citizens. At present, there is something of a deficit of evidence as to this claim – systematic surveys of public sector innovation are only just being developed, and what few studies are available fail to confirm the thesis. The picture is bound to be mixed. Organisations of such scale as public services have numerous opportunities to invest in and roll out innovative solutions to service problems. They can also gain economies of scale unavailable to smaller organisations – and indeed the public sectors were early pioneers in the use of information technology (IT) for back-office functions. On the other hand, their fragmentation into many local organisations and specialised professions, and the complex bureaucratic structures that govern them, may mitigate against innovation – and against the diffusion of those innovations that are created in the course of KISA practice. While the public sector is often criticised as non-innovative, the evidence for this is very mixed; but it could be argued that many innovations that are developed here remain largely 'invisible' and/or fail to be reproduced and scaled-up.[7]

NPM proponents have tended to be convinced that public services are non-innovative, and that the solution is simply to introduce market-like practices and pressures into the public sector. Some of the results have lacked much visible success – efforts to encourage University and hospital employees in the UK to take out patents on their inventions are not known to have achieved a great deal (it could even be suggested that this might restrict the development and diffusion of some types of innovation). Tellingly, recent years have seen a number of initiatives in the health services to stimulate the innovation that has not blossomed as a result of NPM moves. Thus we have seen such interesting organisational innovations as the NHS Institute for Innovation and Improvement, its National Innovation Centre and regional Innovation Centres.[8]

The Professional KISA Worker

Äijälä (2001) – writing for the Organisation for Economic Co-operation and Development (OECD) before the economic crisis led to moves to downsize the public sector in many countries – was concerned with the ability of public services to recruit and retain sufficient, and sufficiently capable, employees, in the context of decreases in the number of new employees entering the labour market. Skills shortages of various types were reported by public sector organisations. The most commonly experienced shortages were those of IT specialists, but a wide range of other professional staff were in short supply in other countries. Sometimes shortages of very specific capabilities could be very important – perhaps relevant to the economic crisis high-level competences in banking and multinational business affairs were noted.

Though the public sector may be seen (in some countries, at least) as offering a secure and even prestigious career, a number of less attractive features were noted. In some countries, and for some public services, there are negative images of these as dull and bureaucratic activities. Wages are often lower than comparable jobs in the private sector, with less opportunity to influence take-home pay by outstanding performance. Similarly for careers, there are often relatively unclear career paths and slow promotion rates, with seniority seen often to be more important than performance and insufficient efforts to support career planning and professional development. Work arrangements are seen as rigid and hard to adapt to employee needs. These were commonly expressed concerns – even though it is possible to find exactly the reverse being asserted in other contexts. One of the lines of attack on public services in the current economic crisis repeatedly claims that many public service jobs are much more comfortable than private sector equivalents.

Among the ways in which public sector organisations can address these problems, and recruit and retain highly professional KISA employees, Äijälä notes:

- Improving human resource management systems (for example ensuring high quality leadership and professional recruitment systems);
- Developing pay and other incentives (taking into account work requirements, individual competence and performance);
- Applying human resources fully (creating workplaces based on equal opportunities in terms of gender, age, ethnic origin, and so on; prolonging the working life of older employees);
- Knowledge management (retaining critical skills in organisations as ageing employees retire, securing institutional memory by transferring tacit knowledge to younger generations);
- Regular monitoring and evaluation (as a tool for continuing development and improvement).

KISA and the 'Public Service Industries'

While KIBS are by definition 'business services', the point is that they support business processes in all types of organisation, not just private businesses. Some types of KIBS have been highly dependent on public procurement of their services – for example the 'think tank' consultancies (such as RAND) that grew up in support of American military planning in the post-war period. These latter examples are also interesting because they developed many of the tools and techniques that have entered into public management over the years

– PPBS (Planning, Programming, and Budgeting System) and the systems approach in general. Strategic and management consultancy firms have been extremely active with public sector clients in many parts of the world.

Across Europe, the UK has been in the vanguard of attempts to establish new ways of using external providers (private firms and non-profit bodies) to supply public services. In the 1980s, competitive tendering was implemented as a central policy of the Thatcher government, largely with goals of efficiency and cost-saving, underpinned by a visceral belief in the superiority of private sector management. Though the wider impacts of this shift have not been well-documented, an extensive review of the 'private service industry' by Julius (2008) provided an overview of many developments here, and can provide some insight as to the implications for external provision of KISA to the public sector.

Julius defines the Public Services Industry (PSI) as comprising private and third sector enterprises that provide services to the public on behalf of government (examples cited are: private sector prisons, NHS referrals to private health care providers, training of military pilots, private and third sector childcare) or services to the government itself (examples cited are: IT and payroll services, consultancy services such as research and policy advice, catering and cleaning services, property management services). These enterprises 'depend in whole or in part on revenues contracted through government and in turn derived from taxation. For the PSI, more than any other industry, the government, as both policy-maker and purchaser, plays a central role in shaping the market' (Julius, 2008:5).[9] She cites research suggesting that some 44 per cent of the PSI is accounted for by 'Managed Services', that is, services provided directly to users (in addition to the examples cited above she notes providing employment services in Jobcentre Plus and medical services in NHS funded independent treatment centres) (Julius, 2008:21). These vary from extremely knowledge intensive activities to much more basic operational services.

Exploring the size of the PSI for a sample of OECD countries in the period 2005–2008, Julius noted huge variations. The PSI accounts for just over 6 per cent of GDP in Sweden and Australia, and 5.7 per cent in the UK (in 2007/8, up from 4.2 per cent in 1995/96) – slightly higher than its share in the US (5.3 per cent) and nearly double that of France and Spain (both less than 3 per cent). Australia has a particularly low share of public sector expenditure in GDP, whereas Sweden has a particularly high share. The US, with its much larger economy overall, has by far the largest PSI market in terms of the absolute size, with the UK, following well behind (about a fifth of the US market), having a substantially larger PSI market than the other OECD countries considered.

Understanding the substantial cross-national variations picked up in

COFOG statistics would require a much more substantial analysis than possible here. But some points can be made. The differences need first to be related to the varying extents to which consumers pay privately for health and education, as opposed to these being acquired as public services. In health services, the US diverges from Europe, with private healthcare spending accounting for 14 per cent of consumer spending (compared with around 4 per cent elsewhere). The UK has very low private spending and relatively low public spending on health – but a substantially larger health PSI as a share of GDP than the other countries. In education the proportions range from 3.5 per cent of consumer spending in Australia (followed by Spain, and only then the US) to a little under 1 per cent for France and 0.5 per cent in Sweden. But it is Sweden and the US that have the largest share of PSI provision of education, with the UK in third place.

Other COFOG categories of public services are less easy to compare, but still use of the PSI can be seen to vary considerably across countries. Thus: 'Sweden channels relatively more of its public spending though the PSI than other countries, with the exception of spending on social protection. The UK ranks close to Sweden in terms of its overall use of the PSI but is low on general public services. France and Spain utilise the PSI less than other countries across the whole range of government activities' (Julius, 2008:65).

The Julius report naturally explored the UK PSI in most detail and among the key results are:

- In 2007/8 its revenues totalled £79bn, generating £45bn in value added and employing over 1.2 million people. In terms of value added this makes it twice the size of many familiar sectors like Communications, Public Utilities and Hotels and Restaurants;
- The PSI more than doubled over the twelve years to 2008, with growth at 6.8 per cent per year in real terms for 1995/96 through 2003/04, though this later levelled off to 2.9 per cent per year;
- Health constituted the largest sector of UK PSI spending in 2007/8 totalling £24.2bn; it was followed by social protection (£17.9bn), defence (£10.1bn) and education (£7.3bn);
- The fastest growing sectors of PSI were education (8.1per cent per year), environmental protection (7.9 per cent) and health (7.0 per cent). In contrast, the slowest growing areas were general public services (–0.3 per cent), economic affairs (2.3 per cent) and defence (3.6 per cent).

What does this mean for KISA? Much of the services supplied by the PSI consist of more or less operational and non-knowledge-intensive activities, such as refuse collection, hospital cleaning, school catering and the like.

But there are many activities that correspond more to our understanding of

KISA, though the report does not single these out for statistical analysis. What Julius does do, however, is provide some information about a set of activities that give us some insight into KISA and non-KISA. We already noted that 'Managed Services' are a mix of KISA and other activities, and constitute around 44 per cent of PSI expenditure. Other categories are (text and data mainly quoted from Julius, 2008:21):

- ICT services – including 'both the building of IT systems and the ongoing management of databases, servers, applications and communication', where some 49 per cent of sales of the top twenty firms is to the public sector (total public expenditure on such services estimated at over £12bn). Much of the work here will be the sorts of KISA associated with computer service and similar KIBS;
- Business process outsourcing – 'the contracting out of an area of business activity, while the client retains strategic and governance control. Examples include back office outsourcing, which includes internal business functions such purchasing, payroll or records management, and front office outsourcing, which includes customer-related services such as call centres'. UK public sector expenditures for 2007 were put at over £5bn. These categories include managerial and administrative work, together with the more clerical and even sales work associated with data entry and call centres;
- Construction services – including the lead contractor role in Private Finance Initiative projects, and other design, engineering and surveying work. The service component on a typical construction project was estimated as costing around 5 per cent of the total expense, and total PSI turnover in construction services in 2006 as around £2-3bn;
- Facilities management (FM) – 'managing facilities after they have been built. The sector is typically divided into support services, building operating and maintenance services, environmental services and property management'. Over £3bn is attributed to UK PSI outsourced FM services. It is likely that only a minority of this will go toward KISA – though probably more than the 5 per cent of construction associated with construction services;
- Professional services – 'a vast range of consultancy or advisory service activities in the areas of human resources, financial, legal and general management consultancy.' These are predominantly KIBS, supplying KISA services. The estimate is that public expenditure on consultancy was in the order of £2.8bn. The National Audit Office reported that the National Health Service alone accounted for around a fifth of the expenditure on consultants, spending some £0.6bn on them in 2005–6.[10]

Across these activities, then, we see a substantial acquisition of KIBS-type inputs by the public sector. Perhaps a quarter of PSI activity represents KISA of these types – and if we add in the KISA associated with 'managed services' (for example private supply of knowledge intensive medical and educational services) the figure may be higher still. The share would seem to be growing, as external provision is increasingly used for strategic management and core front-line services in areas like education and health.

Better documentation, analysis and understanding of such activities is thus of considerable practical significance as well as theoretical interest. While the UK may be a particularly marked case of the development of the PSI, developments here will be of interest elsewhere, since these KISA do exist in some form in most countries – and political choices about them need to be well-informed. (For example, a substantial set of new services are being explored in the area of health care and eldercare around the theme of 'Ambient Assistive Living' technologies. The case for using such systems is extremely strong, but the appropriate business models are still being explored, and the types of mix of public and private KISA that could be instituted are multifarious.)[11]

The Julius report notes some difficulties and risks associated with outsourcing of public services, and some literature highlights such issues. For instance, a survey of public sector managers across several countries (comparing them to professional and financial service managers) noted that experience from the 1990s was that they were more prone to report that outsourcing was associated with losses of: knowledge and skills in provision of particular services; technology and R&D capability; operational flexibility and effectiveness; and opportunities to recognise and respond to organisational and community needs. Staff were also likely to be less motivated, and various problems in the relationships between the public service and suppliers were also documented (more adversarial and disrespectful, less flexible) (Kakabadse and Kakabadse, 2000).

Just as there is management advice on outsourcing for private industries (especially those using IT-related KIBS), so the public sector has a body of advice on public procurement. In the UK, the National Audit Office (NAO) has oversight on the efficiency of public expenditure, and issues guidelines concerning procurement. One of the key issues it raises is the Management, Personal and Technical Skills required for efficient procurement, and this activity constitutes a KISA in its own right. As Julius points out, the NAO has identified a number of skills critical for commissioning and project management where the PSI is being employed. The management and Personal Skills include those skills related to: developing relationships with customers; negotiating with customers and suppliers; developing relationships with other professional groups in government departments; applying best practice and encouraging others to do so. The Technical Skills include the abilities to apply public procurement principles and conform to legal requirements; to prepare tender and contract documents; to understand how prices are arrived at, estimate costs, understand markets, and identify and manage risks. Such staff are doing more than just selecting PSI suppliers – they may well need to discuss strategies with policy makers, public and private suppliers, and specialist advisers such as lawyers, competition experts and so on (Julius, 2008:52). Evidence reviewed by Julius suggests that skill shortages are a major source of those problems that are encountered when the PSI is engaged in provision of public services. The skills for working with KISA are liable to be of especially high levels, given the difficulties in selecting service designs, assessing service performance, and negotiating with professionals.

A particular and longstanding concern focuses on the commissioning of services by the NHS – which has been subject to much attention and reorganisation since the NHS was set up in the late 1940s. In 1991, a set of market reforms were introduced based on a demarcation between purchaser and provider (the purchaser-provider split). The idea was that commissioning bodies would be able to address population needs, whereas providers (hospital doctors and the like) might act to further their own interests. Just who the commissioners were has undergone considerable change, with Primary Care Trusts (PCTs) being central in the twenty first-century (to date). They were awarded budgets to buy health care from 'providers' such as hospitals and ambulance services. In the face of accounts of poor quality commissioning, in 2007 the Government unveiled its *World Class Commissioning* initiative, consisting of (among other things) a specification of 11 Organisational competencies required for effective commissioning: the necessary knowledge base of these particular KISAs.

Also in 2007, a *Framework for Procuring External Support for Commissioning* (FESC) was introduced, aimed at overcoming the lack of relevant skills in PCTs such as data analysis and contract management. Fourteen private sector companies (that is parts of the PSI) were procured centrally, and at the beginning of 2010 there were around £50m of signed contracts with these firms. But PCTs were also able to engage others from the PSI – and in practice, most PCTs appear to be using methods other than FESC. This is one of the points noted in the House of Commons Health Committee's (2010) detailed enquiry into NHS commissioning. This enquiry drew on studies and collected evidence that indicated, among other things, that over three-quarters of PCTs reported using external support in early 2009; contracts ranged in value from several thousand pounds (short-term consultancy work), to several million pounds (for more ambitious schemes); they mainly involved PSI firms or freelance consultants (30 per cent). PCTs were using external support as a means of boosting their commissioning capacity, though a trade union is reported as arguing that the skills purchased from external consultants were not being transferred to PCT staff, and concerns about how well money was being spent were prevalent. In other words, the PSI had to be brought in to support knowledge deficits connected with the introduction of market mechanisms into the NHS (the purchaser-provider split). But then problems arise with commissioning and using the PSI. Knowledge deficits and other organisational issues associated with the role of these consultancies (for instance, they might be used to reduce the burden of responsibility on commissioners) mean that funds are being wasted here. The House of Commons Health Committee report concluded that the purchaser/provider split led to an increase in transaction costs, notably management and administration costs – quite possibly constituting as much as 14 per cent of total NHS costs (and almost a quarter of staff costs). The NHS traditionally reported low administrative costs (an NHS historian is reported as estimating these as around 5 per cent of expenditure until 1981).

At the time of writing, a new government has announced major changes in the structure of the NHS, including the abolition of PCTs with the intention that doctors themselves will do the commissioning. While this could be seen as a reaction to weaknesses in PCTs, and a welcome shift of power down through administrative hierarchies, concerns are being voiced that this will actually mean even more privatisation of health services in the UK, as the management of consortia of doctors and decisions about commissioning are actually undertaken by the PSI (Milne, 2010). With other promised initiatives including moves to 'liberate' hospital trusts from the NHS, a major experiment is about to be launched. Similar moves are apparent in education, where schools are being encouraged to become 'academies', free of local authority control, and where the PSI is looking to supply a much wider range of services to schools (for example preparing lessons for teachers to deliver). These developments are liable to reshape the organisation of KISA in public services and the associated PSI in the UK; and they will almost certainly call for new KISA (just as past initiatives in commissioning have done). It remains to be seen how far the drivers of profit-making enterprises (and even third sector organisations) can really bring about the revolution in public service costs, quality and innovation that is hoped for – and how far they will really be more effective in so doing than would be the members of organisations primarily oriented to services for the public. In either case, experience is likely to be far less monochrome as political ideology, and rapid learning from success and failure is imperative.

CONCLUSIONS

Given the scale of public services, and their high reliance on KISA, this chapter has inevitably only scratched the surface of this topic. It would be valuable to examine the experience of countries other than the UK, and sectors other than health and education. Hopefully this chapter has helped put these issues onto the agenda for further research.

This KISA analysis of public services has nevertheless highlighted a number of important general features, and perhaps casts light on some of the major political issues of our time. First, the KISA approach suggests that it is important to consider just what sorts of knowledge are being employed in these services, how this is organised (for example, in terms of workforce location, compositions, skills and training), and how it is managed. Numerous forms of knowledge management were noted, though not all of these formally go under this name. This is a challenging area for any organisations that are highly dependent on professional knowledge workers, and becomes even more so when these employees are delivering services to individual citizens, whose long-term quality of life may be critically affected by their encounters with the public services (public services may be knowledge intensive, but of course they are dealing with people's lives in very material ways – through medical treatments, educational interventions, channelling financial flows and administering justice). Public services are also important for business and economic affairs, and may play roles in stimulating innovation and promoting standards across the economy. There is certainly much scope for learning across public service organisations, across sectors and countries as to how to accomplish this.

The approach also bears a great deal on the innovation processes in the public sector, for we see the complexity of professional knowledge as representing both opportunities and problems for innovation in these large-scale organisations. There are many lists of barriers to public sector innovation,[12] but a KISA analysis suggests that we should look specifically at how knowledge is mobilised – and whether it is integrated or fragmented, diffused or compartmentalised, related to experience and experiment or treated as something static and to be transmitted from above. In this light, the ways in which the PSI and other external providers of KISA (for example Universities, the third sector, other public sector organisations) can be part of the mobilisation of knowledge in support of innovation that improves public service, are also subjects of considerable interest. Ideologically driven initiatives have been the bane of many public services, where constant reorganisation has practically been the norm. Manuals of good practice (for example, in commissioning) are one thing that will remain of value. But also, the social context of public services is undergoing huge changes – demographic shifts, new demands on the parts of consumers and citizens, information technologies and emerging techniques for dealing with medical, psychological and other challenges, to name just a few. The public sector will also be critical for dealing with the 'grand challenges' that we confront – from environmental sustainability and food and energy security issues, to overcoming social exclusion and poverty within and across countries. Tackling these challenges will require private sector initiative, to be sure. But many of them can be largely attributed to failure to take into account the limits of market structures. Public sector KISA are an essential part of the response to the challenges, and it must be a priority to enable them to operate more effectively.

There will be much opportunity to extend the evidence base on how different organisational structures can confront such challenges. Hopefully, such evidence can be shared with the 'informed consumers' of public services, just as information on the performance of individual service units within a specific organisational structure is part of the current NPM package. The public can be more than just consumers: they can be innovators, and they can actively play roles in the design and selection of designs for the public services of the future.

NOTES

1. Statistics Denmark's Statbank is available at http://www.statbank.dk/ (accessed 20/10/10).
2. Earlier work by Scott (1982) introduced a classic analysis of the organisation of professional work, examining health service organisations. He contrasted autonomous, heteronomous, and conjoint forms of professional organisation, looking at their rationales, functioning, and determinants. Rather similar approaches are still being developed, and these studies are liable to contribute to the understanding of KISA as professional activities in private as well as public sectors. Examples include Adler et al (2008), Currie et al, (2009), and Leicht and Fennell (1997).
3. A helpful overview is Dunleavy and Hood (1994). See Common (1998) for a critical account of the global diffusion of NPM practice, Diefenbach (2009) for a critical examination of the construct and its implications, Page (2005) for a discussion of the extent to which NPM is rebadging of established practices and to what extent it is really novel.
4. We shall not seek to ascertain just how closely these images about private sector practice actually correspond to the reality, but just note that it is not unknown for either politicians or social scientists to set up an exaggerated dichotomy, and act as if this is a sufficient guide to practice.
5. The quotation is taken from the NICE website, at http://www.nice.org.uk/aboutnice /about_nice.jsp (accessed 15/07/2010).
6. There are tools that are moderately effective in converting speech to text, and others that can process semantic information using dictionaries and thesauri, but these are as yet a far cry from the interpretative capacity of human beings.
7. There has been a remarkable growth in the literature on public service innovation in the recent past. Three good starting points are the website of the PUBLIN project (http://www.step.no/publin/), the *Innovation Journal* (http://www.innovation.cc/) and NESTA's work on public services (http://www.nesta.org.uk/assets/documents/ready_or_not and numerous other publications at NESTA's website). The ServPPIN project is an interesting recent effort to explore public-private innovation networks – see http://www.servppin.com/ (all accessed 20/07/2010).
8. The NHS Institute for Innovation and Improvement is at http://www.institute.nhs.uk/, the National Innovation Centre http://www.nic.nhs.uk/

9. Julius notes further (2008:5) that there are '...inevitably grey areas around the PSI definition used for this Review. For example, regulated industries such as water utilities are excluded. These mostly operate in the private sector without government subsidy, although their prices and investment strategies are largely determined by the government's regulatory policy. Where there is a subsidy to franchised services, such as trains, this subsidy element is included in the PSI. Transfer payments, such as state pensions, are excluded although they are tax-financed... In some cases, definitional decisions had to be taken. For example, the activities of General Practitioners (GP), whose salaries totalled £5bn in 2007/8, are treated by this Review as part of the public sector rather than the PSI despite the fact that GPs' surgeries are typically run as private businesses and GPs are considered self-employed for tax purposes....'

10. Quoted by the House of Commons Health Committee (2009), in a report which critically scrutinises the payments made to consultancy firms and asks for evidence as to their effectiveness. Interestingly, the NHS representative suggests that most of the ideas for reorganisation of services came from the public sector employees, but that the consultancies were very helpful in designing the implementation of these ideas. Sensitive to such criticisms, the consultancy business has sought to demonstrate the value for money it provides; the Management Consultancy Association (MCA) claims on the basis of its survey evidence that consultancy studies generate financial returns of between two and 20 times their cost (MCA, 2010).

11. For a straightforward introduction, see http://en.wikipedia.org/wiki/Ambient_Assisted_Living (accessed 20/07/2010).

12. There are many studies that have built on case studies and the like to set out lists of barriers to public service innovation, but efforts to develop systematic survey information are beginning – see the network for measuring public innovation (MEPIN) at http://mepin.eu/ for this and much other interesting work. On a related issue, NESTA's work on the 'Innovation Index' is of interest: http://nestainnovation.ning.com/forum/topics/measuring-innovation-within (both websites accessed 20/07/2010).

REFERENCES

Adler, P.S., Kwon, S.-W. and Heckscher, C. (2008), 'Professional Work: The Emergence of Collaborative Community', *Organization Science,* **19** (2), pp. 359–376.

Äijälä, K. (2001), *Public Sector – an Employer of Choice? Report on the Competitive Public Employer Project*, Paris, OECD, available at: www. oecd.org/dataoecd/37/29/1937556.pdf (access 20/10/10).

Cedefop (2008), *Future Skills Needs in Europe — Medium-term Forecast Synthesis Report* Thessalonika, CEDEFOP, available at: http://www. trainingvillage.gr/etv/Upload/Information_resources/Bookshop/485/4078_e n.pdf (accessed 20/10/10).

Common, R.K. (1988), 'Convergence and Transfer: a Review of the Globalisation of New Public Management', *International Journal of Public Sector Management,* **11** (6), pp. 440–50.

Consoli, D. and Hortelano, E. (2009), *Variety in the Knowledge Base of Business Service Sectors* Valenciua, CSIC-UPV Universidad Politécnica de Valencia (INGENIO) Informes y documentos de trabajo Working Paper no 2009/09 available at: http://digital.csic.es/bitstream/10261/20390

/1/Variety_in_the_Knowledge_base_of_Business_Service_sectors%5b1%5
d.pdf (accessed 20/07/2010).

Currie, G., Finn, R. and Martin, G. (2009), 'Professional Competition and
Modernizing the Clinical Workforce in the NHS', *Work Employment and
Society,* **23**, pp. 267–83.

Department for Education (2010) *School Workforce in England (Including
Pupil:Teacher Ratios and Pupil: Adult Ratios) January 2010
(Provisional),* London, Department for Education SFR 11/2010 available
at: http://www.dcsf.gov.uk/rsgateway/DB/SFR/s000939/index.shtml
(accessed 20/10/10).

Department of Labor (2010), *O*NET – Beyond Information – Intelligence,*
Washington, D.C.: Employment and Training Administration, U.S.
Department of Labor available at http://www.doleta.gov/programs/onet/
(accessed 20/07/2010).

Diefenbach, T. (2009), 'New Public Management in Public Sector
Organizations: The Dark Sides of Managerialistic "Enlightenment"', *Public
Administration,* **87** (4), pp. 892–909.

Dunleavy, P. and Hood, C. (1994), 'From Old Public Administration to New
Public Management', *Public Money & Management,* **14** (3), pp. 9–16.

House of Commons Health Committee (2009), *The Use of Management
Consultants by the NHS and the Department of Health* (Fifth Report of
Session 2008–09), London: Her Majesty's Stationery Office.

House of Commons Health Committee (2010), *Commissioning* (Fourth
Report of Session 2009–10), London: Her Majesty's Stationery Office
available at: http://www.publications.parliament.uk/pa/cm200910/cmselect/
cmhealth/268/26802.htm (accessed 20/07/2010).

Julius, D. (2008), *Public Services Industry Review – Understanding the
Public Services Industry: How Big, How Good, Where Next?,* London:
HMSO (BERR – Department for Business Enterprise & Regulatory
Reform).

Kakabadse, A. and Kakabadse, N. (2000), 'Outsourcing in the Public
Services: A Comparative Analysis of Practice, Capability and Impact',
Public Administration and Development, **21**, pp. 401–13.

Leicht, K.T. and Fennell, M.L. (1997), 'The Changing Organizational Context
of Professional Work', *Annual Review of Sociology,* **23**, pp. 215–31.

MCA (2010), *The Value of Consulting: An Analysis of the Tangible Benefits
of Using Management Consultancy,* London, Management Consultancies
Association available at: http://www.mca.org.uk/reports/insight/value-of-
consulting-report (accessed 20/07/2010).

Miles, I., Kastrinos, N., Bilderbeek, R., den Hertog, P. with Flanagan, K.,
Huntink, W. and Bouman, M. (1995), 'Knowledge-intensive Business
Services: Their Role as Users, Carriers and Sources of Innovation', *Report*

to the EC DG XIII Luxembourg: Sprint EIMS Programme.

Milne, S. (2010), 'We cannot allow the end of the NHS in all but name', *The Guardian* (London) 15 July 2010, p.29, online at: http://www.guardian.co.uk/commentisfree/2010/jul/14/the-end-of-the-nhs-in-all-but-name (accessed 20/07/2010).

National Health Service [NHS] (2005), *The NHS Knowledge and Skills Framework (NHS KSF) and the Development Review Process,* London: Department of Health, available at http://www.dh.gov.uk/en/Publicationsandstatistics/Publications/PublicationsPolicyAndGuidance/DH_4090843 (accessed on: 05/07/2010).

National Health Service [NHS]2009), *2009 Non-Medical Workforce Census,* London: The Health and Social Care Information Centre, available online at: *http://www.ic.nhs.uk/cmsincludes/_process_document.asp?sPublication ID=1269441596432&sDocID=6179* (accessed on: 05/07/2010).

National Health Service [NHS] (2010), *NHS Occupation Code Manual v.8* London, The Health and Social Care Information Centre, available online at: http://www.ic.nhs.uk/statistics-and-data-collections/data-collections/information-supporting-our-data-collections (accessed 20/07/2010).

Organisation for Economic Co-operation and Development (OECD) (1997), *Classification of the Functions of Government [Third Redraft by the OECD Secretariat: 30th April 1997],* Paris: OECD, STD/NA/RD(97)4 available at: http://www.oecd.org/dataoecd/18/0/2666146.pdf (accessed 20/10/10).

Organisation for Economic Co-operation and Development (OECD) (2009), *Government at a Glance 2009*, Paris: OECD.

Page, S. (2005), 'What's New about the New Public Management? Administrative Change in the Human Services' *Public Administration Review,* **65** (6), pp. 713–27.

Scott, W.R. (1982), 'Managing Professional Work: Three Models of Control for Health Organizations', *Health Services Research*, **17**, pp. 213–40.

Scott, W.R. (2008), 'Lords of the Dance: Professionals as Institutional Agents', *Organization Studies*, **29** (2), pp. 219–38.

Tepe, M. (2009), *Public Administration Employment in 17 OECD Nations from 1995 to 2005*, Edinburgh: University of Edinburgh, Reconciling Work and Welfare in Europe – A Network of Excellence of the European Commission's Sixth Framework Programme RECWOWE Publication, Dissemination and Dialogue Centre, *Working Papers on the Reconciliation of Work and Welfare in Europe* REC-WP 12/2009 available at: http://www.socialpolicy.ed.ac.uk/recwowepudiac/working_papers/ (accessed 05/07/2010).

9 The New Green Deal and KISA: a Global and Australian Perspective

Tavis Potts[1]

The combined impacts of the financial crisis and climate change are driving the evolution of 'sustainable' business and changing the way that governments plan for development. Despite the policy drive towards change, a deficit exists in knowledge and skills that would support the move towards markets for environmentally orientated products and services. National governments are debating and formulating policy and investors are taking an interest in fledgling green economies as one of the responses to the global financial crisis. Many of the political and economic drivers have been focused at the macro-economic scale, and while critical for setting the national framework for development, it often neglects the key role that regions and localities can play in innovation for ecological modernisation. As a result there is a demand for knowledge and skills that support the transition to the green economy. This paper examines two regional case studies in New South Wales (NSW), Australia, that are initiating shifts towards networks of sustainable businesses and facilitating the growth of KISA that supports green innovation.

INTRODUCTION TO THE CHAPTER

In the turbulence of the recent financial crisis, there has been significant debate around the notion of a 'new green deal' to be implemented across global economies. This debate has arisen primarily from a perfect storm of three drivers: the credit crisis, concerns over energy security, and the changing of the earth's climate. In 2009, governments around the world allocated more than US $430bn, lead by China and the USA, to climate related mitigation and adaptation measures and investment in the shoots of an emergent green economy (Robins et al, 2009). The question remains, despite this unprecedented investment, will nations, regions and communities, make the transition to low carbon economies despite the pressures inherent in the international system? The answer is uncertain. This chapter will explore the empirical research that looks at the foundation of such economies and a necessary, if not critical missing ingredient, the role of local business and authorities in generating the knowledge services and activities that underpin innovation and green economic development.

As stated by the Organisation for Economic Co-operation and Development: (OECD, 2008): 'For environmental technologies to penetrate and succeed in global markets, it is important that they succeed domestically. Thus, well-designed environmental policies that spur innovation .... contribute to creating and consolidating domestic markets for environmental technologies constitute a basis for success in global markets.'

This chapter goes one step further. In order to develop green economies at the domestic and by extension global level, investment and policy frameworks must focus on the scale of the region and community and increase the growth, integration and output of KISA. KISA (Knowledge intensive service activities) as defined by OECD (2006) and elaborated in this book, refers to the development and integration of service activities undertaken by firms or public actors in combination with manufactured outputs or services. KISA is a driver of innovation, and examples of activity include research and development, legal and financial services, marketing activity, and in the case of green businesses, community and political engagement. KISA are core parts of sustainability orientated small to medium enterprises (SMEs) and act as a source and driver of innovation. Critically, KISA can act as a carrier of innovation to broader actors and can facilitate the development of knowledge to reform regional policies. The chapter argues that a broader view of innovation that engages communities and firms and can unleash the knowledge intensive activities that drive sustainable business development. Regional specialisations and diversity form the basic economic building blocks of a national green economy, and move in line with community aspirations, employment opportunities and ecologically sustainable regions.

The global degradation of ecosystem services including the provisioning of fresh water systems and biodiversity, and the impacts of climate change, are driving debates about what are appropriate forms of development. Environmental and economic policy must decouple environmental impacts from development processes, and increasingly policy formation is turning to green manufacturing and services as a means of meeting the challenges from the economic downturn in terms of providing employment, addressing climate change. This confluence of pressures essentially refreshes the notion of sustainable development – reducing the ecological footprint from economic activity while promoting development that increases the quality of life – into a modern economic context.

This chapter explores the challenges that face the development of 'green'

KISA in SMEs. Its focuses upon recent research that analysed the opportunities for green growth in two Australian regions and provided advice for the expansion of local green economies as a step in a larger framework to national sustainable economic recovery. The research investigated the knowledge intensive activities of sustainability orientated small businesses and how these can link together with policy to develop regional green development opportunities.

THE GLOBAL FRAMEWORK: AN INTERNATIONAL CALL FOR ACTION?

As a result of the economic crisis, there has been an unprecedented public investment in stimulus packages to refresh and renew domestic economies. Table 9.1 highlights investments in the order of US$ 2.8 trillion. US$ 436 billion or 15.6 per cent globally has been dedicated to a 'green' fund dedicated to a transition to a low carbon economy.

Several trends can be taken out of the stimulus figures. China and the USA dominate in terms of overall stimulus and pledge significant proportions into a 'green fund'. China commits an estimated US$ 586.1 billion with 37.8 per cent or US$ 221 billion towards energy and water efficiency. The USA commits US$ 485 billion with a 12 per cent or US$ 94 billion contribution towards a green economy. While China's contribution is larger with a focus on transport, the US has committed resources towards a balanced portfolio across clean energy, efficiency measures, and water. While committing a smaller total stimulus, US$ 38 billion, South Korea has dedicated 80.5 per cent of the stimulus across low carbon power, energy efficiency, water and waste sectors. The EU has contributed 59 per cent or US$ 22 billion with the balance going towards research in carbon capture and storage (US$ 12 billion) and grid research. In comparison, Australia has committed US$ 26.7 billion to the stimulus with a 9.3 per cent or 2.5 billion emphasis on building energy efficiency.

The stimulus heralds a shift towards mainstream recognition and action on climate change by domestic governments and begins to lay the foundation for ecological modernisation of mainstream economies. The link for many policy makers is emerging – between the failures in the financial system and risk management that led to the financial crisis; and between the catastrophic risk and impacts from a warming global environment on the global society and economy. It is within this context that green stimuli have emerged, meeting the objectives of boosting employment and creating economic growth and to create the foundations of a low carbon economy.

9.1 Financial stimulus and green investment

	Fund USDbn	Period Years	Green Fund USDbn	% Green Fund	Low-Carbon Power		Energy Efficiency (EE)				Water/
					Renewable	CCS/Other	Building EE	Lo C Vech+	Rail	Grid	
Asia Pacific											
	26.7	2009–12	2.5	9.3%	-	-	2.48		-	-	
	586.1	2009–10	221.3	37.%	-	-	-	1.5	98.65	70.00	
	13.7	2009	0.0	0.0%	-	-	-	-	-	-	
	485.9	2009 onwards	12.4	2.6%	-	-	12.43	-	-	-	
South Korea	38.1	2009–12	30.7	80.5	1.80	-	6.19	1.80	7.01	-	
	3.3	2009	0.0	0.0%	-	-	-	-	-	-	
Asia Pacific	**1,153.8**	**0.0**	**266.9**	**23.1%**	**1.8**	**0.0**	**21.1**	**3.3**	**105.7**	**70.0**	
	38.8*	2009–10	22.8	58.7%	0.65	12.49	2.85	1.94	-	4.85	
	104.8	2009–10	13.8	13.2%	-	-	10.39	0.69	2.75	-	
	33.7	2009–10	7.1	21.1%	0.87	-	0.83	-	1.31	4.13	
	103.5	2009	1.3	1.3%	-	-	-	-	1.32	-	
	14.2	2009 onwards	0.8	5.8%	-	-	-	1.38	-	-	
	30.4	2009–12	2.1	6.9%	-	-	0.29	1.38	0.41	-	
	308.7	2009	6.2	2.0%	1.9	-	0.4	3.9	-	-	
	325.5	**0**	**54.2**	**16.7%**	**3.5**	**12.5**	**14.7**	**7.9**	**5.8**	**9.0**	

9.2 *(cont.)*

	Fund USDbn	Period Years	Green Fund USDbn	% Green Fund	Low-Carbon Power		Energy Efficiency (EE)				W
					Renewable	CCS/ Other	Building EE	Lo C Vech+	Rail	Grid	
	31.8	2009–13	2.6	8.3%	-	1.08	0.24	-	0.39	0.79	
	4.0	2009	0.0	0.0%	-	-	-	-	-	-	
US ARRA	185.0**	10 Years	18.2	9.8%	10.25	2.6	3.34	0.76	0.33	0.92	
	787.0	10 Years	84.1	12.0%	22.53	3.95	27.40	4.00	9.59	11.00	
	1,007.8		**114.9**	**11.4%**	**32.8**	**7.6**	**31.0**	**4.8**	**10.3**	**12.7**	
	2,796		**436**	**15.6%**	**38.0**	**20.1**	**66.8**	**15.9**	**121.8**	**91.7**	

(* Only EUR30bn from direct EU contribution considered for calculation as the rest (EUR170bn) is contributed by member states; **USD700bn under TARP not considered for calculation as the fund is mainly for bank bailouts not for fiscal stimulus) + Low Carbon Values. Table sourced with permission from: Robins et al, 2009

HSBC estimates

To limit the chance for global warming and remain within the (challenged) two degree envelope that minimises the risk of adverse global impact, emissions need to peak before 2020 and be reduced to a minimum of 50 per cent of 1990 levels (Allen et al, 2009). Given the inertia in the climate system and the inertia in the political and economic system, urgent actions are required to progress the transition, particularly in the context that one degree of warming has been locked into the system by existing emissions.

In this context, the transition from the current trajectory of increasing emission to a low carbon trajectory in 2020 is an immense social and economic challenge. Any transition to a low carbon economy requires investment in renewable platforms, infrastructure, energy efficiency measures, and low carbon technologies. It is a challenge that requires innovation in its broader sense, political support and investment.

Proceeding along the no mitigation path will lead to significant environmental, social economic impacts upon Australian biodiversity, agriculture, infrastructure and ecosystems. The Garnaut Climate Change Review (Commonwealth of Australia, 2008) highlights, amongst other issues, that a 'no mitigation' scenario could result in a 92 per cent reduction of agricultural production in the Murray Darling basin, destruction of the Great Barrier Reef and Australian Alpine region, a lack of water supply to urban areas and metropolitan centers, and damage to buildings and infrastructure in coastal regions. This important policy milestone is due to be updated in May 2011.

This chapter now turns to examine the critical role of regions and communities in term of ecological modernization, and the role that is played by small to medium enterprises.

REGIONS, INNOVATION AND SUSTAINABILITY

The notion of region has evolved as a unit of innovation, economic growth and the appropriate scale to resolve the global challenges of sustainable development (Bellamy et al, 2003; Martinez-Fernandez and Potts, 2008; Potts et al, 2007). Issues such as climate change require an integrated response from the global community through the United Nations (UN) Framework Convention on Climate Change in order to regulate carbon pollution and focus on cleaner development. At the same time, climate change, mitigation and adaptation will impact and influence regional development and bioregional systems. In several interesting examples, regions have responded earlier, quicker or with more vigor than national political systems to the climate challenge. In the US, it is widely acknowledged that California has for many years led US climate related policy (Arimura et al, 2007). The development of state wide energy efficiency measures and investment in renewable energy has led to no net increase in electricity use from 1975 against a national rise of 50 per cent (Arimura et al, 2007). One adopted climate policy in California is the California Global Warming Solutions Act. The Act establishes a Greenhouse Gas (GHG) Emissions target for California and requires that GHG emissions be lowered to 1990 levels by 2020 (Arimura et al, 2007). Although this is far less than what is required to restrict future warming to two degrees, it is a positive step forwards.

Regional innovation and industry clustering activity (Porter, 1990) suggest how clusters of related industries exist in networked, competing, and complimentary relationships and are able to create income and exports. Critically, clusters are embedded in a regional context and specialisation, usually derived in part from a regions social and economic history and are entities that develop through support from their constituent firms, governments, and communities (Porter, 1990; Hargraves and Smith, 2005). While at the forefront of national economic policy, industrial clusters and knowledge based development has a clear extension into regional sustainability and the development of 'green' clusters. A green cluster is where a region can move towards an economy based on its unique features including regional ecosystems, social systems and adapting the existing economic base (Gibbs, 2000; Burstrom and Korhonen, 2001).

Ecological modernisation is a key part of the regional governance debate, it argues that economic and environmental issues can be reconciled to form a new model of development (Brand and de Bruijin, 1999; Janike, 2008). It is a technology, innovation and market based approach to addressing environmental problems, driven by 'smart regulation' and pressures on polluting industries (Janike, 2008).

With regional planning high on the policy agenda the region can be considered an appropriate scale for linking environmental and economic initiatives and processes (Hargraves and Smith, 2005; Shaw and Kidd, 2001). Regional sustainability governance provides a framework where traditional smaller scale sustainability programmes at the firm or organisation level are scaled upwards to a regional focus. This links businesses, universities, municipal authorities and citizen groups together in a regionally focused effort (Brunckhorst, 2002). This requires resources for coordination and addressing inadequate institutional coordination, mismatches between ecological and jurisdictional boundaries and cultural differences between stakeholders (Berger, 2004).

The shift towards green KISA drives efforts to reconcile economic growth and the restoration of natural systems (Krehbiel et al, 1999; Koschatzky and Kroll, 2007. Innovation and sustainability are complementary issues but this relationship has traditionally been informal, segregated and underfunded.

Departing from this tradition in public policy, following is a discussion of the emerging relationship between innovative environmental businesses, local innovation processes and regional governance. The paper identifies emerging networks of knowledge exchange as a means of developing KISA to support innovation that addresses environmental problems.

COMMUNITY PARTNERSHIPS AS A DRIVING FORCE FOR KNOWLEDGE INTENSIVE SERVICE ACTIVITIES

For sustainability to re-orientate behaviour there must be a marriage between government policies and community action (Smith and Scott, 2006). Glass (2002) surmises that sustainability must involve change in lifestyle patterns including patterns of consumption and production. Influencing the choices of individuals to purchase environmentally friendly products can significantly impact national and industries and organisations, but deeper than this is a fundamental change in behavior towards a sustainable society.

Partnerships are tools that promote dialogue, cooperation and education across different community sectors. Gibson and Cameron (2001) identify partnerships as a unifying approach to manage interactions between formal government agencies and individuals. As voluntary initiatives, partnerships compliment and implement national policies and boost support for green strategies. Importantly, the notion of partnership is important for integrating different types of KISA within and between organisations and driving innovation. For example, while research and development is traditionally associated with innovation, the use of network orientated and compliance orientated KISA is critical for moving firms through a rapidly advancing social and political agenda. For example, while technical knowledge of renewable energy is critical for innovation, so too is understanding the policy drivers, social acceptance, and regulatory framework. Often SMEs lack the capacity to develop all three forms of KISA – partnerships are important mechanisms to capture this information and exchange with other firms or actors.

The literature on partnerships identifies the productive links between local government and communities (Armstrong and Stratford, 2004; Feichtinger and Pregernig, 2005; Frame and Taylor, 2005; Smith and Scott, 2006; Potts et al, 2007). Examples exist of public agencies, particularly local government, moving towards considering citizens as 'partners' rather than 'clients' or 'customers' (Vigoda, 2002). This evolving nature of partnerships is extending toward collaboration with other sectors such as the private sector or academia (Vigoda, 2002) and was documented at the UN Summit in Johannesburg in 2002. Local government partnerships with community are not anything new, but the emerging innovation lies in the collaborative arrangements between government, community, business, and academia focused on developing and exchanging green KISA to enhance regional sustainability (Potts et al, 2007).

Recent practice suggests that regional partnerships are seeking greater participation from business and universities. Business groups are increasingly recognising the need to consider the triple bottom line and corporate social responsibility and view partnerships as a tool to achieve this goal (Loza, 2004).

An example of a recent Australian partnership is the Macarthur Regional Environmental Innovation Network (REIN) that links together a regional university, community groups and local businesses in the Macarthur region of South West Sydney, NSW.[2] The mission of the Network is to contribute and communicate ideas, strategies, and research for achieving a sustainable region through environmental innovation. In one sense, this is a public market place for the exchange of KISA. The partnership evolved from a research project titled 'Innovation at the Edges' that highlighted the critical, often overlooked, roles of environmental and social influences on innovation (Martinez-Fernandez and Potts, 2008). The network has provided a focal point for action on regional environmental innovation by facilitating information sharing between partners on the 'how to' questions that surround environmental innovation, developing collaborative research, finding common ground between business, community and government and disseminating information on issues such as water and energy efficiency, climate, transport and food production. Through replicating partnerships such as REIN, regional support for ecological modernisation can be built at the local scale and firms and public organisations can access the elements of KISA that they do not have internally.

RESEARCH ON THE NATURAL ADVANTAGE

In 2006, pilot research was carried out to explore the dynamics of ecological modernisation and knowledge transfer in SMEs and communities in two outer metropolitan regions of Sydney, NSW (Figure 9.1). Twenty-one organisations were interviewed in combination with document analysis to define a policy agenda based on understanding what motivates and concerns sustainability orientated businesses, what can improve their operations and how they contribute to their localities. The research explored the following four themes:

1. What is the Natural Advantage concept? Is it a useful construct for exploring sustainability, and innovation?
2. What role can the Natural Advantage play in building regional sustainable development?

3. What are the activities, drivers, and barriers to local organisations implementing sustainable business activities?
4. What are the mechanisms that can boost environmental innovation through regions?

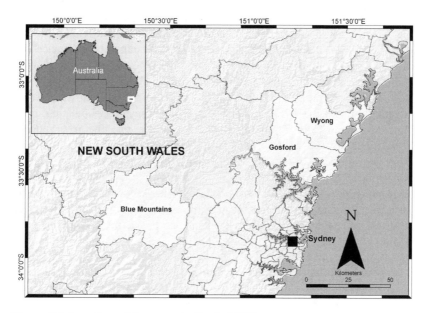

Figure 9.1 Location of the case studies in NSW

The two regions are major population zones on the fringe of the metropolitan region of Sydney. Both have unique natural systems and are renowned for scenic quality. Both regions have experimented with initiatives for sustainable development with varying degrees of success and are identified as regions of population growth. The local economies are dominated by small to medium enterprises.

The Central Coast region of NSW (Wyong and Gosford) is a rapidly growing coastal area on the northern fringe of Sydney. It is characterised by residential growth, sensitive coastal catchments and a mixed economic base of commercial, retail, manufacturing and service industries. The Central Coast is recognised for its natural ecosystems including beaches and estuaries; coastal lowlands that contain significant wetlands, waterways and forests; and elevated valley and mountain systems with a mix of wet and dry temperate ecological communities. The environment of the Central Coast is an attractor of residents and business with a growing population. In 2006 the estimated population was 307,766 with an annual growth rate of 0.8 per cent, concentrated in the Wyong Shire. By 2021 it is estimated that there will be 368,000 people living in the region (Central Coast Research Foundation, 2007).

The Blue Mountains region is located on the western fringe of the Sydney Metropolitan region. The region is internationally recognised for its biodiversity and aesthetic values, as well as providing ecosystem services for the Sydney basin. The Greater Blue Mountains World Heritage Area (GBMWHA) is an area of international natural and cultural significance with the 1.03 million hectare Greater Blue Mountains Area has listed as World Heritage because of its outstanding biodiversity. The local administration is the Blue Mountains City Council with the local government area (LGA) covering an area of 143,000 square kilometers. The total population of the Blue Mountains was 74,067 in 2006. It remains one the most popular destinations in Australia for tourism with a turnover of 2.4 million visitors in 2006 with tourism contributing to approximately 13 per cent of the regional employment. Fifty-seven per cent of the workforce commutes outside the area, predominantly to Sydney (BMCC 2002a). A dominant feature of the business structure is the high proportion of small to medium enterprises (SMEs) with 90 per cent of Blue Mountains businesses considered to be SMEs.

Theme 1: Defining the Natural Advantage

The Natural Advantage is defined as: the advantages and benefits that a public, private or community organisation can obtain by applying cleaner production and environmental innovation principles and processes to its operations.

The initial debate on the Natural Advantage conceived the issue at the scale of the nation and large firm. This is important because domestic implementation requires cohesive national vision and policy coordination. The application at the firm scale has traditionally focused on large companies, many of a multinational character with the capacity to develop and implement sustainability strategies and KISA. Implementing sustainability strategies and developing green KISA may be beneficial to large firms. In a recent report, companies that placed an emphasis on efficiency, green innovation and strong governance are, according to the report, showing above average performance during the financial downturn (Mahler et al, 2009). The practice of Corporate Social Responsibility (CSR) has been an important voluntary mechanism used by many industries to build for a 'community license to operate' and to identify and respond to environmental issues in their operations (Benn and Dunphy, 2004). In fact, CSR appears to be a mechanism that drives internal KISA related to R&D, compliance, standard setting and knowledge exchange.

Despite CSR being an increasingly common feature in larger firms it has failed to manifest at the scale of small to medium enterprises (Potts et al, 2007).

In the context of small to medium firms the natural advantage brings a set of potential benefits including:

- Resource productivity in energy, water, resources and waste;
- New markets and increased consumer demand;
- High quality processes and products;
- Support of local communities;
- Integration of local business needs and local policies;
- Increased social capital and partnership;
- Local environmental restoration;
- Improved local identity;
- Leveraging of resources for sustainability strategies and actions; and
- Knowledge production and exchange.

Traditional manufacturing industries have the capability to employ Natural Advantage concepts and contribute to KISA. A recent Commonwealth Scientific and Industrial Research Organisation (CSIRO) study (Hatfield-Dodds et al, 2008) highlighted the critical role of 'green collar jobs' to address the challenges in Australia relating to climate change. The report found considerable growth potential in traditional sectors that have high environmental impact. These sectors could be converted into green collar jobs to restructure the Australian economy towards a low-carbon future. The report found that the creation of at least 33,000 new jobs in manufacturing, 77,000 jobs in transport, and 145,000 jobs in construction over ten years would present an opportunity for re-training into greener industries (Hatfield-Dodds et al, 2008). This would be in addition to re-skilling of 2.9 million workers already employed in these sectors further underscoring the opportunities for existing industries to develop education, training and skills in low carbon industries.

Sustainable industries can be new companies or originate from the traditional industry base such as manufacturing or services. Sustainability orientated industries pursue the social, economic and political changes that are necessary to advance sustainability in society and go beyond the call of regulatory requirements. They are leading innovators and risk takers in cleaner production, conservation, and environmental management and engage with their communities over their core business.

To frame the discussion on applying the natural advantage concept a conceptual framework was developed (Figure 9.2). The model allowed the approach to be integrated within a local case study, frame the debate, and encourage further analysis and reflection. The model has a temporal basis, outlining a series of drivers and transformative measures over time with the result an improvement in integrated economic and environmental outcomes for a region. It this sense it is can be considered a normative framework that establishes goals or desired states.

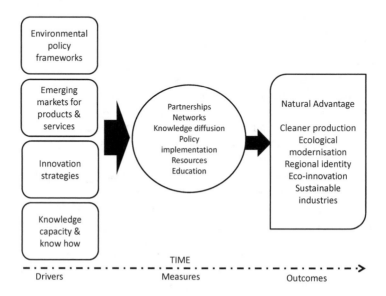

Figure 9.2 Conceptual natural advantage model

The drivers for developing regional natural advantage include policy frameworks, markets for products and services, innovation strategies and the development of knowledge capacity, KISA and 'know-how'. The drivers are the baseline and informal conditions and plans that need to be developed to move towards more synergistic and effective outcomes. At this stage they are considered to be disconnected instruments that do not integrate into a cohesive policy development process.

Policy frameworks and regulation play a significant role in stimulating the development of new markets for environmental products and services (Tukker and Emmert, 2008). Instruments may manifest at the regional or national scale and take the form of regulations such as energy efficiency regulations, market based instruments such as subsidies or emissions trading schemes, and educational tools, strategies or networks that increase knowledge diffusion. Policy instruments support the development of markets for sustainable products and account for ecosystem services. The development of local innovation strategies through KISA exchange is another important driver. There are some local attempts in Australia to increase the dialogue between businesses, communities, and universities around environment and innovation as typified by the REIN described above. Often the technical and R&D capacity in SMEs is not matched to KISA relating to policy frameworks and networks, SMEs may also be limited in accessing research developments due to resource or manpower constraints and will seek out partnerships to improve knowledge flow and innovation activity. Voluntary initiatives, driven by local stakeholders, are an important element in building local capacity, but require other supporting measures. A 'whole of society approach' with contributions from civil institutions, business, government, and the public is necessary for developing the 'know-how' or embedded knowledge that supports widespread integration of natural advantage drivers through a region.

As the baseline conditions evolve and integrate, they become more effective over time through a series of 'transformative measures' (Figure 9.2). This moves a region from a set of disparate activities to a platform for regional transformation. Transformative measures build capacity, transfer knowledge, and create new opportunities. Sharing information, expertise and resources and increasing the understanding of the role of different sectors leads to new initiatives and outcomes. The outcomes include the strategic objectives of cleaner production processes, new waves of environmental innovation, industry development and the development of a regional identity – all measurable by a set of agreed regional indicators.

Theme 2: What Role Can the Natural Advantage Play in Building Regional Sustainable Development?

The case studies explored questions concerning the development of the organisation, its relationship to the region and the links to sustainable development. The interviews highlighted a diversity of views regarding the motivation of the business and its contribution to the region. Results reveal that several firms and organisations from heterogeneous sectors consider themselves as 'sustainable businesses' and sustainability forms a core part of their daily operations and operating ethic.

On the Central Coast, the responses suggested entry into a sustainable business came from many backgrounds. When asked about the drivers of the business, views included:

> Originally money until we found out how bad the world was and how much help it needed. It definitely was an area that had a massive gap. Trades people need help…with business skills. The participants in our classes were a driver towards us learning more…as our knowledge has grown, the business has evolved and changed. [Case 9]

It was the area I was skilled in…it wasn't that I wanted to make a difference or change the world's climate; it was the area I was trained in so it was naturally the best business I could go into. I wanted to work for myself and this was the business I knew. [Case 11]

Sustainable businesses evolve from several sources: trades, small business, concerned citizens, and entrepreneurs. This has policy implications to reach to target audiences and strategies to improve the generation of KISA. Traditional as well as new sectors can be incentivised to 'convert' to a sustainability focus but the issue of skills is important (Hatfield-Dodds et al, 2008).

The Central Coast as it is home to a diverse and growing base of SMEs, with the dominant sectors across the retail, community services, construction, manufacturing, business services and hospitality. The shift in the region from primary industries to service orientated industries underscores the growth in knowledge based services and the potential for growth in sustainability orientated firms.

In the Blue Mountains, interviewees equated drivers for the creation of a business with previous education and experience in sustainable development a common factor. Interviewees expressed opinions relating to a growing sustainability influence in previous businesses and changed when an opportunity presented itself, such as a new business idea, change in direction or relocation to the region with its high quality natural environment. This underscores the role that KISA may play in generating new businesses or spin-offs as well as supporting innovation within firms.

It seemed like an idea at the time that met our altruistic and values needs and an opportunity to move into another career. We were both in a fork…finding out about sustainability and seeing its opportunities aligned with all the things that we thought we wanted in our career, it was a life change and a coming together of the knowledge that drove it. [Case 17]

We didn't say we were going to create this environmental business…it was just a gradual process… I do have a background in accommodation and combining my knowledge in that area we structured the property to accommodate various markets we created something that would suit groups, families and couples…we already had an environmental bent. [Case 15]

Environmental education and practical knowledge are clearly important in developing natural advantage. Community education may lead to awareness and opportunities for individuals in organisations to 'change tact' or develop entrepreneurial output. Statistics show the Blue Mountains is home to an educated workforce and has a high proportion of small businesses existing within a World Heritage designated area (BMCC, 2002b). This situation could support KISA and innovation amongst small businesses and develop sustainable products and services. When asked about the role of the business in relation to sustainability within the region, Central Coast firms revealed a variety of motivations.

> ...there is awareness in some sectors and I compare it to four years ago when we first started out, there was no understanding. The only money to be made up here was in real estate, clearing land and the like. When I look at where we have come... it's actually a term which is in use now, people say 'I'm looking at setting up a sustainable business' the term is more widely used. [Case 6]

> We are looking at the end user. To get the end user or the person who makes the choice, asking for the right thing rather than relying on someone to push the right thing towards them. This puts less pressure on the builder to have to do the right thing, less pressure on the supplier to do the right thing because the customer is asking from the start. That's our theory, if we can convince them, then everyone above will have to follow suit. [Case 3]

Some businesses saw themselves educating customers and the community to preference sustainable products, acting as agents for developing markets. Other businesses felt their role was limited or the sector did not have critical mass. Several respondents felt that 'something was happening' in the community and in the market in terms of sustainability and that the publicised environmental issues concerning water quality and climate change were responsible for this change. Several respondents felt that it was 'early days' for developing a sustainable region and that business, community, and government had a long way to go in terms of education. Many firms identified that the key challenges in the region were changing the values of the public but government was lagging in developing sustainable industry policies and there was a need for industry support.

The Blue Mountains identified consistent issues that affected regional business. These included the development of the local economy within the context of the World Heritage listing and the influence of the listing on the regions image; the role, extent and evolution of the tourism sector; and opportunities that could drive the sustainable business sector through the region. Several respondents noted that they felt more emphasis was required across business and the community about the advantages and opportunities of living within a World Heritage area.

Theme 3: What Are the Activities, Drivers, and Barriers to Implementing Sustainable Business Activities?

The Central Coast faces competing demands for employment generation and maintenance of the coastal environment. Results in Table 9.2 reveal a number of activities spanning the industry base with a focus on the development of products and services, education and partnerships.

Table 9.2 Sustainable business activities on the Central Coast

Sustainable Business Activities	Environmental Products	Environmental Services	Green Purchasing Policy	Education or awareness	Partnerships	Research & Development	Monitoring	Conservation Activities	Examples
Case 1				X	X				Business Incubation Activities Networking support, Knowledge transfer
Case 2	X	X	X	X		X			Manufacture and sale of recycled products. Education of community
Case 3	X	X		X	X			X	Green home building & design, partnership with TAFE, schools Greensmart member
Case 4	X		X	X		X			Produces solar panels and wind turbines. Export based. Support for customers in Pacific
Case 5						X			R&D into new and drought proof products
Case 6		X	X	X	X		X	X	Community awareness and education, projects, govt / private partnerships
Case 7	X	X	X		X	X			Home audits, solar devices, schools outreach and partnerships
Case 8	X					X			Manufacture of solar hot water
Case 9		X		X	X	X			Education & training of trades, research into green design, business outreach
Case 10		X		X	X		X		Cleaner production, Partnerships with schools & community, regulatory and voluntary monitoring
Case 11	X	X	X	X	X				Manufacture, installation, service & training of remote renewable systems
Case 12	X	X		X		X		X	Rehabilitation, native species supply, specialised local knowledge and services
Case 13	X	X		X	X	X		X	Primary and sec. education, industry partnerships, local studies, environmental management

On the Central Coast organisations developed a mix of environmental products or service activities. Several organisations developed both products and services and found this to be a complimentary and reinforcing activity. For example, Case 11 manufactured remote renewable energy systems for an international market but focused on complimentary long term education and training about the product, its service and repair:

> We maintain a support service network in specific island nations – capacity, products, knowledge… there are thousands of solar panels in this region with many not working. Believe this is due to a hardware only approach to renewable development, rather than a technology service – whole system, holistic, hardware, software and knowledge. [Case 11]

Another operator discussed the innovation benefits of supplying environmental products (native plants) and services (a database and ecological knowledge on regional vegetation). This allowed for a degree of specialisation as a knowledge provider, allowing access to new development and rehabilitation projects and driving innovation within the SME.

> I've got a computer database for local native plants – second to none. I do a lot of research and development…I have to because the plants that I grow aren't grown by anybody else in the industry. [Case 12]

The involvement of firms in education and the development of partnerships was a feature of Sustainable Business Activities (SBAs) on the Central Coast. Most organisations engaged in this activity to generate business, provide information about products and services, and access knowledge about products. Developing networks to share knowledge was seen as a useful activity, but most partnerships were not developed in a way that directly benefited the firm and were short term. The activities that were least supported by firms and organisations were monitoring and reporting and field based conservation. In terms of monitoring and reporting, it was clear from the interviews that sustainability indicators and triple bottom line were beyond the reach of small business. The concept was found to be useful to improve internal performance, but the time and resources associated with this activity was problematic. One firm noted:

> …reporting is time consuming, would be good to have time to sit down and do analysis, and would be nice to get grants for reporting and work with the universities doing reporting. [Case 3]

Firms were asked to identify the drivers of their activities. Regulations were cited as a high driver for developing sustainable activities. Regulations and policies were viewed in two ways. The first is that regulation caused a firm to act in accordance with a particular ruling such as an emissions standard. The second view was that regulations provided new opportunities for businesses. The most frequently cited reform was BASIX (the NSW Building Sustainability Index) that requires new developments in NSW to incorporate sustainable design into residential and commercial buildings to gain development approval. Environmental awareness of the firm was another driver of SBAs that resulted in pressure for action or a willingness to act. Several businesses were familiar with the concept of sustainability and actively incorporated it into their business model and/or development. Interestingly, community pressure was listed as a driver of low importance. This suggests for establishing sustainable business activities, businesses and organisations may respond more towards internal awareness developed by KISA than to external community pressure. Cost savings, efficiencies, competitive advantage and the development of new markets were all identified as drivers of high importance. Organisations were able to save costs for themselves and for customers, develop efficient practices and use sustainability as a source of competitive advantage. Competitive advantage was seen an important driver, but was viewed as a likely future state rather than a present advantage. This argument is backed by Porter and van der Linde (1995) who discuss that the fastest emerging markets are increasingly in the area of sustainable products and services.

Respondents identified the issues that were a barrier to developing sustainable business activities. The issues that were raised as major obstacles to developing activities were cost of research, lack of adequate funding and a lack of time. Several interviewees noted a lack of government assistance and a difficulty in accessing and generating research and development on their products and services. This highlights the fact that more support is required to develop research in SMEs.

> The companies that are already set up and are wealthy, they hire people to do all of that stuff and throw resources into it. But if you're starting from scratch it's very expensive to do that, the amount of time (it takes) to develop. [Case 9]

> Research is what I really want to get moving but it's very difficult for a small business. Accessing grants and partnerships is difficult. I could just use our own money...but I'm not terribly inclined to do that. I'm looking for a cheaper way through a grant. [Case 4]

Sustainable business activities: the Blue Mountains
The Blue Mountains region has a small but significant base of sustainability orientated businesses in the services sector, including firms that have developed activities using the World Heritage listing as a means of increasing business activity. There was a distinct difference in the mix of SBAs in the region as compared to the Central Coast as displayed in Table 9.3.

The regional expertise is focused in three areas. The first relates to the development of environmental services such as environmentally friendly accommodation and ecotourism. The second focuses on the development of partnerships and networks. The third relates to environmental education and covers formal and informal activities that contribute to the growth KISA. The focus on services and education was a clear distinction from the more mixed activities of the Central Coast.

Table 9.3 Sustainable business activities in the Blue Mountains region

Sustainable Business Activities	Environmental Products	Environmental Services	Green Purchasing Policy	Education or awareness	Partnerships	Research & Development	Monitoring	Conservation Activities	Examples
Case 14	X			X		X			Selling energy products, research into design & application, community education
Case 15		X	X	X			X		'Green' accommodation, environmental education, monitoring programmes
Case 16		X		X	X		X	X	Regional ecolabel (BMBA programme), community education, partnerships with business
Case 17		X		X	X	X			Organisational sustainability strategies, business partnerships, community education
Case 18	X	X							Development of green hospitality products, green retreats, design, education
Case 19		X			X				Networking, ecolabel, organisational strategies
Case 20		X		X	X			X	Eco-tourism, client education, professional courses, advocacy
Case 21		X		X	X	X			Research and advocacy on regional issues

There are two dominant, if slightly contradictory influences for the development of sustainable industries and activities. One is the need for the diversification of the industry base as a strategy to shift from over-reliance on tourism. This would open space for new businesses, encourage employment growth in the region to reduce travel times to centers in Sydney, and harness the high educational standard in the region. The other influence for developing a sustainable industry base is the dominance of tourism. Development of high quality sustainable accommodation and eco-tourism services is a regional goal but must be responsive to supply and demand. The World Heritage listing plays an important regional role through awareness, education and research, branding and creation of new businesses. Some interviewees felt that the importance of the World Heritage message was not resonating within the broader community and translating into environmental action.

An innovative approach in region was the Blue Mountains Business Advantage programme which establishes an accredited brand identifying firms that have participated in a sustainable business training course. The brand is owned by Blue Mountains Tourism Limited and administered by the regional Chamber of Commerce and assisted by the Blue Mountains City Council. Accredited organisations receive a licence to use the logo for their marketing. The initiative appears to be catching on in the local business community and is a facilitator with KISA within firms (developing internal awareness and technical capacity) and between firms (sharing experiences and knowledge).

There are clear links between the provision of environmental services, networking and partnerships, and environmental education – all elements of developing KISA that supports sustainable innovation. For example, environmental education at a community level may increase general awareness on issues such as energy and climate. Increased awareness can lead to a greater demand for products and services such as energy efficient appliances, solar hot water and heat pump technology. Education can also work for the firm, contributing to understanding the merits and impacts of different technologies (R&D orientated KISA) and aid in the creation of informal knowledge networks (network orientated KISA). Not only is the demand for products increased, but new services such as green design, conservation activities, and eco-friendly tourism and accommodation move from niche to mainstream practice.

In discussing their business operations, several respondents identified in open discussion various drivers and obstacles that affect them. For one firm, the commitment to sustainability practices offered customers a clear choice. These practices were not seen as widespread through the sector, with the result that the firm believed it gained a competitive advantage. Through marketing and an international accreditation scheme specifically for the sector (eco-tourism), significant benefits flowed to the firm. However the cost of accreditation was an obstacle unless the benefits were clearly identified.

> Through being accredited we've had some advantage. It is standing us alone and saying we have done the hard yards... it has given us a reputation that precedes us wherever we go. We have people who know about us in America, England, Japan, Singapore, Asia, and Europe. But the cost of becoming sustainable and staying sustainable is high, the product value becomes high and therefore you reduce your client base. [Case 20]

For some firms accreditation was a means to establish competitive advantage and potentially new markets through sustainability orientated product differentiation and recognition. However, not all businesses were open to the idea of accreditation serving their needs. In reference to the local accreditation scheme, the BMBA (Blue Mountains Business Advantage), several operators believed the programme required reform. While the role of a regional accreditation programme may increase KISA, more evidence is required on policy tools, knowledge creation and innovation.

> I cannot say that I have seen concrete results from accreditation. I certainly don't think it hurts...If it is there, use it and join it. And the more of us, I think if the whole community got onboard it would make a difference. But there are so many people out there that just don't understand the value, and it is probably not going in the right direction now. [Case 15]

The role of environmental awareness and the status of World Heritage was clearly a factor in driving business activities.

> One (issue) for me would be to try and get the city accredited as a sustainable city and stand as a benchmark for education and make the Blue Mountains an icon...so that universities, TAFE, the council, National Parks could engage...could set up the city as the first city in the world that has been accredited as minimal impact. That would be a large community step forward... we need to be able to have the Blue Mountains community stand up and recognise that they are in a world heritage area [Case 21]

In terms of constraints, the issue of acquiring new knowledge and technical 'know-how' was raised by interviewees. Similar to the Central Coast, the means of accessing new knowledge and finding personnel with skill sets that supported the business was difficult. Often SMEs were busy running the day to day tasks of the business with little time to invest in broader KISA activities such as R&D, networking and policy development. For example:

> [An obstacle is] the availability of the latest technology. I was looking at some sort of solar panels, but then (name removed) said there was a new solar panel in the market. And so I don't know where to get the most up to date information. It might be there, but there is a time limitation for us to for doing research [Case 14].

This underscores the importance of establishing mechanisms such as networks and partnerships to assist SMEs in accessing appropriate information and knowledge concerning business activities. Community and business attitudes to sustainability were identified as another barrier. Respondents felt that attitudes across the region were generally positive and changing, but resistance and a lack of awareness was present in many parts of the community, including many businesses. As one commentator noted:

> One of the biggest issues in my mind...is where sustainability needs to be put to the broader community almost as much or at the same time as it is put to the industry

sector...this is big picture stuff...but if we link into everything down the chain so that the milk bar wants to be accredited (to the BMBA). It is not meant to put one against the other.

Theme 4: Boosting Environmental KISA Through Regions

Implementing the natural advantage is a strategy for business, environmental education, and innovation that is linked to environmental improvement. The concept should not operate in isolation – the focus is an integrating strategy to link regional economic and environmental planning. The case studies highlight that there are benefits to planning regional economic strategies in line with sustainability and opportunities are emerging as the regions engage in predominantly preparatory, and to a minor extent, transformative activities. While both regions have firms that specifically identify as sustainable businesses, the natural advantage concept can apply to all activities across the economic landscape. While many sustainable businesses are innovators and early adopters, this sector is still small as a proportion of total firms. As natural advantage takes hold both the sustainable industry sector and the activities of other traditional sectors will co-develop.

The main recommendation is that local and regional authorities should explore the linking of sustainable development, KISA and economic development in their regions through the development of Natural Advantage action plans. Plans should transform local businesses, grow the sustainable industry base, expand and support KISA orientated capacity and activities, focus on local issues and regional strengths, and support the development of environmental products and services. Policy instruments from the case studies to drive KISA include:

- Strengthening of sustainable business networks – Sustainable business networks provide a means for knowledge transfer and building of KISA between stakeholders. A sustainable business network would have partners from SMEs, local chamber of commerce, government, education, research and community organisations. A network encourages collaboration and exchange of knowledge and resources, ideas and opportunities, policy feedback, and building new business opportunities. Members of a sustainable business network should be committed to the development of a sustainable industries sector and driving the social change necessary for pushing sustainability into civil society;
- Support the role of environmental education – The case studies consistently identified the critical role of public, private and community environmental education in generating support and ideas that lead to the

growth of KISA. Education plays an important role in developing awareness in the community of sustainable lifestyles and can increase the demand for environmental products and services. It is recommended that environmental education strategies and programmes extend to cover local businesses communities and SMEs;

- Develop local accreditation schemes – The evidence from the research suggests that regional accreditation schemes can provide an incentive for organisations to explore sustainability in the context of their operations and promote knowledge activities for practical improvements. Although further research is required on the effectiveness of the accreditation process and outcomes, the study notes that regional branding, marketing, promotion and support from local government and businesses create incentives for engagement. It is important that any accreditation scheme is robust, exclusive, transparent, and provides clear benefits;

- Regulatory reform and policy integration within government to support the sustainable industry sector. Policy support and integration from local, state and federal authorities is necessary for the growth of the sustainable industry sector and the development of KISA to boost innovation. The sector, while creating employment in local areas, also contributes to broader societal goals through producing environmental goods and services and reducing environmental impacts. Supporting this sector therefore achieves multiple policy goals for environment and employment. A policy reform agenda could move forward on several fronts within local and regional decision making bodies. Key areas of action include:

  • Building KISA into regional environment and sustainability strategies;
  • Integration of economic development, employment and sustainability strategies;
  • Updating State of the Environment reporting to include sustainable business and innovation performance;
  • Identify resources for sustainable business networks, open days, accreditation schemes, and business incubators;
  • Develop and reform the innovation agenda to ensure SMEs are getting appropriate support and assistance with KISA to compete in the knowledge economy;
  • Support community demand for resource and energy efficiency and explore links to schemes such as emissions trading, subsidies and research grants.

CONCLUSION

The results from the case studies demonstrate the potential social and economic benefits of developing sustainable business activities. While limited to two Australian regions, green innovation is emerging as a field of competitive advantage through increasing resource efficiency, reducing waste, opening new markets and boosting knowledge capacity and 'know-how' through communities and regions.

KISA and the natural advantage can play a significant role in progressing regional development. Knowledge activities provide the foundation for business development, environmental education, and regional innovation that is linked to environmental improvement. The natural advantage should not operate in isolation – the approach emphasised here is an integrating strategy that can link economic and environmental planning that for many years has progressed in separate silos. The case studies demonstrate the benefits to planning regional innovation and economic strategies in line with sustainability principles and the effort now should be to replicate, grow and monitor these strategies across different economic and geographical contexts.

This chapter aims to advance the practice of green networks and highlight that KISA can be at the heart of regional development and change for sustainability. It anticipates that this message will increasingly resonate with policy makers, business leaders and the community but to do so, requires significant preparation and resources. The message however is clear – the old environment versus development debate is redundant.

NOTES

1. Scottish Association for Marine Science: tavis.potts@sams.ac.uk
2. http://www.mcsl.org.au/rein-meeting-080910.html

REFERENCES

Allen, M., Frame, D., Frieller, K., Hare, W., Huntingford, C., Jones, C., Knutti, R., Lowe, J., Meinshausen, M., Meinshausen, N. and Raper, S. (2009), 'The Exit Strategy', *Nature*, **3**, May, pp. 56–8.

Arimura, T.H., Burtraw, D., Krupnick, A. and Palmer, K. (2007), *US Climate Policy Developments. Resources for the Future Discussion Paper.* 07–45. Washington D.C. p. 39, Available from: http://www.rff.org/documents/ RFF-DP-07-45.pdf.

Armstrong, D. and Stratford, E. (2004), 'Partnerships for Local Sustainability and Local Governance', *Local Environment*, **9**, pp. 541–61.

Bellamy, J., Meppem, T., Goddard, R. and Dawson, S. (2003), 'The Changing Face of Regional Governance for Economic Development: Implications for Local Government', *Sustaining Regions*, **2** (3), pp. 7–17.

Benn, S. and Dunphy, D. (2006), 'Can Democracy Handle Corporate Sustainability? Constructing a Path Forward', *Innovation: Management, Policy and Practice*, **6** (2), pp. 141–55.

Berger, G. (2004), 'Reflections on Governance: Power Relations and Policy Making in Regional Sustainable Development', *Planning Theory and Practice,* 5(3), pp. 219–34.

BMCC (Blue Mountains City Council) (2002a), *Towards a More Sustainable Future: Working in the Blue Mountains. Paper No. 14e.* Katoomba, Australia. Available from: http://www.sustainablebluemountains.net.au/our-city-vision/city-vision-publications/.

BMCC (2002b), *Blue Mountains City Council. Blue Mountains Our Future. Where are We Now? Issues and Trends for the Blue Mountains. Background Paper 6.* Katoomba, NSW, Available from: http://www.sustainablebluemountains.net.au/our-city-vision/city-vision-publications/.

Brand, E. and de Bruijin, T. (1999), 'Shared Responsibility at the Regional Level: the Building of Sustainable Industrial Estates', *European Environment*, **9**, pp. 221–31.

Brunckhorst, D.J. (2002), 'Institutions to Sustain Ecological and Social Systems', *Ecological Management and Restoration*, **3** (2), pp. 108–16.

Burstrom, F. and Korhonen, J. (2001), 'Municipalities and Industrial Ecology: Reconsidering Municipal Environmental Management', *Sustainable Development*, **9**, pp. 36–46.

Central Coast Research Foundation, (2007), *The Central Coast at a Glance.* Available from: http://www.hvrf.com.au/pages/design/links/uploaded/CCAAG_07.pdf.

Commonwealth of Australia. (2008), *The Garnaut Climate Change Review. Commonwealth of Australia*, Available from: http://www.garnautreview.org.au/2008-review.html (Accessed April 2011).

Feichtinger, J. and Pregernig, M. (2005), 'Imagined Citizens and Participation: Local Agenda 21 in Two Communities in Sweden and Austria, *Local Environment*, **10** (3), pp. 229–43.

Frame, B. and Taylor, R. (2005), 'Partnerships for Sustainability', *Local Environment*, **10** (3), pp. 275–99.

Gibbs, D. (2000), 'Ecological Modernisation, Regional Economic Development, and Regional Development Agencies', *Geoforum*, **31**, pp. 9–19.

Gibson, K. and Cameron J. (2001), 'Transforming Communities: Towards a Research Agenda', *Urban Policy and Research*, **19** (1), pp. 7–24.

Glass, S. (2002), 'Sustainability and Local Government', *Local Environment,* **7** (1), pp. 97–102.

Hatfield-Dodds, S., Turner, G., Schandl, H. and Doss. T. (2008), *Growing the Green Collar Economy: Skills and Labour Challenges in Reducing our Greenhouse Emissions and National Environmental Footprint. A Report to the Dusseldorp Skills Forum,* Canberra: CSIRO Sustainable Ecosystems.

Hargraves, K. and Smith, M.A. (2005), *The Natural Advantage of Nations: Business Opportunities, Innovation and Governance in the 21st Century,* London: Earthscan.

Janicke, M. (2008), 'Ecological Modernisation: New Perspectives', *Journal of Cleaner Production,* **16**, pp. 557–65.

Koschatzky, K and Kroll, H. (2007), 'Which side of the coin? The regional governance of Science and Innovation', *Regional Studies,* **41** (8), pp. 1115–27.

Krehbiel, T., Gorman, R., Homer Erekson, O., Loucks, O. and Johnson, P. (1999), 'Advancing Ecology and Economics Through a Business–Science Synthesis', *Ecological Economics,* **28** (2), pp. 183–96

Loza, J. (2004), 'Business–Community Partnerships: The Case for Community Organisation Capacity Building', *Journal of Business Ethics,* **53**, pp. 297–311.

Martinez-Fernandez, M.C. and Potts, T. (2008), 'Innovation at the Edges of the Metropolis: An Analysis of Innovation Drivers in Sydney's Peripheral Suburbs', *Housing Policy Debate,* **19** (3), pp. 553–72.

Mahler, D., Barker, J., Belsand, L. and Schulz, O. (2009), *'Green Winners': The Performance of Sustainably Focused Companies During the Credit Crisis.* A.T. Kearney Inc. Available from: http://atkearney.com/shared_res/pdf/Green_Winners.pdf.

OECD (Organisation for Economic Co-operation and Development) (2006), *Innovation and Knowledge Intensive Service Activities – Executive Summary,* OECD, Paris: 179pp. Available from: http://www.oecd.org/.

OECD (Organisation for Economic Co-operation and Development) (2008), *Environmental Innovation and Global Markets,* Working Party on Global and Structural Policies, OECD. ENV/EPOC/GSP(2007)2/FINAL, 22 Feb 2008. Paris: OECD.

Porter, M. (1990), *The Competitive Advantage of Nations,* New York: The Free Press.

Porter, M. and van der Lindem, C. (1995), 'Green and Competitive, Ending the Stalemate', *Harvard Business Review,* **September–October**, pp. 121–34.

Potts, T., Merson, J. and Katchka, M. (2007), 'Multi-stakeholder Partnerships for Sustainability'. In: Nelson, A. (ed.) *Steering Sustainability: Policy,*

Practice, & Performance in an Urbanising World. London: Ashgate Publishing.

Potts, T. (2010), 'The Natural Advantage of Regions: Linking Sustainability, Innovation, and Regional Development in Australia', *Journal of Cleaner Production*, **18** (8), pp. 713–25.

Robins, N., Clover, R. and Singh, C. (2009), *A Climate for Recovery. The Colour of Stimulus Goes Green*, HSBC Global Research, Available from: http://www.research.hsbc.com.

Shaw, S. and Kidd, S. (2001), 'Sustainable Development and Environmental Partnership at the Regional Scale: The Case of Sustainability North West', *European Environment*, **11**, pp.112–23.

Smith, G. and Scott, J. (2006), *Government and Sustainability in Australia: Living Cities, An Urban Myth?* Dural, Australia: Rosenburg Publishing.

Tukker, A., Emmert, S., Charter, M., Vezzoli, C., Sto, E., Andersen, A.A., Geerken, T., Tischner, U. and Lahlou, S. (2008), 'Fostering Change to Sustainable Consumption and Production: An Evidence Based View', *Journal of Cleaner Production*, **16** (11), pp. 1218–25.

Vigoda, E. (2002), 'From Responsiveness to Collaboration: Governance Citizens, and the Next Generation of Public Administration', *Public Administration Review*, **62** (5), pp. 527–40.

10 Venture Capitalists as Knowledge Intensive Service Activity Providers

Samantha Sharpe[1]

This chapter investigates the role of venture capitalists as knowledge intensive service activities (KISA) providers. Venture capital (VC) funds invest in high growth potential, and usually high technology firms, that would otherwise lack financial resources for their firm development. In addition to the provision of capital, venture capital funds also provide their portfolio firms with non-financial inputs, in the form of strategic advice and monitoring, introductions to customers and suppliers and assistance with recruitment of management team. These non-financial inputs are rarely analysed and evaluated of their own accord, VC funds are evaluated in terms of financial performance alone. However the increasing involvement of the public sector in directly investing public money into early stage VC funds has provided an impetus for these non-financial inputs to be evaluated more fully. Public sector investors are interested in other returns from early stage VC activity in addition to financial returns, for example the commercialisation of technology and encouraging high technology entrepreneurship. The KISA framework is used as a potential mechanism for assessing these non-financial inputs.

INTRODUCTION

The aim of this chapter is to investigate the role of venture capital funds as knowledge intensive service activity (KISA) providers. Venture capital is a form of private equity investment and a specialised part of the financial services industry. VC is defined as independently managed, dedicated pools of capital that focus on equity or equity linked investments in privately held, high growth companies (Lerner, 2009).

VC is credited with a catalytic role in innovation because VC activities finance new technology-based firms (NTBFs) who are actively translating research and development (R&D) activities into commercial outcomes

(Christofidis and Debande, 2001). NTBFs and are defined as firms '...where its products and processes are the commercial result of investment in the research and development of new scientific and technology applications' (Haywood, 2008:3). The importance of new firm creation is well noted in the literature (Acs and Audretsch, 1990) but NTBFs play a further role in creating wealth by their ability to create new markets and industries (Sainsbury, 2007).

The relationship between a VC fund and their portfolio firms is usually addressed in terms of a financial relationship. The VC fund provides capital investment to the firm in return for a share of ownership (equity). The VC fund then works with the portfolio firm, providing strategic as well as financial support to the firm, to develop the business to such an extent that the VC fund can make a profitable exit from their investment, usually through a trade sale.

The VC fund therefore provides portfolio firms with both financial capital and non-capital inputs. This type of relationship has been ongoing since the beginning of the venture capital industry. The non-financial components of VC investments have been widely acknowledged as a crucial part of the success of firms who receive this kind of investment. Indeed this support was seen as the unique contribution of VC activity, even from the first VC firm set up in the wake of the Second World War in the US.[2]

These non-financial inputs are not standardised across portfolio firms, support naturally needs to be tailored to suit individual firm requirements and the timetable of firm development. Portfolio firms also have differing views on the VC funds provision of these activities, and the success, relevance and usefulness of the provision of such knowledge intensive services to the development of their NTBFs.

The difficulty in analysing these non-financial inputs is two-fold. Firstly, as noted, these activities are non-standardised knowledge inputs and are individually tailored and exchanged with individual firms. There is some generality in the strategic knowledge that is provided and exchanged with portfolio firms, and also in the way in which this strategic advice is applied (that is portfolio firms are new technology based firms, and face similar challenges with proof of concept, market and organisational development) but the individual context of each portfolio firm heavily shapes the way in which this knowledge is used. Secondly, VC funds and portfolio firms differ in their interpretation of the value of these activities to portfolio firm development. They differ both as separate groups, but also within their group, individual VC fund managers have different ideas about what non-financial inputs is part of the VC portfolio firm relationship, and individual firms depending on their particular experience of these non-financial inputs have differing views on their value to the development of their business.

The focus of much of the literature examining venture capital activity is concerned with how VC funds select their investments and less concerned with analysing the non-financial aspects of VC fund contributions to portfolio firms over the term of their investment. This is despite the fact that these non-financial inputs are as critical to portfolio firms as the financial capital inputs; and arguably as critical an activity for VC fund managers as selecting investments.

These non-financial inputs align with the definition of KISA, and categorising non-financial inputs into the KISA framework provides a mechanism to analyse in a systematic way the non-financial contributions that VCs make to their portfolio firms. The KISA framework provides the ability to analyse types of knowledge intensive activities, but also the location of these activities. VCs sit in a unique position in relation to their portfolio firms, in having access to both internal and external sources of KISA that their portfolio firms use. Through this unique position further investigation of the boundaries of KISA and how external knowledge is translated into the internal setting within the portfolio firm and vice versa can be achieved. This chapter looks at the use of KISA in a different way than has been previously discussed. Instead of using KISA as a measurement methodology for innovation, using it as an assessment technique for aspects of firm development, specifically to assess the intangible contributions of venture capitalists. This chapter examines whether the knowledge intensive service activity framework can provide a mechanism through which to investigate these non-financial inputs.

One reason why VC monitoring activities have not received the analysis that they deserve is because of the mythology surrounding VC and 'blockbuster' NTBFs that developed in size and revenue quickly and then achieved enormously successful Initial Public Offerings (IPOs), exemplified in the 'tech boom' of the late 1990s. This mythology is also reinforced by the need for secrecy and protection of commercial-in-confidence information that NTBFs possess.

This mythology is countered by the actual experience of portfolio firms. Most VC investments will fail or significantly underperform. The VC portfolio model dictates that the majority of profits created by and for the funds come from a small number (2–3 per fund) of investments.

In recent years a need for an understanding of how this process of firm development works has emerged from increased public investment in the early stage venture capital environment. Public policy has always played a role in the development of VC industry. During the 1980s and 1990s the emphasis of public support was on encouraging investors into venture capital, through tax breaks and concessions to investors; and providing incentives to NTBFs such as R&D tax credits. Public policy has also played a major role in creating new pools of capital through regulations relating to employee funded pensions, and then regulations and guidelines which have allowed these pools of capital to be invested in venture capital funds.

However in the past ten to fifteen years public policy has switched from the direct provision of capital support to NTBFs to public sector investment in private sector managed funds (Lerner, 2002; Leleux and Surlemont; 2003; Da Rin, et al, 2006; Jaaskelainen et al, 2007). These funds are variously known as government-backed funds or hybrid funds and involve public sector agencies investing capital as limited partners (in addition to other private sector investors) into privately administered venture funds.

The reasons for this increasing prevalence of public sector money in early stage venture capital are three-fold:

1. To support technological development;
2. To support high growth potential firms;
3. Respond to market failure of private funds to provide early stage investment (due to the changing structure of the equity environment (more money, more institutional investors and professionalised participants), but also the poor returns of early stage VC compared to other stages.

These three reasons do not necessarily produce mutually beneficial results for VC funds or for the portfolio firms. It is clear that government activity in the early stage VC environment is seeking outcomes beyond the financial returns that the privately managed VC funds may or may not deliver.[3]

If governments are investing significantly in early stage VC activity and if they are seeking beyond financial returns (such as maturing technology, stimulating entrepreneurship, providing start-up experience to management teams, and regional development) understanding how this process happens becomes critical to evaluating the effectiveness of this policy position. An analysis framework for characterising and assessing the non-financial inputs that VCs make to portfolio firms is an important part of this overall evaluation. This is because one of the things distinguishing early stage VC investing from other forms of new business finance (such as bank loans (putting aside the difficulties firms face in accessing debt finance) and other government spending on new technology development (that is grants) is the provision of this highly specialised strategic and commercial business advice that is provided to portfolio firms, in addition to capital.

This chapter sets out to use the KISA framework to evaluate these non-financial inputs by VCs to their portfolio firms. The rest of the chapter proceeds as follows. First, an overview of venture capital activity with a specific focus on early stage VC activity in the UK is presented. The three case study portfolio firms that make up the empirical component of the chapter are presented next. All the three firms are UK based firms, hence the focus on a UK context. The case study analysis enables the KISA framework to be trialled in characterising the non-financial inputs that are provided by VCs to be assessed. For comparative purposes, all of the portfolio firms are investments of the same VC fund manager. The purpose of this chapter is to trial the KISA framework, and while some conclusions of this analysis are presented at the conclusion of the chapter, a broader sample of firms and funds would need to be analysed before these conclusions could be considered more than tentative.

OUTLINE OF VENTURE CAPITAL ACTIVITIES[4]

Venture capital is an important source of funding for a small number of firms. European Union figures note that VC finance is used by only 2 per cent of the Small and Medium Enterprise SME firm population (ECB, 2010). In the UK, successive surveys of SME firms in the period from 1991–2004, Cosh and Hughes (2007) established that approximately four per cent of small and medium enterprises (SMEs) sought external equity financing. However, the firms that did rely on equity finance considered it as an important source of finance; this was particularly true for micro firms[5] where the importance of equity finance increased in the survey period. The firms that need to access VC investment are typically rich in intangible assets such as technology and specialist knowledge but lack the sort of assets that help them to access other forms of external finance, such as debt finance.

The analysis of venture capital in the literature proceeds from two directions – venture capital as a financial asset class; and venture capital as a means of supporting NTBFs who in turn act as vehicles for the commercialisation of innovative activity. The link between new business formation and economic development is well established (Hughes and Story, 1994; Denis, 2004). Small and new firms are recognised as important drivers of innovations (Acs and Audretsch, 1990) and employment (Lerner, 1994). The creation of new and high technology firms plays a further role. These firms are associated with higher levels of innovative activity, radical innovation, and higher usages of research and development. They form the core of the knowledge-based economy and the products and services that emanate from these firms create the markets and industries of the future (Sainsbury, 2007). VC is linked to debates on economic development at the national, international and regional level. The linkage of VC activity and maturation of technology and economic development is long held and is increasingly given as the reason for public policy activity in supporting and encouraging the supply of venture capital.

Figure 10.1 shows the amount of US$ currently invested in venture capital in 26 OECD (Organisation for Economic Co-operation and Development) member countries. The United States accounts for 49 per cent of total venture capital investments in 2008 in OECD countries. The United Kingdom was the only other country with a share that exceeded 10 per cent of the OECD total (OECD, 2009).

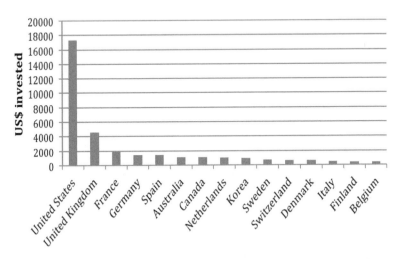

Source: OECD, 2009

Figure 10.1 Venture capital investment (US$ millions) in 2008 for top 15 OECD member countries

Figure 10.2 shows the increasing levels of venture capital activity across Europe as a percentage of gross domestic product (GDP) in the past three decades. The VC industry in Europe really only emerged in the late 1980s however by 1989, VC industries were in existence in most European countries but particularly in the UK, France, Belgium and the Netherlands. The industry increased throughout the 1990s and 2000s. Specific areas of policy intervention are behind the increases in VC activity in Belgium, Sweden and the Netherlands in the 1990s and Denmark and Finland in 2000 (Maula et al, 2007).

VC has both a supply and demand cycle (Christofidis and Debande, 2001). The supply side is concerned with the raising of funds and the process of making and exiting from investments. The demand cycle comes from high technology firms who are seeking equity investment to support the successive stages of development of their firms. The supply side of venture capital activities are guided by the venture capital cycle (Gompers and Lerner, 2004). The venture capital cycle has five phases – fundraising, screening, negotiating, monitoring and exiting. Each of these phases is briefly discussed in further detail.

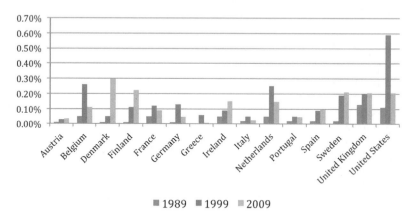

■ 1989 ■ 1999 ■ 2009

Source: Christofidis and Debante, 2001; OECD, 2009

Figure 10.2 Venture capital investment as a percentage of GDP 1989–2009

The Supply Side of VC Activity – The Venture Capital Cycle

Fundraising

This phase of activity is concerned with the processes of raising funds. Activities include deciding on management fees and negotiation of contracts between investors and the fund managers, concerning the timings of investment disbursements and distribution of profits over the course of the fund management period (Gompers and Lerner, 2004). The increasing level of support and sponsorship by government of venture capital funds (otherwise known as hybrid funds) highlights differences that exist in fundraising according to fund type. Government sponsorship usually entails various conditions designed to meet policy objectives and to encourage private investors (although both of these conditions may be mutually exclusive). Conditions can include government investors subordinating their investment position despite the fact that they may be lead investor in the fund, and also agreeing to 'first loss' status (having any fund losses taken from their investment first). Government sponsored funds can also negotiate a longer time period for the operation of the fund, so fund managers have a longer time period to realise their investments.

Public funding into both publicly and privately managed funds targeting the early stage has increased in the past decade and considerably in the aftermath of the financial crisis in 2008. This policy activity is in response to two supply issues; lack of early stage VC for NTBFs due to what is variously described as the 'equity gap' and a focus on increasing the supply of NTBFs to stimulate economic development. Public funding can significantly change the dynamics of investor behaviour because the risk-return trade-off is changed. This changes the behaviour of fund managers in how they deal with government agencies as limited partners, but also how they screen and select portfolio firms.

Screening

The second part of the venture capital cycle is generating and assessing investment opportunities. Screening activities need to highlight good investment opportunities that have the potential for excellent returns within the lifespan of the fund and to meet any other conditions where public funding is involved. Cultivating good deal flow is an essential activity for the venture capital firm, but is largely completed through informal channels and principally through referral (Langeland, 2007). There is an extensive literature assessing screening and selection techniques of venture capital fund managers (Macmillan et al, 1987; Hisrich and Jankowicz, 1990, Diaz de Leon and Guild, 2003; Lange et al, 2007). The literature emphasises the importance of three groups of information. Firstly information from intermediaries, such as bankers, accountants and lawyers, other venture capital funds, investors and university contacts are all relied upon for providing investment opportunities (Shane and Cable, 2002). Secondly, VC fund managers consider the network status and position of the potential portfolio firms within a wider community of firms, and the entrepreneur and/or management team's position within an entrepreneurial community. Thirdly fund managers coɪsider the past experience of the entrepreneur and/or entrepreneurial team. From these sources of information fund managers develop 'rules of thumb' that shape their assessment behaviour (Hisrich and Jankowicz, 1990).

Deal flow and screening activities are also influenced by the investment objectives of the fund. Traditional mainstream venture capital typically makes the majority of profits from a few highly successful investments. Screening is therefore focused on identifying investment opportunities that have a very high growth potential, but also the ability for this potential to be realised within the lifespan of the five to seven years fund life. Hybrid funds on the other hand may have less capital at their disposal, but may have longer time periods over which to realise their investments. Screening would be more focused on identifying a balanced portfolio, shifting the risk of identifying very high growth firms, to ones in which they can invest and monitor over a longer time period, compared with mainstream VC.[6]

Negotiating investments

This stage of the VC cycle involves the venture capital manager valuing the firm. This is done with regard to market conditions and future prospects. The fund manager will also complete a number of background checks on the entrepreneur and management and analyse the firm's proposition and technology base. This is referred to as the due diligence period (De Clercq, et al, 2006).

The negotiation process is reliant on information gathered through personal and professional networks of the fund manager. Aspects of the literature point to similar uses of informal and intangible methods of firm evaluation that were used in screening investments (Macmillan et al, 1987; Hisrich and Jankowicz, 1990). Similar comments can be made on the 'rules of thumb' methods used by venture capitalists to make firm valuations.

The due diligence process is time-consuming and costly. Due diligence costs are also relatively fixed and not related to the size of the investment in the firm, therefore larger investments in portfolio companies are more cost effective in relation to their due diligence costs. When negotiations are complete, a written document, a 'term sheet' is produced, it summarises the main terms and conditions and, if the due diligence checks turn out positive, then the 'term sheet' will provide the basis for contracts to be drafted.

Monitoring

Once an investment is made then the monitoring phase begins. This is the stage at which non-capital value is added to the portfolio firms through the monitoring, advice and guidance of the fund managers. In the classic VC model, strategic business support was part of the package. VC investment was considered 'more than money' (Bygrave and Timmons, 1992; Lange et al, 2007). Support extended to portfolio firms includes fund managers occupying board positions within new firms, providing advice on strategic direction, assisting in recruiting management executives and providing introduction to customers and other key contacts. Research has also shown that venture capitalists play a role in highlighting unconscious and ill-considered decision making behaviour in their portfolio firms by questioning assumptions that the firm may make (Berglund et al, 2007). Some commentators claim that this provision of non-capital value is overstated. Fund managers will still take positions on the boards of these companies but, as research from Norway (Berg-Utby et al, 2007) suggests, many portfolio firms' expectations about even modest levels of involvement of the VC fund managers in the business are unmet.

Exit

Exit is the final stage of the VC cycle and is an obligation taken on when the limited partnership was formed, but may not always be taken at a time that is in the best interests of the firm, the economy, or even the investors. There are five different types of exit: exiting through an IPO, trade sale, secondary sale to another financial institution or fund, buy back by the entrepreneur or write off. The first of these exits methods, the IPO is perhaps the most celebrated and prominent in the literature, yet the second method, the trade sale is the most common successful exit method for VC funds (Soderblom, 2006).

The entire length of the investment process for early stage ventures is estimated to be on average about six to seven years, from the first capital investment to the final exit (Manigart et al, 2002), although this can vary significantly by industry. Research also shows that early stage specialist funds generate lower rates of return (Gottschlag et al, 2004). This demonstrates the inability of early stage funds to realise successfully their investments over a six to seven year period.

The Demand Side of VC Activity – New Technology-based Firms

Venture capital firms invest in new (usually technology based) firms that exhibit high growth business potential than can be developed and exploited within the medium term (five to eight years). They take equity holdings in these companies in return for financial capital that they provide to the firm. Individuals and companies invest in venture capital funds in order to capitalise on the extraordinary returns that a small number of these firms make.

The number of firms demanding equity finance is a relatively small percentage of the total firm population. These firms are particularly rich in intangible assets, usually of a technological and knowledge intensive nature, but few tangible assets. The long periods of R&D these firms need to complete also means that significant periods of negative cash flow are anticipated. These characteristics make securing more traditional means of finance for their business, such as debt finance, unlikely.

There are a number of well known characteristics of firms that seek venture capital, and firms that venture capital funds prefer to invest in. Between these two spheres of activity we have areas of cross over, but also gaps. These gaps have variously been described as equity gaps[7] (early stage and expansion equity gaps).

Not everyone accepts that there is an equity gap (Library House, 2006). Dissenters point out that the supply of equity capital is less the issue than the limited number of viable propositions, the so called 'investment readiness gap'. However, a recent OECD report on SME financing (OECD, 2006:10) concluded that 'most OECD countries perceive that a lack of appropriate financing has been a hindrance to the expansion of innovative SMEs (that is firms, often in technology sectors, with new business models and high growth prospects)'. It is for this reason that these gaps in activity have been a catalyst for the increasing role being played by government in the supply of venture capital funding.

Public Policy and VC Activity

Public policy activity in the venture capital industry is stimulated by the link between NTBFs and their demand for equity based financing to support technology and firm development, and the link between NTBFs and economic development (nationally, internationally and regionally) through the translation of R&D into technology and the maturation of technology into new products, processes and businesses which in turn create profits and employment. The link between NTBFs and increased economic activity is well established. The link between venture capital and NTBFs is more complex – more venture capital does not necessarily mean more NTBFs, as the maturation of technology requires many other factors to be in place in addition to finance.

VC, particularly capital focused on early stage portfolio firms (early stage VC) has declined sharply in the UK in the last decade. This decline in activity is in response to poor European early stage VC performance and the 'two tyrannies' of early stage VC (Murray and Marriott, 1998); project risk and scale related costs. Project risk concerns adverse selection problem in assessing 'a technology that is unproven, incorporated into products not yet demonstrated, for markets not yet developed' (Murray and Marriott, 1998:954). The scale related costs are the fact that successful fund managers are able to raise progressively larger funds from investors. The relatively fixed costs associated with due diligence and deal negotiation and the relatively modest capital demands at the early stage compared with later stages, inevitably lead to a concentration on larger and later stage deals.

The performance issues are arguably the most critical for private sector investors involved in early stage VC. Poor investment returns of early stage investments in the UK and Europe more broadly over the past twenty years, relative to risk, have significantly reduced the appetite for early stage venture capital investing.

These three factors: performance, project risk and scale related costs, have led to a situation of perceived market failure. The term 'perceived' is used because there is no consensus on the motivations for public policy activity; there are arguments supporting market failure in the provision of a public good (the development of NTBFs, creation of entrepreneurs, new knowledge based employment and so on). There are also arguments supporting public policy interventions to provide a 'demonstration effect'; early stage VC can be profitable for private sector investors if different models are used. Public subsidies are therefore used to demonstrate these models.

VENTURE CAPITAL ACTIVITY IN THE UK

The UK private equity market has been overwhelmingly driven by equity investment in large scale management buy-out and buy-ins and not early stage investments. Management buy-outs and buy-in MBO/MBI investments accounted for 58 per cent of the more than £8.5 billion in equity investment in the UK in 2008, whereas expansion and early stage capital accounted for 24 per cent and 4.1 per cent respectively.[8] The VC market refers to the expansion and early stage categories. The early stage category of the venture capital market has a number of aspects to its activity.[9] The common call is that early stage VC activity has decreased in the past decade – this is not the case, but the role of early stage investing in the UK VC market has changed significantly.

As shown in Figure 10.3, early stage investment accounted for 18 per cent of £ amount of VC investments in 2002, but only 14.8 per cent in 2008. If we take a longer view, looking at activity over the past decade, the decline is more marked, in 1997 the early stage made up 85 per cent of the VC market. In the post-tech bubble period (2001 onwards) the early stage has not recovered its role in the UK VC market.

There has also been a significant increase in the reliance on the UK public sector as a provider of early stage funds in terms of both stand alone investments and combined public/private co-investments. In a sample of early stage deals from Library House, public and public private co-investment deals accounted for 57 per cent of early stage deals and 46 per cent of early stage investment in 2007. This is compared with 2002 when they accounted for 30 per cent of deals and 14 per cent of amount invested in early stage firms. Stand alone early stage private sector venture capital declined significantly between 2002 and 2007 from 86 per cent of £ amount invested to 54 per cent respectively.

This is a trend that looks likely to continue. The BVCA in its report on Investment activity in 2008 (BVCA, 2009) reported on funds raised by source. The funds raised by UK government sources over the past three years are shown in the second column of the below table (Table 10.1). The figures are prone to annual fluctuations, but in 2006 Government sources accounted for 4.8 per cent of all UK funds raised, growing to 5.9 per cent in 2008.

These may seem small percentages, but when they are compared with the figures for funds raised by expected stage of investment, the importance of government activities in the early stage equity environment becomes apparent. Government funds because of their mandate and small (relative) size are limited to investing in the early stage. Putting these two facts together we can see that government funds in 2006 accounted for 38 per cent of the total raised to be invested in early stage and in 2008 accounted for all of the funds raised for the early stage.

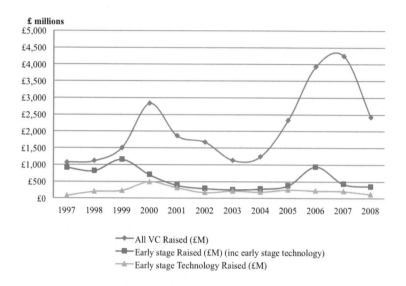

Source: BVCA, 2009, Pierrakis and Mason, 2008

Figure 10.3 Venture capital activity in the UK 1997—2008

Table 10.1 Sources of early stage venture capital investment 2006—2008

	Funds raised by UK Government sources (£M)	Funds raised by expected stage of investment	
		Early stage	Technology (subset of early stage)
2008	£334[10]	£243	£109
2007	£59	£830	£658
2006	£470	£1,235	£549

Source: BVCA, 2009

KNOWLEDGE INTENSIVE SERVICE ACTIVITIES IN THE VC CONTEXT

As noted as the beginning of this chapter, the aim is to use the KISA framework as a mechanism to analyse non-financial inputs that VC funds make into their portfolio firms and to assess how and in what way VC fund managers are KISA providers. This chapter applies KISA in a different way than has been so far presented in this book. KISA traces its evolution from sectoral studies of innovation. Despite this difference, the approach is still complementary and the link between this and other KISA studies is provided by the NTBFs.

New technology-based firms, by definition, display numerous constantly evolving innovation processes. Technological innovation is at the forefront, as these firms are attempting to commercialise new technology into new products and services. Process innovation is an essential part of technological innovation, as part of commercialising new technology is developing the ability to produce, in volume, quality and for a viable price the new product or service. This means productions and supply systems need to be developed and implemented. Organisational innovation is also a prominent activity of new firms as organisational structure are designed and implemented and business and revenue models are developed and tested.

In other studies of KISA in the innovation process there are slight variations in the categorisations; this is to allow for further differentiation of types of activities within a sector. Table 10.2 gives the categorisations used in this study, with a short description of the knowledge intensive service activities involved.

Case Study Analysis of Three VC/Portfolio Firm Relationships[11]

Case study firm 1

Firm 1 is a communications software company, founded in 2005 by three technology professionals. The three founders previously worked together for the same technology manufacturing firm when they were made redundant when their employer closed their UK operations.

The three founders decided to create a company using their combined financial reserves (from redundancy payments) and technical experience in high volume hardware development. The product offering was a software/hardware packaging of integrated telephony functions with customer relationship management (CRM) software.

The resources of the firm in the first few years of operation were primarily technical. The firms secured initial external financing from a prominent business angel. This provided commercial and entrepreneurial experience to the firm, as well as providing access to the network and reputation benefits of the prominent business angel.[12] Therefore with the addition of a first round of external finance from the business angel, KISA in the form of strategic development services and business planning services.

Table 10.2 NTBF KISA

KISA	Internal
Strategic development services	Activities associated with the strategic direction of the firm including business and revenue models and product offerings.
Business planning advice	Activities that are mapped out to achieve the strategic direction of the firm, including sales channels, unique product offering, and conduct and organisation of the firm.
Marketing and promotion	Activities concerned with developing paths to market for product offering. Market development and identifying customers (especially early adopters) and partners (for complementary activities that is content provision) are critical activities.
Research and development	Research activities are essential for NTBFs, but the development side of R&D is just as critical. Activities include developing a technology into a commercially viable product, that is product prototyping and testing.
Accounting and Financial services	Finance, particularly external finance is critical for NTBFs because they can lack internal financial resources for long periods of time. Identifying, pitching and negotiating external finance is a time consuming but critical activity for NTBFs.
HR/Recruitment services	The primary activity of HR/Recruitment services is the recruitment of new staff. NTBFs can grow quickly and at unstable rates, correct HR decisions can have an enormous impact on the success of the firm. Recruitment services will also be needed at the senior management and board level as the firm progresses.
Legal/IP services	These services relate to the protection of intellectual property and the strategy regarding whether the patent, what to patent and what intellectual property to share in collaborative research arrangements.

VC funding followed soon after, but the earlier lack of market focus at the early stages was not so easily overcome. The firm's first group of products was not well received into the market, not due to technical deficiencies but poor analysis of customer demand. A new managing director was appointed, with the three founders remaining in technical and sales related roles. The company's product offering was refocused in line with market demand and expectations, and became a software service product offering rather than a software/hardware offering. This in turn resulted in major changes to the business and revenue models, software services cost less to produce than a physically manufactured product but also had to be priced accordingly.

Without a physical product for customers to purchase, the firm had to integrate the software service with other product offerings to encourage take up. This was done through a process of strategic relationships with distributors and critically a partnership with a downstream hardware manufacturer. This relationship developed into a partnership manufacturing and distribution agreement, in that the hardware firm sold product including the firm's software. The agreement opened up a number of distribution channels through which future sales opportunities could be generated. It gave the firm a physical product to point to in sales conversations plus also gaining user feedback and sales data from their partners.

When the role of VC fund managers in the development of the firm is analysed, they are associated with all of the activities of the firm, as a representative of the fund was a member of the board. However when VC activities are analysed in terms of the previously outlined KISA categories, the primary areas of valuable input, in this case by the VC fund to the portfolio firm, are captured primarily within three categories:

- Strategic development services – with the realignment of the firm from a hardware/software firm to a software service firm and the associated changes to the business and revenue models;
- Business planning advice – with the development of sales channels for the new product offering and the development of the strategic partnership with a downstream hardware manufacturer;
- HR/Recruitment services – with the selection and appointment of a new Managing Director at a critical time in the firm's evolution, who had the skills and experience (start-up and major contract negotiation experience) needed by the firm at that point in time.

Table 10.3 summarises all of the KISA activities mentioned in the earlier section and which group of people primarily provided the KISA in these areas.

Table 10.3 Case study firm 1 KISA

KISA	Internal	VC	Other external
Strategic development services	X	X	
Business planning advice	X	X	
Marketing and promotion	X		X
Research and development	X		
Accounting and Financial services	X		
HR/Recruitment services	X	X	
Legal/IP services	X		X

Case study firm 2

The second case study firm is a medical diagnostic device firm. The firm was founded in 2002 as a corporate spin-out. The firm acquired worldwide licences to develop a diagnostic device from original research completed in a hospital lab. As part of the spin-out both the managing director and technical director left the parent company to take up the same positions with the new spin-out firm. The spin-out was located on the same premises as the parent company.

Initial seed funding was accessed from the founders and business angels. Three further rounds of funding have been received in the following six years, including the involvement of further business angels, three VC funds and one corporate investor. The external financing arrangements needed to cover a more extended period of product development than was anticipated at the outset due to technical difficulties with the diagnostic product. Although the firm had acquired the technology under licence, the technology did not work in the same way as established in the patent. The scientists and engineers involved with the initial R&D did not become part of the new firm and therefore critical 'know-how' knowledge about how the diagnostic product operated was lost. As a result the diagnostic device took longer in development.

One member of the equity investment team and a member of the board provided extensive financial negotiation skills and experience in selecting, pitching to and gaining new financial backers that allowed the firm to overcome this long than expected period of technological development. As a result of this longer development time line and more external finance the business and revenue models changed.

Initially the business model for the firm was to develop a simple, relatively inexpensive manual diagnostic device for the healthcare market in the developing world. However due to the long development time further financing was needed. This created a dilemma for the firm, in order to be attractive to potential investors and on the advice of potential distributors (customers) the firm was advised to refocus on the US market. The US market was the largest single market, however entry into this market would require a fully automated product and Food and Drug Administration (FDA) approval. Both of these would require further product development, time and resources.

> ...In terms of getting additional finance after our seed finance we needed to have the pull of the US market...so we had one manual instrument that we had to put on the shelf and then we turned our attention to the additional things we needed to do to get into the US market...we still have not lost the vision of fully developing a system for the developing world, because the market for that instrument is at least as big as the US, but this (fully automated product) had to be our focus first (Firm interview).

At this time various new hires were made including a new Managing Director to drive the period up to and after FDA approval. FDA approval was achieved eighteen months later. The intention of the firm after FDA approval had been achieved was to license the product to medical device manufacturers but negotiations with the device manufacturers resulted in product that would not achieve the revenue projections expected. The firm therefore made the decision to set up a small manufacturing facility to produce the product and the associated consumable (test capsules) themselves, with the aim of initially selling in low volumes and attracting more favourable terms from licensing deals when manufacturers could see and touch the product and see sales figures.

The KISA provision by the VC fund managers to the portfolio firm in this case study was more extensive. Table 10.4 shows the areas where the VC fund provided major non-financial inputs into the firm. They included:

- Strategic development services – with the realignment of the product offering, target market and associated revenue model;
- Business planning advice – including the change of production and sale mechanisms from a licensing model to internal manufacturing model;
- Marketing and promotion – the change in production and sale mechanisms also affected the marketing and promotion strategies. New strategies had to be developed for a new set of customers (direct product purchasers rather than potential licensee manufacturers);
- Accounting and Financial services – through the identification and negotiation of external finance resources from both VCs and corporate sponsors for the long R&D programme;
- HR/Recruitment services – the selection and recruitment of a new MD (replacing the founding MD) in order to drive the US regulatory process of the product development.

Table 10.4 Case study firm 2 KISA

KISA	Internal	VC	Other external
Strategic development services	X	X	
Business planning advice	X	X	
Marketing and promotion	X	X	X
Research and development	X		
Accounting and Financial services		X	
HR/Recruitment services	X	X	
Legal/IP services	X		X

Case study firm 3

Case study firm three is a software company within the internet content market. The company was founded in 2003 with the two founders having already worked together in their own games consultancy firm. The idea behind the foundation of this new firm was to commercialise into a product a small program they had developed through their own consultancy. The product would be extended and offered for sale as a 'boxed' product available to purchase in retail outlets.

The early business strategy of the firm was to access a small amount of capital (£100,000) to produce an early stage product. Revenue from this product would then fund the development of further versions. This strategy was reinforced when the emerging market for user-generated internet content expanded rapidly in 2004–2005. Viral marketing and user referral have been prominent in online activity, but really came into their own in the late 1990s.

> ...The best way in which we can capture the enthusiasm of our early users is through internet community spaces, including web forums... (We) need to be able to create more effective and sticky community spaces on the web for our users...We would put extra effort into building the online community and forum space for our earliest users, as a catalyst for marketing, PR and product improvement (firm interview).

Reflecting on this comment –

> ...in software businesses today there is a minimum quality threshold – I ignored advice to get early revenues by putting out an early bit of product, you cannot cheat this business and you only get one chance (firm interview).

The internet content market significantly altered in the early 2000s as user generated content from websites such as YouTube and Facebook began generating huge interest. Innovation and product development in the internet content market became strongly influenced and directed by user activity. This movement in the industry was compound by increasing access to high speed broadband, which makes it possible to transfer large amounts of data online and diminished the marketability of physical computer products (namely game CDs) that were brought form retail outlets; games and other content could now be delivered online.

This industry shift meant that the initial business and revenue model of the case study firm (develop small product for immediate sale, then use revenue to fund later generation products) was no longer viable. Also competition in the industry meant that is was also not viable to offer a small, 'limited featured' product for sale, even if available online; it would simply not be competitive. The firm was in a situation that required a longer development time scale, more resources, and in an environment where physical product sales were being replaced by online ones (and at a lower sale price). One clear advantage that emerged from all this industrial evolution was that users could be part of the development process in a much more effective way, and that the firm could access market feedback before a product was finalised through beta testing and user forums.

External financial resources from VC funds had been brought into the firm early on. However, more so than in the other two case studies, the founders continued to play the leading role in establishing the strategic direction and business planning of the firm. A new Managing Director was appointed after two years, this allowed the founders to concentrate full time on the technological development of the product. The product that is currently in beta testing is a software-as-a-service (SAAS) online program with associated user forums and user developed content. The path to market is now more direct, without the need for a video games developer to produce and market the game. This meant that the firms marketing and promotions strategy also needed to change, and resources both internal and external in marketing and advertising needed to be developed to market the online product.

Table 10.5 outlines the KISA activities of the case study firm and the role internal, VC and external sources played in providing these services. As in the other two case studies, VC provides services in strategic development, business planning and HR/Recruitment activities. In this case the VC firm also provided study firm, marketing and promotion activities. Detailing each in term:

- Strategic development services – in the movement from a physical to an SAAS product;
- Business planning advice – through the development of direct user sales channels;
- Marketing and promotion – market development and creation of user groups and the use of networks to create 'buzz' about the product;
- HR/Recruitment – recruitment of MD to allow founders to concentrate on technical development.

Table 10.5 Case study firm 3 KISA

KISA	Internal	VC	Other external
Strategic development services	X	X	
Business planning advice	X	X	
Marketing and promotion	X	X	X
Research and development	X		
Accounting and Financial services	X		
HR/Recruitment services	X	X	
Legal/IP services	X		

SOME CONCLUSIONS ABOUT VENTURE CAPITALISTS AS KISA PROVIDERS

The aim of this chapter is to investigate the role of venture capital funds as knowledge intensive service providers. The VC–portfolio firm relationship is a unique one, because the VC is not an internal or external source of knowledge but rather a hybrid of the two. The VC has intimate knowledge of the internal workings of the portfolio firm and can use this knowledge to draw in external resources and knowledge that the portfolio firm needs. This knowledge exchange and matching process comes in addition to financial resources that the VC fund provides the firm, and they represent the non-financial inputs of VCs into their portfolio firms.

These non-financial inputs have always been part of the VC/portfolio firm relationship; however they have not been the subject of critical evaluation as to their type and value to the portfolio firm and its development. There is no doubt that they are valuable, but both VC funds and portfolio firms have acknowledged that the distribution of these non-financial inputs can be mixed and in some cases ineffective (Berg-Utby et al, 2007). The difficulty in analysing these non-financial inputs comes from the very specific and customised nature of the knowledge services that are exchanged between the VC and the portfolio firm.[13] This together, with the mysterious profile of VC fund activity that developed in the late 1990s, has made it very hard to talk with authority about these non-financial inputs.

The recent increase in government funding for early stage venture capital has created an incentive to understand the mechanics of the VC/portfolio firm relationship in more detail. Public policy activity in encouraging the supply of early stage VC activity has policy objectives (support technological development, encourage entrepreneurship, regional and national development) in addition to financial returns from their investments in funds. Therefore understanding VC non-financial inputs is important to evaluate the success of these policy interventions, in contrast to other policy options that could achieve the same objectives (that is R&D grant, subsidised loans, government loan guarantees and so on).

From the case studies we can conclude that the core areas of KISA provision by VCs to their portfolio firms are in strategic development services, business planning advice and HR/Recruitment. VCs also provide other specialised, customised knowledge intensive services in other areas – such as financial services and marketing and promotion, at specific times and in response to specific events in the firms' development. A next step in fully developing a KISA framework for VC non-financial inputs would be to see how these KISA provision categories change over the course of the portfolio firms' development, and how KISA provision varies between VC funds.[14]

NOTES

1. Research Fellow, Centre for Business Research, Judge Business School, Cambridge University, Trumpington Street, Cambridge CB 21AG UK, ss798@cam.ac.uk
2. The first VC firm, established in 1946 in the US, was American Research and Development (ARD). The founders were MIT President Karl Compton, Harvard Business School Professor Georges Doriot and other local business people keen to commercialise promising technology emerging from MIT (Gompers and Lerner, 2004). The ARD founders believed that investment

in new technology-based start-up ventures would make a good long term investment, and with the business management advice that ARD could offer the new firms along with capital infusions, these small firms should be able to develop into successful large firms, and this in turn would underpin sustained economic and employment development (Bygrave and Timmons, 1992). After a rocky start ARD proved to be a success. The majority of the return to the fund however resulted from one $70,000 investment in Digital Equipment Company (DEC) in 1957. Ultimately this investment grew in value to $355 (Gompers and Lerner, 2004).

3. To emphasise this point, most government investors subordinate their investment position, taking a 'first loss' status (any losses that the fund makes come out of the public investment first) and capping their returns from the funds (that is receiving as a return money invested, plus a certain percentage) to allow other private investors a larger share of the profits.

4. The equity environment is broadly segmented into three categories; start-up or early stage finance, expansion finance and buy-out finance. The early stage or start-up finance is equated with venture capital.

5. Micro firms were defined as firms with fewer than ten employees.

6. Although this can lead to what has been called a 'catch-22' (Dimov and Murray, 2008; Sharpe, et al, 2009), with successful portfolio firms exhausting investment resources of these small hybrid funds, but still requiring further follow-on financial resources to reach full potential. The catch-22 arises when early stage investors must dilute their equity investment by taking on later investors to provide the capital to allow the portfolio firm to develop.

7. The early stage equity gap is where firms seeking relatively small amounts of equity investment for start-up and early commercialisation and development cannot access equity funds because investors prefer larger and later stage deals. Nominally this equity gap exists for firms seeking funding in the range of £500,000 − £2million (Hurley, et al, 2005; Dimov and Murray, 2008). The expansion stage equity gap sees NTBFs facing difficulties in accessing funding up to £5 million.

8. All figures from BVCA (2009) Private Equity and Venture Capital Report on Investment Activity 2008, unless otherwise stated. Another category; secondary buy-outs and refinancing bank debt accounted for 13 per cent of PE industry.

9. A considerable difficulty with assessing 'early stage' activity comes from the different ways data sources define 'early stage'. The BVCA define early stage as funding for product and business development prior to the firm achieving profitability. BVCA split this financing into two categories; *Start-up* defined as 'financing provided to companies for use in product development and initial marketing. Companies may be in the process of set up or may have been in business for a short period of time but have not yet sold their product commercially' and *Other early stage* defined as 'financing provided to companies that have completed the product development stage and require further funding to initiate commercial manufacturing and sales. They may not yet be generating profits (BVCA, 2008:46). Other data sources categorise on the basis of funding rounds – seed round, first round and so on. Early stage is taken as an amalgamation of a number of rounds. In the NESTA 'Shifting Sands' report, using Library House Data, early stage was defined as firms with up to three rounds of finance, with rounds sizes of less than £2m and still in product development.
A certain number of funding rounds does not necessarily correspond with the stage of development of a venture backed firm. For this reason actual deals and value of investment differs for 'early stage' data from different sources.

10. The higher figure of funds raised by government sources in 2008 in comparison with the fund raised by stage of investment could be explained by the ability of some funds to invest in expansion activity of their portfolio firms. The *Enterprise Capital Funds* are able to invest up to £2m in a portfolio firm. However the relatively small size of these government-backed funds (compared to private funds) prevents them from larger volumes of expansion stage investing.

This shows that going forward; the vast majority of new early stage investment is going to come from UK government sources.

11. The case studies were conducted in 2008–2009. Data were collected at this one point of time, and looking backwards to the foundation of the firm. Data sources include interviews with the firms and VC fund managers, documents including; business and financial plans, board meetings and reports and marketing and advertising material.

12. Business angels are wealthy individuals who invest in firms either individually or alongside VC funds. These individuals usually have specialist knowledge and skills in the industries of the firms in which they invest. They also may be serial entrepreneurs with previous start-up experience. Business angels are a critical part of the early stage equity investment environment.

13. This knowledge exchange is also not one way, VC funds receive valuable knowledge on new technology and market and industrial development from their portfolio firms. This knowledge is valuable as it increases their available resources that can be exchanged with other portfolio firms, with the aim of successful developing these firms.

14. The case study firms analysed in this chapter were all portfolio firms of the same VC fund.

REFERENCES

Acs, Z. and Audretsch, D.B. (eds) (1990), *The Economics of Small Firms: A European Challenge*, Netherlands: Kluwer.

Berg-Utby, T., Sorheim, R. and Widding, L.O. (2007), 'Venture Capital Funds: Do they Meet the Expectations of Portfolio Firms?', *Venture Capital*, **9** (3), pp. 23–41.

Berglund, H., Hellstrom, T. and Sjolander, S. (2007), 'Entrepreneurial Learning and the Role of Venture Capitalists', *Venture Capital*, **9** (3), pp. 165–81.

BVCA (2009), *BVCA (British Venture Capital Association) Private Equity and Venture Capital Report on Investment Activity* 2008, London: BVCA.

Bygrave, W.D. and Timmons, J.A. (1992), *Venture Capital at the Crossroads*, Boston, MA: Harvard Business School Press.

Cristofidis, C. and Debande, O. (2001), 'Financing Innovative Firms through Venture Capital', *European Investment Bank Sector Papers*, Brussels: European Investment Bank.

Cosh, A. and Hughes, A. (eds) (2007), *British Enterprise: Surviving of Thriving?*, Cambridge, UK: Centre for Business Research, Cambridge University.

Da Rin, M., Nicodano, G. and Sembenelli, A. (2006), 'Public Policy and the Creation of Active Venture Capital Markets', *Journal of Public Economics*, **90** (8-9), pp. 1699–723.

De Clercq, D., Fried, V.H., Lehtonen, O. and Sapienza, H.J. (2006), 'An Entrepreneur's Guide to the Venture Capital Galaxy', *Academy of Management Perspectives*, **20** (3), pp. 90–112.

Denis, D.J. (2004), 'Entrepreneurial Finance: An Overview of the Issues and

Evidence', *Journal of Corporate Finance*, **10**, pp. 301–26.

Diaz de Leon, E. and Guild, P. (2003), 'Using repertory grid to identify intangibles in business plans', *Venture Capital*, **5** (2), pp. 135–60.

Dimov, D. and Murray, G. (2008), 'Determinants of the Incidence and Scale of Seed Capital Investments by Venture Capital Firms', *Small Business Economics*, **30** (2), pp. 127–152.

European Central Bank (ECB), (2010), *SME Access to Finance Survey Report*, Brussels: European Commission.

Gompers, P. and Lerner, J. (2004), *The Venture Capital Cycle*, Cambridge, MA: MIT Press.

Gottschlag, O., Phalippou, L. and Zollo, M. (2004), 'Performance of Private Equity Funds: Another Puzzle?', *Working Paper*, Fontainebleau: INSEAD.

Haywood, J. (2008), *High Technology Cluster in the Greater Cambridge Area*, Cambridge, UK: Cambridge Investment Research Ltd.

Hisrich, R.D. and Jankowicz, D. (1990), 'Intuition in Venture Capital Decisions: An Exploratory Study Using a New Technique', *Journal of Business Venturing*, **5**, pp. 49–62.

Hughes, A. and Storey, D.J. (eds) (1994), *Finance and the Small Firm*, London: Routledge.

Hurley, B., Herriot, W. and Parnell, H. (2005), *Improving the Funding and Successful Commercialisation of Innovation in the East of England*, Cambridge, UK: Report to the East of England Development Agency.

Jaaskelainen, M., Maula, M. and Murray, G., (2007), 'Profit Distribution and Compensation Structures in Publicly and Privately Funded Hybrid Venture Capital Funds', *Research Policy*, **36**, pp. 913–29.

Lange, J.E., Mollov, A., Pearlmutter, M., Singh, S. and Bygrave, W.D. (2007), 'Pre Start-up Formal Business Plans and Post Start-up Performance: A Study of 116 New Ventures', *Venture Capital*, **9** (4), pp. 237–56.

Langeland, O. (2007), 'Financing Innovation: The Role of Norwegian Venture Capitalists in Financing Knowledge-intensive Enterprises', *European Planning Studies*, **15** (9), pp. 1143–61.

Leleux, B. and Surlemont, B. (2003), 'Public Versus Private Venture Capital: Seeding or Crowding Out? A Pan-european Analysis', *Journal of Business Venturing*, **18**, pp. 81–104.

Lerner, J. (1994), 'The Syndication of Venture Capital Investments', *Financial Management*, **23** (3), pp. 16–27.

Lerner, J. (2002), 'When Bureaucrats Meet Entrepreneurs: The Design of Effective "Public Venture Capital" Programmes', *The Economic Journal*, **112** (477), pp. 73–84.

Lerner, J. (2009), *Boulevard of Broken Dreams: Why Efforts to Boost Entrepreneurship and Venture Capital Have Failed and What to Do About it*, New York: Princeton University Press.

Library House (2006), *Beyond the Chasm: The Venture-backed Report UK 2006*, Cambridge UK: Library House.

Macmillan, I.C., Zemann, L. and Subbanarasimha, P.N. (1987), 'Criteria Distinguishing Successful from Unsuccessful Venture in the Venture Screening Process', *Journal of Business Venturing*, **2**, pp. 123–37.

Manigart, S., Desbrieres, P., De Waele, K., Wright, M., Robbie, K., Sapienza, H.J. and Beckman, A. (2002), 'Determinants of Required Return in Venture Capital Investments: A Five Country Study', *Journal of Business Venturing*, **17** (4), pp. 291–312.

Maula, M., Murray, G. and Jaaskelainen, M. (2007), *Public Financing of Young Innovative Companies in Finland*, Finland: Ministry of Trade and Industry.

Murray, G. and Marriott, R. (1998), 'Why has the Investment Performance of Technology-specialist, European Venture Capital Funds Been so Poor?', *Research Policy*, **27**, pp. 947–76.

OECD (2006), *The SME Financing Gap (Vol. 1): Theory and Evidence*, Paris: OECD.

OECD (2009), *Science, Technology and Industry Scorecard 2009*, Paris: OECD.

Pierrakis, Y. and Mason, C.M. (2008), *Shifting Sands: The Changing Nature of the Early Stage Venture Capital Market in the UK*, London: NESTA.

Sainsbury, Lord (2007), *The Race to the Top: A Review of Government's Science and Innovation Policies, The Sainsbury Review*, London: HM Treasury.

Shane, S. and Cable, D. (2002), 'Network Ties, Reputation and the Financing of New Ventures', *Management Science*, **48** (3), pp. 364–81.

Sharpe, S., Cosh, A., Connell, D. and Parnell, H. (2009), *The Role of Micro Funds in the Financing of New Technology Firms*, London: NESTA (National Endowment for Science, Technology and the Arts).

Soderblom, A. (2006), *Factors Determining the Performance of Early Stage High-technology Venture Capital Funds: A Review of the Academic Literature*, London: Small Business Service Research, Department of Trade and Industry.

PART THREE

Strategic Policy Implications

11 Implications for Skills, Employment and Management

Ian Miles and Cristina Martinez-Fernandez

This chapter discusses the broader implications of the increasing significance of Knowledge Intensive Service Activities (KISA), especially in relation to skill requirements, skills upgrading and employment generation, and to management strategy, government policy, and the responses of educational institutions. We consider the nature of KISA occupations and the skills they deploy and report arguments that there are widespread trends towards the broadening of competences needed in these.

INTRODUCTION

It is well-known that there is huge variation across service firms and sectors in terms of the skills and knowledge they employ. Some of the most professionalised service sectors are those where KISA are the main business, notable KIBS (Knowledge Intensive Business Services) – while sectors like retail, hotels, catering, depend on high levels of input from relatively unskilled workers (often on low wages and insecure contracts). But even if we focus only on KISA, there are considerable variations. Of course, the types of knowledge in which these activities are intensive will be highly differentiated. One would not expect a software engineer to readily prepare a sophisticated legal brief, or an architect to provide marketing advice. The different knowledge domains suggested by these examples correspond roughly to occupational categories and industrial (KIBS) sectors, but this is just the beginning.

For one thing, there are typically different depths of knowledge that can be possessed, and a deep understanding may be acquired by higher education, professional training, extensive work experience or even life experience – and often by a mixture of several or all of these. Occupational statistics often give us a crude differentiation between professional and the associate professionals who support them, but it is apparent that the depth of knowledge possessed about a given domain may vary widely within such categories. Furthermore, exactly what parts of a given domain are known well are liable to vary, and it is widely reported that interdisciplinary and inter-professional knowledge that spans more than one domain is more and more needed. The types of knowledge that may require integration can be relatively technical domain-specific knowledge, but also there are requirements for people to have good capabilities in various managerial activities and interpersonal relationships. There are also requirements for staff that can work with and manage teams that span several knowledge bases.

These developments are more or less inevitable consequences of the growing role of KISA in economic life. As more KISA are engaged in support of business activities, so it becomes necessary to call on specialist knowledge – and to have capabilities to bring together the contributions from professionals of different types. In addition KISA's role in learning and skills development requires greater attention to this function, as complementary to formal training.

But the precise ways in which such trends unfold is liable to be highly influenced by several key factors. Work organisation may impose a high division of labour, or rely on more multi-skilled staff. Production may be modularised with many processes outsourced – in ways that could require more or less managerial oversight – and, as discussed in earlier chapters, KISA can be produced in-house or bought in.

This chapter will explore the validity and implications of the assertions made above. We first discuss the data with which we can assess the skills required for KISA and within KIBS, and then outline implications for employment, skills, and innovation policy and management.

KISA WORK ACROSS THE ECONOMY

KIBS specialise in producing services to support the business processes of other private firms and public organisations. Most earlier work, and most statistical analyses of KIBS, followed Miles et al (1995) in differentiating between two types of KIBS sector. These are: technical KIBS (computer support, R&D, engineering, industrial product and process design, and so on) and more traditional professional services (accountancy, legal services, market research). Some more recent work has argued for identifying a third KIBS category of business-related creative services (within the standard business service groups these include advertising, design, and some elements of architecture; and also there are business-related design, media and the like that are lumped together with entertainment and 'other' services in statistical series). Other external KISA may be supplied in relation to financial and telecommunication services, furthermore. These are not counted as KIBS because the broad sectors involved have large consumer markets as well as more specialised business ones, and correspondingly they also often feature large shares of relatively low-skill employees in sales and related occupations. Statistical analysis reveals the KIBS included in the business services sectors to be among the most knowledge-intensive parts of the economy, as measured in terms of such indicators as the share of University graduates in the workforce. The KIBS, located in Figure 11.1 within the 'business services' group, are rivalled in this respect only by health and education services, with financial services somewhat behind.

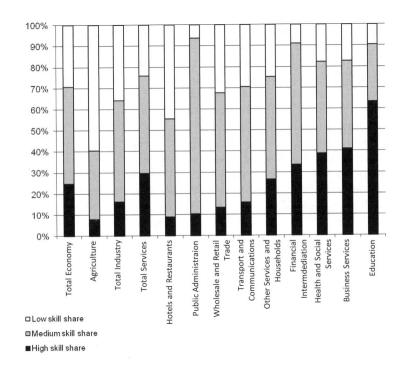

Notes: Low skill is defined in terms of attainment of less than upper secondary education (below level 3 in the International Standard Classification of Education (ISCED) classification); medium skill involves attainment of upper secondary education (ISCED level 3). High skill is an attainment of higher education (ISCED levels 5, 6, and 7)

Source: Developed from data in annexes to CEC (2005)

Figure 11.1 Skill composition of economic sectors in the EU-15, 2000

In terms of statistical classification systems, the main KIBS sectors are usually taken from the standard industrial classification set of 'business services', excluding various operational services like security, cleaning and (perhaps controversially) secretarial support and some related functions. This gives us a core set of KIBS among activities belonging to NACE 72-74: **IT services** (72,1– Hardware consultancy; 72,21 – Publishing of software; 72,22 – Other software consultancy and supply; 72,3 – Data processing; 72,4 – Database activities; 72,5 – Maintenance and repair of office, accounting and computing machinery; 72,6 – Other computer related activities); **R&D services** (73,1– Research and experimental development on natural sciences and engineering; 73,2...on social sciences and humanities); **Architectural and technical services** (74,2 – Architectural and engineering activities and related technical consultancy; 74,3 – Technical testing and analysis); Professional and market-related services); **Professional services** (74,11 – Legal activities; 74,12 – Accounting, book-keeping and auditing activities; tax consultancy; 74,13 – Market research and public opinion polling; 74,14 – Business and management consultancy activities; 74,15 – Management activities of holding companies); and 74,4 – Advertising.

The statistics under these categories provide information on KIBS sectoral employment, value-added, and so on. But what can we say about KISAs more generally, including those not taking place within KIBS? For some of the KIBS, there are clearly specialised occupations conducting the main professional work (of course, not all KIBS employees are professionals – there are many clerical and data entry staff). For example, corresponding to IT services are professional and associate professional occupations such as IT hardware and IT software professionals, Hardware consultancy professionals, Data processing and Database managers, and IT maintenance and repair staff. For R&D services (an important but relatively small sector) the corresponding occupations are R&D personnel. For Architectural and technical services are professional and associate professional occupations such as Architects, Engineering and engineering design professionals, Technical testing and analysis professionals. For Professional and market-related services there are Lawyers and other skilled legal workers, Accountants, auditors and related professionals, Market research, marketing, and advertising professionals – and managers (though we suspect that management consultancy skills and activities are rather different from those expressed in management more generally).

Marja Toivonen (unpublished paper) has examined the distribution of such KISA occupations in the Finnish economy (Figure 11.2). What is striking is that in all cases except one – computer professionals – only a minority of the profession is employed in the relevant KIBS industry. KISA are pervasively distributed, even if there are KIBS firms that specialise in them.

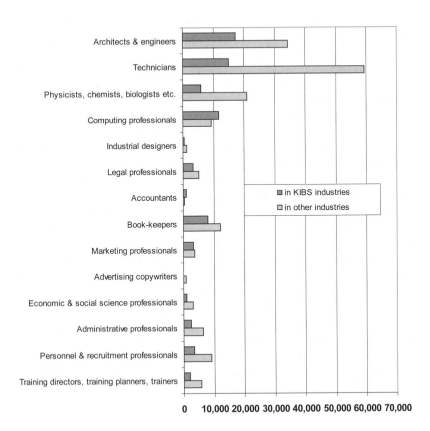

Architects & engineers

Technicians

Physicists, chemists, biologists etc.

Computing professionals

Industrial designers

Legal professionals

Accountants

Book-keepers

Marketing professionals

Advertising copywriters

Economic & social science professionals

Administrative professionals

Personnel & recruitment professionals

Training directors, training planners, trainers

■ in KIBS industries
□ in other industries

0 10,000 20,000 30,000 40,000 50,000 60,000 70,000

Source: Data from Statistics Finland, elaborated by Marja Toivonen, unpublished paper (Helsinki University of Technology) 2003

Figure 11.2 KISA professions in KIBS and the wider economy: Finland in 1995, thousands of employees

A similar UK study (Higgs et al, 2008) focused on professions associated with financial and creative services. Two-thirds of the financial specialists worked outside the core Financial Services industry in 2001, and almost 40 per cent of all of the UK financial services workforce was estimated to be employed outside of the financial services industries. Similarly, 35 per cent of the total 'creative' workforce (a very broad definition, including computer software) were employed in non-creative sectors (especially, financial services, and also in manufacturing, real estate, business services, and wholesale and retail trade). Such detailed occupational data tends to be worked on in single countries only, since there are problems comparing the detailed categories internationally. The International Standard Classification of Occupations (ISCO) does identify three broad groups that span the KISA occupations outlined above. These are ISCO 1 – **Legislators, senior officials and managers** (11 Legislators and senior officials; 12 Corporate managers; 13 Managers of small enterprises); ISCO 2 – **Professionals** (21 Physical, mathematical and engineering science professionals; 22 Life science and health professionals; 23 Teaching professionals; 24 Other professionals), and ISCO 3 – **Technicians and associate professionals** (31 Physical and engineering science associate professionals; 32 Life science and health associate professionals; 33 Teaching associate professionals; 34 Other associate professionals).

Occupational statistics provide evidence about the number of people in these roles, and about the sectoral distribution of KISA work – as evidenced by occupational gradings. These are indicators of KISA work of course. Just as KISA can be undertaken and even sold by organisations that are not strictly KIBS, so KISA can be undertaken by people who are not in one of the three 'KISA' occupational groups. On the other hand, at least some of the time when KISA professionals are at work they will be engaged in non KISA activities, as the queues around photocopiers demonstrate!

Figure 11.3 presents data on the sectoral distribution of professional occupations in Europe in 2006. Several striking points emerge.

First, across all sectors, these occupations account for a striking share of employment: not far below 40 per cent of the total. We may expect that managers of small businesses who also engage in a good deal of non KISA work themselves (for example in transport firms like taxi services) may inflate these figures somewhat. Indeed, in Primary sector and Utilities, Manufacturing, Construction and the service sectors of Distribution and Transport, the shares of legislators, senior officials and managers in employment are higher than those of professionals. If we look solely at the professional category, this accounts for 13 per cent of employment overall – from 3 per cent in primary and distributive sectors, to around 17 per cent in business services and almost 30 per cent in non-marketed services. If we add in associates, the overall figure is around 30 per cent, ranging from less than 10 per cent in some sectors to 37 per cent and 50 per cent in business and non-marketed services respectively. It seems reasonable to estimate that at least a third of all work across the economy currently consists of KISA.

Two of these grand sectors feature particularly high levels of KISA – non marketed services (health, education, and so on) and business services (which will include KIBS). Between them, they account for the lion's share of KISA occupations in Europe – almost exactly 75 per cent of the three occupational groups are employed in these two sectors.

(a) Contributions to overall employment

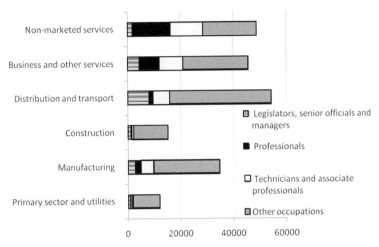

(b) Shares of sectoral employment

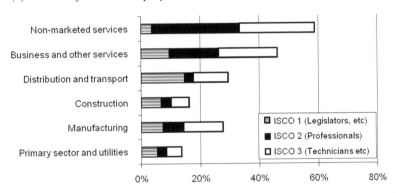

Source: Data from annexes of CEDEFOP (2008a)

Figure 11.3 Occupational distribution across sectors, EU 25+ 2006

The relative sizes of the different KISA groups are also interesting. The ratio of 'technicians' to the ISCO group of professionals and senior managers varies quite markedly. In most sectors it is within the range 0.4 to 0.6 (that is each technician supports around 2 professionals and senior managers); but in manufacturing it is close to 0.75, and in distribution 1.21. Looking at the relative shares of professionals and technicians is equally striking. In non marketed services there are greater numbers of professionals, in business services the numbers are roughly equal – while in manufacturing there are almost twice as many technicians as professionals, and in distribution there are nearly four times as many. The implication is that the organisation of work, and the actual functions that are performed, vary considerably across the broad sectors.

The CEDEFOP report which these data derive from is mainly concerned with forecasting demand for skills and employment over the coming decade. The sector with highest growth rates in the period 2006–2015 was forecast to be Business and Other Services (2 per cent per annum), followed by Non-marketed Services and Distribution and Transport (both 0.7 per cent per annum); Construction grows at 0.3 per cent per annum, while the Primary and Manufacturing sectors decline. In terms of occupations, the three KISA groups are all expected to grow at 1.4 to 1.5 per cent per annum; and elementary occupations by 1.6 per cent (this is largely a matter of growth in 'sales and service elementary occupations'), other occupations grow at less than 1 per cent or actually decline. While all such forecasts have to be treated with a pinch of salt, and certainly cannot be viewed as precise, the general trends that are depicted here correspond to the long-term sectoral and occupational evolution in Europe, and give some guidance as to the sorts of work to be anticipated in the medium-term future.

SKILLS INVOLVED IN KISA

What are KISA workers doing, and what skills and competences are drawn upon? These are complicated topics, not least because of the many varieties of KISA and the many types of knowledge involved. Knowledge and skills can be acquired through various combinations of formal and on-the-job training, through communities of practice and professional networks and from learning-by-doing. Formal training takes place through a variety of institutions, with a wide range of qualifications being awarded. It is not surprising, then, that progress toward cross-national analysis of trends and developments has been slow. Most analysis of skills has simply been in terms of the three levels of educational attainment as used in Figure 11.1. The CEDEFOP (2008a) analysis, for instance, present data in terms of this indicator. Overall demand is expected to shift increasingly toward higher qualifications, as might be expected (2.4 per cent per annum growth for higher qualifications, 1 per cent per annum for medium, and –0.9 per cent for lower qualifications).

But these three levels of educational attainment hardly capture the variety of skills that are in use on a practical basis. Typically, occupations demand a portfolio of skills, which are liable to change over time, with organisational and technological development. There are also liable to be variations across sectors and across specific occupational groupings (even within categories of KISA professional). Bosworth and Wilson (2005) provide one illustration of this. They found major differences in the structure of management across different sectors of the UK economy, for example, the gender composition of the management workforce, with an all industries average of around 35 per cent varied from 11 per cent female in sales and maintenance of motor vehicles and 10 per cent in construction, to over 70 per cent in education and health and social work. As for age just under 40 per cent of managers are aged 45 and over in terms of the all industries average – but this ranges from just over 20 per cent for computer and financial services to just under 60 per cent for mining and quarrying. The share of managers in overall employment, and the proportion of self-employed as opposed to corporate managers, also varies across sectors. There are also strong sectoral variations in the qualifications of managers, reflecting both managerial status – self-employed, corporate manager, and so on – and overall qualification levels of the sector. The authors found that when overall workforce qualifications are low, those of managers also tend to be low, for example as measured by the share of managers without qualifications. Less than 2 per cent of some sectors' managers lacked high-level qualifications in computing services, public administration, and utilities, while agriculture, textiles and clothing, and sales and maintenance of motor vehicles all feature over 15 per cent. The evidence suggests that KIBS and KISA-intensive industries more generally typically have high levels of formally qualified managers. While this was a UK study, we can anticipate cross-national and even regional differences, as well.

Educational attainment is an imperfect measure of knowledge. It neglects all types of learning and knowledge acquired through practice. Further, the multifaceted variations in skills that exist are poorly represented by a single dimension of more or less skill. At the very least we can differentiate between those KISA skills that are technical and job-specific, and those that are more generic and required across many professional occupations. But among these more generic skills, there are also a range of different types of capability that are required – so, for example, as more managerial functions are taken on by other professionals, so more fluency with management skills is likely to be experienced. One solution may be to think in terms of skill profiles, such as is accomplished in the USA's O*Net system, which describes occupations in terms of reports from employees and experts' judgements as to the most important skills that each requires.[1] The degree of sophistication that is required of each of a set of different skills is graded in terms of seven-point scales.

A few survey studies have taken steps toward measuring the skill content actually used within jobs, as assessed from individual employees' reports of their job requirements – rather than in terms of the workers' credentials or professional judgements about what a job requires. An extensive UK study is reported by Felstead et al, (2007). This survey enquired as to the total training time required to do the job, the amount of learning on the job required for full competence, and the qualification level required for new recruits. They used statistical techniques to reduce the answers to some 35 questions about the importance of particular skills to the job performed, to a smaller and more meaningful set of generic skills: literacy, numeracy, technical know-how, high-level communication skills, planning skills, client communication skills, horizontal communication skills, problem-solving, checking skills and physical skills, emotional and aesthetic skills (there are also measures of the importance and sophistication of computer use). The survey actually covers more material, but we focus on these results for present purposes.

Skills are more or less generic, with some skills being required across a wide range of occupations (notably checking skills – 'very important' in 79 per cent of all jobs, with horizontal communication skills next most common). Least common are influence skills, number skills and physical skills (very important in 23 per cent, 28 per cent and 26 per cent of jobs, respectively). Figure 11.4 reports the share of jobs in each category in which the skill is 'very important' (a measure of how generic the skill is), and the average level of each skill required across all jobs. Figure 11.5 displays results in terms of how far the average skill requirement reported for each occupational group deviates from the grand mean – this allows us to see differences between occupations more starkly than the absolute figures.

The tendency is for the three KISA professions (Legislators, senior officials and managers; Professionals; and Technicians and associate professionals) to display greater use of most of the generic skills. The only consistent exception is Physical skills, though Technical know-how is less prominent in Managers and Professionals, while more so in Associate Professionals (these two categories of skills have highest scores among Skilled Trades). Literacy skills and Horizontal communication skills[2] are highest for Professional occupations, Number skills for Managers (and Problem-solving skills are greatest for Managers but also Skilled Trades). Influence skills are highest among 'Professionals' and 'Managers'. Considering other service jobs, checking skills (high for all groups) are most needed by Administrative and Secretarial occupations; Emotional skills by Personal Service occupations; Aesthetic and Client communications skills in Sales occupations. These results are intuitively plausible, but it is welcome to have statistical data to validate our preconceptions.

4a How 'Generic' Skills are   4b Average skill requirement

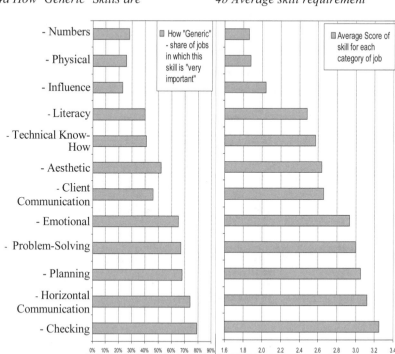

Notes: Definitions of Skills: *Numbers:* adding, subtracting, divisions, decimal point or fraction calculations and so on, and/or more advanced maths or statistical procedures. *Physical*: the use of physical strength and/or stamina; skill in using one's hands. *Influence*: persuading or influencing others, instructing, training or teaching people, making speeches or presentations, writing long reports, analysing complex problems in depth, and planning the activities of others. *Literacy*: both reading and writing forms, notices, memos, signs, letters, short and long documents and so on. *Technical Know-How*: knowing how to use tools or equipment or machinery, knowing about products and services, specialist knowledge and/or skill in using one's hands. *Aesthetic*: looking and sounding the part. *Problem-Solving*: detecting, diagnosing, analysing and resolving problems. *Planning*: planning activities, organising one's own time and thinking ahead. *Horizontal Communication*: working with a team of people, listening carefully to colleagues. *Client Communication*: selling a product or service, counselling or caring for customers or clients, dealing with people, knowing about products and services. *Emotional*: managing own and handling others' feelings. *Checking*: noticing and checking for errors

Source: Felstead et al (2007), from data in Tables 3.8, 3.9

Figure 11.4 How far skills are required in UK Occupations, 2006

5a 'More professional' skill requirements

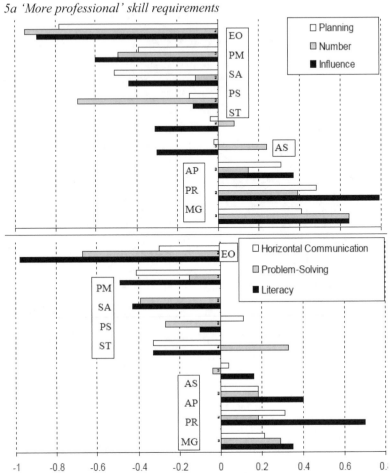

Note: Skills are: *Planning*: planning activities, organising one's own time and thinking ahead. *Number Skills:* adding, subtracting, divisions, decimal point or fraction calculations and so on, and/or more advanced maths or statistical procedures. *Influence*: persuading or influencing others, instructing, training or teaching people, making speeches or presentations, writing long reports, analysing complex problems in depth, and planning the activities of others. *Horizontal Communication*: working with a team of people, listening carefully to colleagues. *Problem-Solving*: detecting, diagnosing, analysing and resolving problems. *Literacy Skills*: both reading and writing forms, notices, memos, signs, letters, short and long documents and so on. The occupations are EO = Elementary Occupations; PM = Plant & Machine Operatives; SA = Sales; PS = Personal Service; ST = Skilled Trades; AS = Administrative & Secretarial; AP = Associate Professionals; PR = Professionals; MG = Managers

Source: Felstead et al (2007), from data in Tables 3.8, 3.9

Figure 11.5 Skills across occupational categories, UK 2006

5b Service and 'less professional' skill requirements

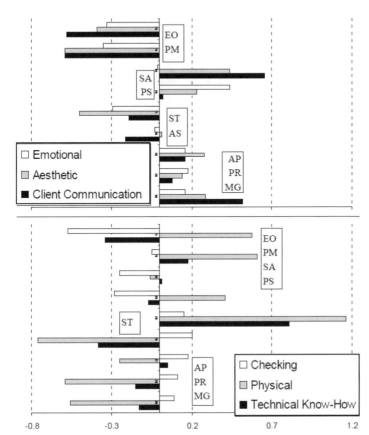

Notes: The skills depicted here are defined as: *Emotion Skills*: managing own and handling other's feelings. *Aesthetic Skills*: looking and sounding the part. *Client Communication*: selling a product or service, counselling or caring for customers or clients, dealing with people, knowing about products and services. *Checking Skills*: noticing and checking errors. *Physical Skills*: the use of physical strength and/or stamina; skill in using one's hands. *Technical 'Know-how'*: knowing how to use tools or equipment or machinery, knowing about products and services, specialist knowledge and/or skill in using one's hands

Source: Felstead et al (2007), from data in Tables 3.8, 3.9

Figure11.5 Skills across occupational categories, UK 2006 (continued)

Further evidence as to use of knowledge at work comes from the European Working Conditions Survey. This asks employees about their experiences at work, including the extent to which they learn at work, solve problems, deal with complex tasks, and so on. Figure 11.5a shows data in terms of the sectors within which the people work; Figure 11.5b presents data in terms of occupations. Again we present data in terms of the sectoral/occupational deviation from the mean for all workers.

6a Sectoral Data

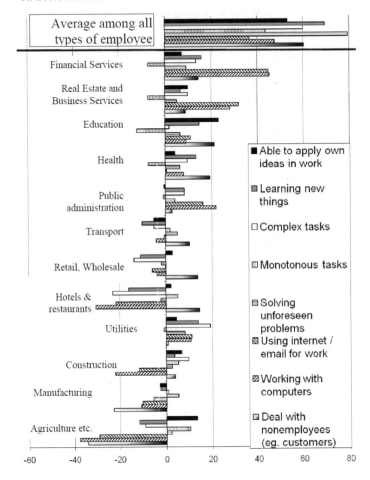

Note: The comparison with the average for employees will not take into account the experience of self-employed people

Source: Based on data in Parent-Thirion et al (2007)

Figure 11.6 European working conditions survey data, European Economy (EU-27+ Croatia, Norway, Switzerland, Turkey), 2005

6b Occupational Data

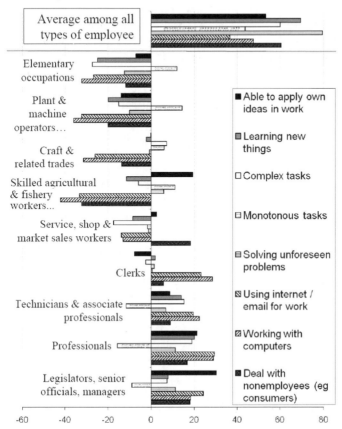

Note: The comparison with the average for employees will not take into account the experience of self-employed people.

Source: Based on data in Parent-Thirion et al (2007)

Figure 11.5 European working conditions survey data, European Economy (EU-27+ Croatia, Norway, Switzerland, Turkey), 2005 (Continued)

Among the evident results sectoral trends are apparent: Service sectors involve more contact with non employees (for example customers); Finance, real estate and business services (within which are KIBS), and public services like education – which of course are the sectors with high levels of high-skill employment as measured by credentials – feature relatively large shares of jobs where the employees report complex tasks, problem-solving, learning new things on the job, computer and internet use, and so on. Conversely they record relatively low shares of people reporting monotonous work. The reverse tends to be the case for some other services – transport and trade services, and HORECA (hotels, restaurants and catering); and these are the sectors with low levels of high-skill employment as measured by educational attainment. In terms of occupations, the three KISA categories[3] feature work that is more complex, demanding, and knowledge intensive. At the same time elementary occupations using 'influence skills' are up to a high degree.

There are other sources of data and approaches that can be taken to statistics such as these. For example, the CEC (2007) presents an interesting clustering of jobs related to working conditions, training, and the like. The study differentiates among jobs in terms of dimensions such as firm-specific human capital (learning on the job), formal training, employment stability, seniority, and the like. KISA occupations fall into a number of clusters differentiated by such factors. There are many detailed studies of specific categories of KISA work, too. These are often sensitive to the dynamics of change.

For instance, Penn and Holt (2000) explored skills in a number of professional KIBS (Management consultancy, Advertising, Market research, Legal services, and Accounting), and reported common features and some blurring of functions (for example, accountants offering management consultancy services); and Information Technology Service firms moving into these professional service areas – and professional service firms offering IT-related KISAs. One common trajectory, very much related to the continuing diffusion and further development of IT systems for supporting KISA, has been growing requirements for IT associate professionals. IT specialists are often moving into the 'professional' roles, acquiring relevant skills; and established professionals are often acquiring new IT skills. On-the-job training is an important way of acquiring relevant skills, but is accomplished in different ways across KIBS sectors it is typically highly company-specific in management consultancy, but less so for advertising and market research). All the sectors were found to be undergoing considerable structural change, and – perhaps especially the 'creative' activities of consultancy, advertising, and so on they – are being reshaped by Internet use.

Rodgers and Waters (2001), focused on Business and Public Service Associate Professionals, examining insurance underwriters, legal associate professionals (legal executives and barristers clerks), personnel officers (including recruitment consultants), market researchers and estate agents. These KISA occupations have different skill needs, entry routes and skill development strategies, but there are also cross-cutting features and trends apparent. The jobs require a complex mix of technical and generic skills and personal attributes to deliver the KISA, and experienced some change in the level and range of technical, generic and interpersonal skills required. Broadly, the number of skills associated with these KISA occupations has risen. Three types of role were distinguished. 'Traditional' Associate Professionals – the majority of the occupations – needed a high level of technical skills with above average generic skills and well-developed personal attributes. The ability of individuals to perform their job is largely determined by the technical knowledge and skills that they possess. The important skill shifts involved increasing importance of generic and interpersonal skills, with greater 'customer handling' skills required for better service – as organisations seek to differentiate their value propositions. 'Transitional' Associate Professionals required an average level of technical skills, but high-level generic skills and well-developed personal attributes. Job roles in this group are most likely to be undergoing some form of reclassification, with additional job tasks being incorporated into the job role; there were increases in the importance, range and level of technical skills required. Finally, 'Generic' Associate Professionals require high-level generic skills and personal attributes but relatively low levels of technical skills. The skills required for these associate professional roles are largely transferable and, as such, these job roles typically have lower entry requirements and higher levels of employee turnover. There was less skill change apparent, with the main development being the introduction of additional generic skills, especially those associated with basic ICT.

As for more technology-based KISA, a huge amount of attention has been paid to skills related to ICT professions, which are distributed across electronics production sectors, computer services, and all sorts of ICT user sectors. Petersen et al (2004) compare the frameworks introduced in earlier studies, synthesising them to identify three categories of generic skills and six types of ICT specialism (with associated technical skill requirements). The skill categories are: 'Behavioural and personal skills': Flexibility, Self Learning, Motivation and Commitment, Stress Resistance and Emotion, Responsibility, Managing Risks, Decision Making, Negotiation, Initiative and Attention, Persuasiveness, Professional Attitude (Business or Technical Orientation and Interests). 'Cross section and basic work and technical skills': Quality Awareness, Commercial and Market Awareness, Entrepreneurship, Customer Orientation and Relationship, Company and Business Organisation, Work and Project Organisation, Business and Work Process Knowledge, Work Safety and Health Protection, Labour Law and Data Privacy, Environmental and Resource Awareness. 'Soft and method skills': Communication and Moderation, Languages and Culture, Collaboration and Interaction, Teamwork and Mentoring, Conflict and Consensus, Creative and Innovation, Analytical and Reasoning, Problem Analysis and Solving, Strategy, Conception and Planning, Context and Causal Connection Thinking, Information Handling, Documentation and Presentation (Petersen et al, 2004:57).

The six specialisms require these skills to varying extents, but also confront specific technical skill needs as listed in Table 11.1.

Table 11.1 Six ICT KISA occupations

---

1) Technical skills in 'ICT marketing, consulting and sales'

'a comprehensive work area covering commercial and consultancy activities with special focus on information and communications technology (ICT) projects, products and services. It applies to both the ICT industry and to companies of the ICT user industries (keyword: Profit Centre Organisation). Successful marketing and sales of ICT products and services requires fundamental analyses of external and internal market and customer needs. Following various consultations these requirements need to be translated into services and products that answer specific customer needs while providing benefits to the own company or department at the same time. These combinations of business and technical tasks ask for specific skills justifying the elaboration and delimitation of a generic ICT work area and corresponding skills at different levels.'

2) Technical Skills in 'ICT Business and Project Management'

'also combines business and ICT skills ensuring the work flow success of an ICT project and business process. Within a wide range of project activities and responsibilities business and project orientated ICT practitioners at different skill levels closely collaborate with internal and external ICT experts, providers and customers in order to ensure that customers' business needs are met when developing and deploying infrastructure and software ICT solutions and services. All together business orientated ICT practitioners constitute the crucial 'interface' between the customer and primary ICT specialists and technicians. Common goal of more business and technical orientated ICT practitioners is a clear description of the business requirements within the 'technical specification' of the ICT solution to be developed. In shared responsibility more business and technical orientated ICT practitioners organise and implement applied support, training and instructions to the customer.'

3) Technical Skills in 'ICT Systems and Application Development'

'covers far more than just mere individual programming or coding. In this work area ICT practitioners at different skill levels work in development teams that design, realise, update, test and document ICT systems and software applications. The work is carried out based on comprehensive analyses and descriptions of what ICT systems and applications are needed by the market, a specific sector or a specific (internal or external) customer. In practise contacts to the project manager and ICT business and technical practitioners within our without the company are important. In the daily work processes the transfer of the technical and business requirements into a consistent 'data processing specification' is crucial for the final success of the ICT systems and application development process. Primary criteria for the software solutions are reliability and usability. Furthermore the work as part of a team often runs under time constraints and must be constantly well communicated and documented. Eventually, the customer and its users often need applied support, training and instructions.'

4) Technical Skills in 'ICT Integration and Administration'

'ICT systems and applications ... need to be professionally integrated, deployed, administered, optimised, supported, and so on, depending on the platform the applications run on. 'ICT Integration and Administration' teams configure, integrate, maintain and administer new developed or already running systems and software applications. The work is carried out based on comprehensive analyses and descriptions of needed or existing systems environments to be finally successful in the integration and deployment process. In daily work processes contacts to the project manager and ICT business and developers within our without the company are important. Eventually, the customer and its users often need applied (Help Desk) support, training and instructions. As part of the (continuing and often contracted) technical support, systems and applications are optimised and up-graded and troubleshooting need to be coordinated and problems resolved at different levels.'

5) Technical Skills in 'ICT infrastructure and installation'

'covers the planning, integration, modification and installation of the wide range of different ICT systems, devices, telecommunications, networks, and so on, summarised as ICT infrastructure. The work is carried out based on problem orientated analyses and descriptions of what type and level of ICT infrastructure is needed by the market, a specific sector or (internal or external) customer. In practise contacts to customers, project managers and ICT business and systems development practitioners within or without the company are important. For the realisation of the projects or project parts and depending on the skill and responsibility level ICT infrastructure practitioners need to consider aspects like cost effectiveness, expandability and upgradeability, reliability, security, and so on. The integration of standard, specific and innovative solutions (for example software applications, wireless network and telecommunication solutions, web based infrastructure) is part of this work. The work, sometimes as part of a team, often runs under time constraints and must be constantly well communicated and documented. Eventually, the customer and its users often need applied support, training and instructions.'

6) Technical Skills in 'ICT support and systems service'

'concerns the analysis, troubleshooting and fixing of ICT infrastructure, systems and application problems. In principle this work covers a wide range of different ICT technologies and services and correspondingly the use of different soft and hardware based expert and diagnosis tools, depending on the level of service and support. In order to narrow the faults down to the concrete technical problem, ICT service practitioners need to well communicate with customers, users and colleagues. As part of the service and maintenance the ICT practitioners must be able to propose possibilities of optimising and upgrading existing ICT systems.'

Source: Petersen et al, (2004) pp. 55–57.

SKILLS DEVELOPMENT THROUGH KISA

KISA develop skills through the projects undertaken by the different professionals, and by stimulating learning that is relevant for the firm at the moment but which can be of long-lasting relevance for finding solutions to complex problems. In this way KISA is also utilised by firms (particularly SMEs) as an alternative way of learning and skills upgrading to that of formal education and training. 'Formal training', here, refers to learning that occurs in an organised and structured environment (for example in an education or training institution or on the job), and is explicitly designated as learning (in terms of objectives, time or resources). Formal learning is intentional from the learner's point of view; it typically leads to validation and certification. 'Informal training' refers in contrast to learning resulting from daily activities related to work, family or leisure. It is not organised or structured in terms of objectives, time or learning support. Informal learning is often unintentional from the learner's perspective (CEDEFOP, 2008b). KISA can be placed within the informal training category although they are typically more reliant on knowledge intensive professionals and interactive skills. Although much attention has been devoted to KISA performed by the high skilled, low skilled employees can also benefit when the environment allows for their participation. The results are increasing capabilities in business areas usually outside the specifications of routine tasks and into new areas of importance such as entrepreneurial skills (OECD, 2010a).

The relevance of KISA for skills development is especially crucial for SMEs (up to 250 employees). A striking characteristic of many SMEs is their lack of participation in formal training activities for skills upgrading. An ongoing OECD project is investigating why smaller firms participate up to 50 per cent less in training, and which skills are more likely to be acquired through formal training and through KISA. This study is using surveys of SMEs to investigate the following group of skills (OECD, 2010b):

- Generic – general IT user skills, oral communication, written communication, numeracy and literacy, office admin skills.
- Routine – repetitive, more basic, low knowledge intensive skills.
- Technical/Advanced – skills required for problem solving; design, operation, rethinking and maintenance of machinery or technological structures; IT professional skills.
- Management – skills for business planning, regulations and quality control, human resources planning (recruitment, training and skills development) and allocation of resources.
- Social – motivation and appreciation of people's characteristics for individual and team working purposes, customer handling; appreciation of networks and value-chain partners.
- Language and cultural – ability to communicate in more than one language, appreciation of cultural characteristics of different ethnic groups.
- Entrepreneurial – specific skills for start-ups such as risk management, strategic thinking, self-confidence, the ability to make the best of personal networks and the ability of dealing with challenges and requirements of different nature.

In relation to the need for training and skills upgrading, a sample of firms from New Zealand noted business skills, social skills and generic skills as the more important areas of development. Fifty per cent of the firms also noted that desired training was not carried out. KISA is acknowledged as an informal, alternative way to acquire skills; chiefly management skills, technical skills and social skills. KISA was also noted by firms as a key factor of productivity in the firm and for increasing market position and competitiveness. Several skills categories are also noted as being better sourced through KISA than through formal training. These are business planning, marketing and promotion, information and technology and entrepreneurship. In general the New Zealand study confirms the high relationship of training and innovation performance; it indicates that 'clients', followed by co-workers, are the most important groups for KISA in both high and low innovation firms. There were six categories where a noticeably larger number of firms reported more participation in KISA than in formal training: marketing and promotion; research and development, legal advice; e-commerce; language coaching; and entrepreneurship. The study also found that more firms reported participation in formal training for job-specific technical skills, for example, than in informal 'KISA' activities/training (OECD, 2010b).

For SMEs to continue being competitive, KISA seems to be a key component of their skills upgrading activities. KISA thus form a complementary instrument to formal training processes. The anticipation of the skills needs liable to be confronted by SMEs is probably especially important in the post crisis context, where access to finance has worsened, and more attention is needed to how KISA can contribute to the competitiveness of the small firm.

FUTURE KISA SKILLS REQUIREMENTS

The long-term trends seem to be toward both higher shares of KISA jobs in Western economies – off-shoring fears notwithstanding – and for a widening of the skill sets required in many KISA, with evolving combinations of business and technical skills. Just how these trends will work out in the future depends on a combination of technological, organisational, and other factors. In addition to growing use of ICT, which may of course be used to automate some KISA functions, key influences are liable to be:

1. Wide introduction of other generic technologies, for example nanotechnology, biotechnology and (perhaps relevant to health and experience services) cognitive/neurotechnology, with demand for associated skills in their production and application;
2. The organisation of the KIBS sector, in terms of the roles of firms (specialisation/integration), firm size, and the use of overseas KIBS and the off-shoring of some functions by KIBS firms;
3. Demand for KISA on the part of clients, related to levels of economic growth and internationalisation, and to strategies concerning internalization

of KISA versus externalising them to KIBS;
4. The availability and quality of training in KISA skills, modes of provision of training (on-the job and in formal institutions, life-long learning, and so on).

There have been a number of scenario studies focusing on the future of KIS and KISA occupations (see Miles and Jones, forthcoming, for a review). RAND-Europe (2006) explored the future of professional work, which has a clear bearing on the KISA with which this volume deals. RAND-Europe identified three main trends shaping future professional skills (they looked ahead to 2015): the decreasing 'half-life' of knowledge, coupled with the increasing amount of information to process; and with concurrent pressures for both generalisation and specialisation in the workforce. Professionals face increasing amounts of data, and are using new tools for their work which demand new knowledge. They are also confronting more turbulent environments, and require access to evolving knowledge across a wide spectrum, to inform strategic decisions. While less specialisation would seem to follow, new sorts of specialist knowledge will also be required as new technologies and techniques are introduced.

RAND-Europe developed scenarios differentiated in terms of two highly important but also uncertain drivers of change. The first dimension relates to the development of science and technology – high versus low user-friendliness of advancing technologies. The second concerns workplace developments – increased/decreased centralisation (sharing of responsibilities and delegation to other practitioners in the organisation versus tighter control on workflows and centralised responsibility). Four scenarios result from cross-cutting these dimensions. 'Autonomy' (decentralised and user friendly) is characterised by 'self-organisation in complex organisations, which implies adherence to professional standards, or a broadening of the knowledge to apply in different realms, creativity to seize opportunities or to solve problems'. 'Control' (centralised and user unfriendly) requires 'specialists to have a deep knowledge of the technologies that they are handling, as well as of the influence that these technologies have on the wider system (value chain) surrounding the professionals: it requires insight in the factors that control their environment as well as the factors that they control'. 'Decision support' (centralised and user friendly): here, professionals' jobs are facilitated by technologies that are tailor-made to fit the context of that job, and simultaneously governed 'by strict guidelines that prescribe actions to be undertaken (… often embedded in the software or technology that is used). This may make professionals' jobs easier, but will also allow a broader range of activities to be undertaken by the same people.' Finally, 'expertise' (decentralised and user unfriendly) requires professionals to possess 'a large amount of knowledge to effectively work in their organisations; furthermore, this knowledge needs regular updating as the half-life of knowledge decreases. Not only are these experts required to know a lot about technical issues, but also organisational and legal issues, which allows them to work efficiently and effectively in a decentralised setting' (RAND-Europe, 2006:36–39).

The study discussed the nature of several professions in each scenario, and is significant for demonstrating that even with the general trends that have been discussed earlier, the future of KISA remains highly uncertain. But it did also note three common features (RAND-Europe, 2006:39–41):

1. In all scenarios, advancing technology creates demand for professionals who 'provide services or supportive jobs to maintain technologies that are used in a specific sector; these professionals would require a multidisciplinary background, or at least they require both insight in the sector as well as in the technologies used; the design of user friendly systems would require knowledge of technology, ergonomics and business processes; likewise, the development of control systems requires knowledge of technology, organisational flows, and legal restrictions.' Specialisation or generalisation (perhaps not surprisingly) is seen as more closely linked to the way in which centralisation/decentralisation evolves than to the direction of scientific and technological development;

2. Lifelong learning is likely to be in demand as a result of the decreasing half-life of knowledge (this will be more severe the more complex the technology). Professionals' state-of-the-art knowledge may become obsolete after a few years. Given this, educators may be advised to focus on more general principles rather than the details of specific technologies, which may be more efficiently acquired in practice in workplace settings;

3. The emphasis on technology above should not be read as underplaying the growing importance of expertise in 'business skills, creativity, systems analysis, organisational understanding, legal skills, negotiation skills', and so on. Exactly which of these are most important is liable to vary across scenarios.

Finally, we should note that survey research suggests a more complex pattern than one of overall upgrading of skills. The picture may well vary across countries, so it is unwise to take UK data as necessarily representative of global trends. Still, it is worth noting that Felstead et al (2007:68) reported that a trend for greater requirements for most generic skills (planning skills, for example) over the previous decade was concentrated mainly in lower-status occupations, that in client communication skills in Sales occupations. There has thus been some convergence across occupations, though Managers and Professionals retain their lead in the usage of skills. Nevertheless, the study suggested that Professionals experienced either a stable usage of skills or in some cases a deskilling (for example in requirement for number skills);

Managers similarly had mainly stable use of skills, with some increase in literacy and horizontal communication skills. We should also note that this study brought to light many important differences across male and female, and full-time and part-time workers, which would merit detailed examination in their own right.

Little is known of the demand for new skills such as green skills or skills for a low-carbon economy. A new OECD report found that small firms have little knowledge of the requirements of the green economy, they participate very little in green training and they use KISA for getting new knowledge (OECD, 2010b).

IMPLICATIONS

Certainly there are specific skills that are associated with particular KISA (accountancy, computing services, design, and so on). These are not going to disappear, though we can expect to see more routine elements of the work automated, delegated to paraprofessionals, and/or off-shored. But KISA occupations also typically demand generic skills – such as those associated with management of people, projects, inter-organisational and interpersonal relations, communications, and so on. It is clear that there is a requirement for an adaptable, multi-skilled and highly knowledgeable workforce across the economy, and especially in high-tech industries and knowledge intensive service sectors. The challenge for Higher Education is to translate that requirement into coherent combinations of abstract and practical knowledge (thus the calls for a new discipline of 'service science'), and the portfolio of curricula that can deliver these. This may imply restructuring some elements of educational systems so that they may be more effective in promoting social and behavioural skills as well as those to do with specific technical and managerial issues. Training and educational institutions should conduct, or at least draw on, future-oriented analyses exploring the most important future needs and potential KISA skill shortages, and the most relevant responses to these perceived challenges.

Chiefly, entrepreneurial education should include KISA skills as part of the curriculum. This is important, given that SMEs and start-ups are highly dependent on KISA for acquiring new and relevant knowledge and applying it to their current operations.

Policy makers face the challenge of enabling Higher (and Vocational) Education systems to adapt flexibly to these requirements, that may involve crossing traditional disciplinary and professional boundaries, and improving interfaces with industry and public service employers of KISA professionals. Strengthening the latter is vital if we are to cope with the acceleration of organisational changes that many commentators believe to lie ahead of us. Policy makers will also do well to continue to promote lifelong learning and mobility of the workforce (including international mobility). Governments will also need to play a role in improving statistical systems that address skills and changing skill requirements, where we have been struck by the very uneven development of useful data. Policy makers, educational institutions and firms will all have roles to play in finding ways of encouraging people of various age cohorts, and in various life contexts, to learn the new skills that are needed. Policy programmes supporting businesses need to consider the evolution of KISA skills, as a potential instrument to boost innovation in firms; funding mechanisms for KISA should be explored so that high skilled employees could benefit from knowledge intensive interactions.

Meanwhile, managers face challenges in recruiting appropriate staff and mobilising them in suitable ways. This is not just a matter of locating people with the right skill sets; it also involves forming and managing teams that can bring different KISA competences to bear on evolving projects and changing circumstances. As well as calling for specific management skills that can handle this sort of cross-professional work, this will also involve use of knowledge management methods and decision support tools of various sorts – and often involve openness to collaborations and team working that extends beyond the boundaries of the individual organisation. Organisations will have to pay more attention to how they invest in knowledge, but the scope of this investment may need to be seen in broader terms.

Finally, we would note that there could be important roles played by professional associations, and similar ways of organising communities of practice, across KISA occupations. Such associations can be important vectors of new knowledge, can help to establish standards and outline good and bad practice, provide opportunities for mentoring and benchmarking, and so on. They can also create entry barriers, which in some cases may inhibit the development of the new skill combinations that are required. Such bodies would do well to consider the future of their professions in the light of changing demand for KISA.

NOTES

1. For details of O*Net, see the web resources available at http://www.onetcenter.org/overview. html (accessed 24/06/2010).
2. See definition in notes for Figure 11.5.
3. Legislators, senior officials and managers; Professionals; and Technicians and associate professionals.

REFERENCES

Bosworth, D. and Wilson, R. (2005), *Sectoral Management Priorities: Management Skills and Capacity* (Report to the Sector Skills Development Agency), Coventry: University of Warwick, Institute for Employment Research.

CEC (Commission of the European Communities) (2005), *Employment in Europe 2005*, Luxembourg: Office for Official Publications of the European Communities.

CEC (2007), *Employment in Europe 2007*, Luxembourg: Office for Official Publications of the European Communities.

CEDEFOP (2008a), *Future Skill Needs in Europe Medium Term Synthesis Report,* Luxembourg, European Commission CEDEFOP.

CEDEFOP (2008b), *Terminology of European Education and Training Policy*, Luxembourg: Office for Official Publications of the European Communities.

Felstead, A., Gallie, D., Green, F. and Ying Zhou (2007), *Skills at Work, 1986 to 2006,* Universities of Oxford and Cardiff, ESRC Centre on Skills, Knowledge and Organisational Performance (ISBN-978-0-9555799-0-5) available at: http://kar.kent.ac.uk/4845/ (accessed 24/06/2010).

Higgs, P., Cunningham, S. and Bakhshi, H. (2008), *Beyond the Creative Industries: Mapping the Creative Economy in the United Kingdom*, London: NESTA (NESTA – National Endowment for Science Technology and the Arts, Technical report) available at: http://www.nesta.org.uk/assets/pdf/beyond_creative_industries_report_NESTA.pdf (accessed 24/06/2010).

Miles, I., Kastrinos, N., Bilderbeek, R., den Hertog, P. with Flanagan, K., Huntink, W. and Bouman, M. (1995), *Knowledge-intensive Business Services: Their Role as Users, Carriers and Sources of Innovation*, Report to the EC DG XIII Luxembourg: Sprint EIMS Programme, available at: http://www.mbs.ac.uk/research/centres/engineering-policy/publications/reports.htm (accessed 24/06/2010).

Miles, I. and Jones, B. (forthcoming), *Innovation in the Service Economy*, Seville: IPTS, Erawatch reports.

OECD (2010a), *SMEs, Entrepreneurship and Innovation*, OECD: Paris.

OECD (2010b), *Leveraging Training – Skills Development for SMEs: An Analysis of Canterbury Region, New Zealand*, OECD: Paris.

Parent-Thirion, A., Fernández Macías, E., Hurley, J. and Vermeylen, G. (2007), *Fourth European Working Conditions Survey*, European Foundation for the Improvement of Living and Working Conditions, Dublin, available at: http://www.eurofound.europa.eu/pubdocs/2006/98/en/2/ef0698en.pdf (accessed 24/06/2010).

Penn, R. and Holt, R. (2000), *Skills Issues in Other Business Services –*

Professional Services, London: DFES (Her Majesty's Stationery Office): Skills Task Force Research Paper 16.

Petersen, A.W., Revill, P., Ward, T. and Wehmeyer, C. (2004), *ICT and e-Business Skills and Training in Europe*, Thessalonika: CEDEFOP.

RAND-Europe (2006), *Changing Professions in 2015 and Beyond*, Luxembourg, European Commission, European S&T Foresight Knowledge Sharing Platform, EUR 21966, ISBN 92-79-02664-X, available at: http://ec.europa.eu/research/conferences/2004/foresight/index_en.html (accessed 24/06/2010).

Rodgers, R. and Waters, R. (2001), *The Skills Dynamics of Business and Public Service Associate Professionals*, London: DFES (Her Majesty's Stationery Office): Skills Task Force Research Report RR302.

Index

KISA skills requirements, future
  key influences 261–2
KISA sourcing, in-house 71
KISA, strengthening of, tools need 37
KISA suppliers, external 125
KISA survey
  design services 102
  employment training 102
  IT services 102
  management consultancy 102
  marketing services 102
  research and development 102
  sales and distribution support 102
KISA, tacit and informal components
  crucial role of 148
KISA types used 27, 33
KISA usage findings
  variety according to firm type 34
KISA use in public sector 159–83
KISA Utilisation in Resource Intensive
  Industries
  mining in Australia 12 63–82
KISA venture capitalists 14
KISA work across economy 242
'knowledge coordinator'
  'dynamic library' of solutions 76
knowledge diffusion 77
knowledge domains 241
knowledge flows within firms 78
knowledge intensive activities
  design activities of firm 93–6
  environmental certification procedures
    93–6
  external training of company 93–6
  firm distribution system 93–6
  group in seven variables 97
  information and communication
    activities 93–6
  marketing functions of firms 93–6
  PR activities of firm 93–6
  R&D relationships of firm 93–6
knowledge intensive services, variables
  92
Knowledge Management 75, 181
  formal training systems 171–2
  importance of, transfer of knowledge
    174
knowledge network formation 152
  equipment suppliers, components

suppliers, data program suppliers
    145
knowledge, practical and experience-
    based 29
knowledge production, link to innovative
    activities
knowledge sharing 90
knowledge transfer mechanisms 9
knowledge variations 76
KS Efficiency Network project, Norway
    121

laboratory and testing activities
  use of R&D institutes 91
labour force statistics, Norway 115
Labour Force Survey 2001 128
leadership, high quality
  in human resource management 174
legal KISA 35
  for protection of inventions 30
Legislators 250
lifelong learning 263, 265
linkage types 90
Linux 149
local associations of citrus firms 47
local networking, role of
  in upgrading firms 43
location of external KISA
  international market 142
low carbon economy, transition to 191
low education profiles
  barrier for technology innovation 47
lower-technology-based KISA
  translation services, technical writing
    146
low-tech industries, agro-food processes
  role of KISA 43
low-tech industries, KISA relevance to
    44

Macarthur Regional Environmental
  Innovation Network (REIN)
  Australia National Nuclear Science
    and Technology Organisation
    (ANSTO) 194
maintenance services 79
management services access, 102
manuals of procedures 77